Lovecraft's Library:
A Catalogue

LOVECRAFT'S LIBRARY: A CATALOGUE

Fourth Edition, Revised & Enlarged

S. T. Joshi

With David E. Schultz

Hippocampus Press
New York

Copyright © 2002, 2012, 2017 by Hippocampus Press

Published by Hippocampus Press
P.O. Box 641, New York, NY 10156.
http://www.hippocampuspress.com

All rights reserved.
No part of this work may be reproduced in any form or by any means without the written permission of the publisher.

Cover design and "Lovecraft's Library" logo by Barbara Briggs Silbert.
Hippocampus Press logo by Anastasia Damianakos.
Cover art by Jason C. Eckhardt.

Lovecraft's bookplate (p. 2) was designed by Wilfred Blanch Talman
c. June 1929.

First published in 1980 by Necronomicon Press.

Fourth Edition
1 3 5 7 9 8 6 4 2

ISBN13: 978-1-61498-217-3

Contents

Introduction 7

Explanatory Notes 13

Lovecraft's Library 19

Weird &c. Items in Library of H. P. Lovecraft 173

Indexes 179

    A. Names 179

    B. Titles 195

    C. Works by Lovecraft 197

    D. Publishers 199

    E. Subjects 199

INTRODUCTION

The reasons for issuing a catalogue of H. P. Lovecraft's personal library may not be immediately evident to the casual reader. To be sure, there is some intrinsic curiosity value in knowing that he owned a 1567 black-letter edition of Ovid, or a complete file of *Weird Tales, The Fantasy Fan,* and other now fabulously rare journals of fantasy fiction, or several issues of *The Rhode Island Almanac,* by a writer (or, rather, a series of writers) disguised by the classic Augustan pseudonym of Isaac Bickerstaff, a pseudonym once used by Lovecraft himself. And yet, the present compilation is far more than a farrago of *curiosa;* for Lovecraft, like Samuel Johnson (to mention only one other whose library has been catalogued), was so thoroughly a man of letters that his library—not greatly distinguished from a bibliophilic point of view—was an essential part of his life and thought: it shaped his intellectual growth; it was one of his most prized possessions; it was a storehouse of ideas that found expression in all aspects of his literary work. To understand the man, we must first understand his books.

Confronted by the glaring and outré covers that adorn the paperbound editions of his stories—now distributed in the millions of copies throughout the world—it is often forgotten that Providence-born Howard Phillips Lovecraft did more than write the greatest horror fiction since Poe. Poems, essays, and, most especially, letters would occupy a far greater proportion of his collected writings than his admittedly great fiction; indeed, his letters may perhaps be his greatest achievement, so full as they are of a stupefyingly diverse erudition. If nothing else, he wrote more letters than almost anyone in this century and, perhaps, in all literary history: an estimated 80,000 letters emerged from his pen, although probably fewer than 10,000 now survive. The letters alone may confirm that Lovecraft, aside from being Rhode Island's greatest native writer, might occupy—or come to occupy—a significant place in modern intellectual history. That he was, intellectually, highly gifted is beyond doubt: from the age of four to his death at forty-six he was an omnivorous reader, thus abundantly making up for the missed opportunity (because of poor health) of attending Brown University. Fittingly for a man who had not the world but the cosmos for his subject of study, his reading tastes were bewilderingly wide, and his library in large measure reflects the *crème de la crème* of his readings—those books that he was satisfied not merely with reading but also with owning.

It is therefore regrettable that I am unable to offer a complete listing of Lovecraft's library, for about 1100 of his 1500 or 2000 volumes have (for reasons outlined in the Explanatory Notes) been here located and catalogued.[1] Though it is possible to estimate the nature of the missing portions of the library, and though certain areas have surely been catalogued with comparative thoroughness, there is nonetheless little chance that these lacunae will ever be filled. To begin with, it seems that many of Lovecraft's volumes on science and philosophy are absent from the present list: of the books by Darwin, Haeckel, Huxley, Margaret Murray, and many others to which Lovecraft frequently referred in his letters there is hardly a trace (possibly he consulted many of these only in libraries); nor do we find much by Santayana, Bertrand Russell, Hobbes, Spinoza, and the other thinkers whom Lovecraft admired. Volumes of history—especially modern history—seem, too, in rather short supply.

But on the positive side we are aware of a great many volumes that Lovecraft proclaimed to be dear to his heart. In particular we note the profusion of Greek and Latin classics, books on ancient history and civilisation, English poetry and belles lettres (particularly of the eighteenth century), New England history and antiquities, and—most important of all to the literary scholar—his holdings of weird fiction, which may be considered virtually complete thanks to the availability of a list in Lovecraft's own hand—"Weird &c. Items in Library of H. P. Lovecraft"—which he prepared late in life, evidently "for the benefit of distant members of the 'weird fiction gang' [i.e., his literary correspondents] who wish to borrow spectral volumes not obtainable in their hometown bibliothecae" (*SL* 5.243–44).

Lovecraft's poverty precluded extensive campaigns of book-buying, and a good many of the volumes in his library—particularly those of eighteenth- and early nineteenth-century imprint—were holdovers from his family library. This

---

1. HPL gives varying numbers to various correspondents of the total number of books in his library, ranging from "1500 or so" (*SL* 2.287) to "1500 volumes . . . with perhaps 200 more in storage" (*DS* 259) to "perhaps 2000 to 2500" (*OFF* 242) and even "present total perhaps 2500 in the house on shelves; 200 or 300 more in attic or stored in a neighbouring stable" (HPL to the "Coryciani, 14 July 1936; "Letters to the Coryciani," ed. David E. Schultz and S.T. Joshi, *Lovecraft Annual* (2017): 137). The 1085 titles recorded herein might come much closer to the 1500 figure if individual volumes of multi-volume sets are counted separately. HPL also admits to owning "about half the entire series" of Haldeman-Julius booklets, usually priced at 5¢ or 10¢ (HPL to Zealia Bishop, 27 July 1927); but it is unclear whether he counted these among the various totals of his books.

may explain the profusion of works by Dickens, Thackeray (who "induceth drowsiness" [*SL* 1.73]), Jane Austen, and others (in particular the totally un-Lovecraftian romances of Mrs Mulock) in which he found little interest. Many other volumes—beginning, perhaps, with the presentation of Lang's *Arabian Nights* by his mother in 1898—were gifts, as the inscriptions on the volumes by Donald Wandrei, Walter J. Coates, Samuel Loveman, and others testify. A small number must have been acquired gratis as a consequence of Lovecraft's being a contributor to the volume: thus we find the Christine Campbell Thomson anthologies published by Selwyn & Blount, Hammett's *Creeps by Night*, Harré's *Beware After Dark!*, and others. But a substantial residue was purchased by Lovecraft himself, either upon publication or through used-book stores, where, as he remarked, "one can obtain astonishing bargains" (*SL* 2.287).

In many ways Lovecraft's library was an enviable one. He possessed a remarkable collection of Augustan and early Romantic poetry, encompassing both the great (Keats, Shelley, Coleridge, Thomson, Gray) and the near-great (Shenstone, Beattie, Trumbull, Crabbe). His statement that "I picked up my peculiar style from Addison, Steele, Johnson, and Gibbon" (*SL* 1.11) is confirmed by his significant holdings of these and other eighteenth-century masters of English prose.

Although Lovecraft knew a smattering of many tongues—though not, as Zealia Bishop would have us believe, of African dialects!—he could read only English and Latin fluently; so that what volumes of French, Italian, German, and Greek literature he owned were almost exclusively in translation. (His copy of Baudelaire's *Lettres* in French was a gift.) Moreover, many of his Latin volumes were in translation or in bilingual editions with interlinear translations (a technique upon which Latinists now look with horror). Needless to say, he owned those celebrated translations of the Latin and Greek classics which have in turn themselves become classics—Dryden's *Aeneid*, Pope's *Odyssey* and *Iliad*, Garth's Ovid, Dryden's Plutarch (revised by Clough), Chapman's *Hymns of Homer*, Murphy's Tacitus, and the like. His volumes on ancient history and civilisation were largely high-school or college textbooks, some rather shoddy and most now outdated; but Lovecraft never claimed to be a specialist, and his knowledge in this field, as in so many others, was admirable for a layman.

The few science books in his library of whose existence we know—largely astronomy, biology, and chemistry—are almost without exception textbooks or general, non-technical manuals. Lovecraft's disinclination for mathematics prevented him from penetrating the mysteries of astronomy and physics as deeply as he would have liked; perhaps a fortunate circumstance, else we might have seen competent if dry astronomy volumes from him rather than the brilliant weird fiction by which he has achieved an universal if tardy fame. It was, in fact, precisely because Lovecraft did not become a specialist in any single field that he could coordinate his multifarious knowledge and distil it into his fiction and essays: without being a geologist he could write such a convincing narrative as *At the Mountains of Madness;* without being a specialist in New England history, he could pen such a tale as *The Case of Charles Dexter Ward.* But had he been a scholar either in one field or the other, we might perhaps never have seen one or the other of these tales. True enough, his knowledge can be picked apart and criticised by any specialist; but could that specialist boast the catholicity of taste, the inveterate curiosity in so many academic fields, and the miraculous integration of this knowledge into a single and coherent philosophy such as Lovecraft achieved? Although the concept of the Renaissance man may be becoming increasingly obsolete with the bewildering expansion of knowledge in all fields, it is hard to doubt that Lovecraft was the latest to attempt and, perhaps, to succeed in filling that role.

But there was perhaps one field in which Lovecraft could justifiably claim authority—weird fiction; for it is the belief of many that Lovecraft's essay on "Supernatural Horror in Literature" is one of the finest studies of its kind, providing not only a succinct history of the genre from antiquity to the present, but also guidelines towards its aesthetic bases and a defence of its worth as a literary form. Lovecraft not only read all types of weird literature, from the best to the worst, but also sought to establish a collection encompassing his personal favourites in the field. Thus Dunsany, Machen, Poe, Shiel, Bierce, Hawthorne, Blackwood, and others who significantly influenced Lovecraft's own writings are heavily represented in his library; but these are just the tip of the iceberg of his holdings. Such tantalisingly obscure volumes as Leonard Cline's *The Dark Chamber,* J. Provand Webster's *The Oracle of Baal,* Henri Béraud's *Lazarus,* James De Mille's *A Strange Manuscript Found in a Copper Cylinder,* and others filled his shelves; and their perusal might unearth literary influences hitherto unknown to scholars.

Lovecraft the *littérateur,* then, cannot be separated from his library; it was as integral to his being as the New England landscape he adored. That Lovecraft would "part with all my furniture and squat and sleep on the floor before I'd let go of the 1500 or so books I possess" (*SL* 2.287) is eloquent enough testimony to a man for whom books were, not an evasion of the "real" world, but the essence of that real world itself. Reality may comprise not only the prosiness of daily existence, but the thoughts of the great minds that have, perhaps more than the conquests of war or the complexities of political manoeuvring, shaped our civilisation. It is this reality that Lovecraft devoted a lifetime in seeking.

—S. T. JOSHI

Explanatory Notes

This listing of Lovecraft's library has been compiled in a somewhat unusual way, in that the compilers have examined only a fraction of the books he actually owned. The fact that Lovecraft's library was dispersed not long after his death in 1937 has made personal recording impossible, and we have almost entirely had to work indirectly in compiling a list of books and editions owned by Lovecraft.

Our major source is a confused, inadequate, inaccurate, and virtually illegible list of books prepared shortly after Lovecraft's death by Mary Spink, Lovecraft's neighbour living in the apartment below him in 66 College Street (now 65 Prospect Street) in Providence. Miss Spink was given the task of cataloguing Lovecraft's library because Lovecraft's aunt and heir, Annie E. P. Gamwell, was under the false impression that she was in need of money; she therefore wished to sell some of the volumes. (Mrs Gamwell actually was quite well-to-do, as her estate upon her death in 1943 was valued at over $10,000.) Spink's list must not be assumed to be complete: not only are a good number of volumes of weird fiction missing (this perhaps because R. H. Barlow, whom Lovecraft named his literary executor, took some of these volumes in accordance Lovecraft's "Instructions in Case of Decease"), but some other facets of Lovecraft's library seem also to be missing. Among them can be mentioned his collection of old farmer's almanacs: these apparently were given to W. Paul Cook (who with Lovecraft had one of the finest private collections of almanacs at the time), and the few recorded by Spink may perhaps be duplicates left behind by Cook.

Mrs Gamwell died, however, before the books could be appraised, and Spink's listing lay untouched for some years. (Lovecraft's volumes gradually were dispersed, many going to H. Douglass Dana's bookshop in Providence, some perhaps perishing in the fire that consumed the store in the 1970s.) Spink seems to have had a friendship with Dorothy C. Walter, a correspondent of Lovecraft in Providence, and Walter upon seeing the list hoped to publish it. Part of the listing had been typed by an unknown hand, but the typist was (not surprisingly) unable to read Spink's handwriting very well, and moreover seemed not of literary bent; among the results is that we find one of Dickens's novels titled *Master Chuzzlewut*, while *Dracula* is, we learn, written by a B. Stokie. Fortunately the whole of Spink's manuscript was preserved. Walter contacted Cook, then editor and publisher of *The Ghost*, an amateur journal containing numerous items about Lovecraft. Cook and Walter set about preparing the text for publication (making, apparently, very little progress), but Cook's death in 1948 confounded the plans. Walter (who died in 1959) then turned the manuscript and typescript over to the John Hay Library for its Lovecraft collection, where they have lain ever since.

The reconstruction of Spink's listing into coherent form is not the simplest of tasks. Aside from her incredible script, she often provides very brief and insufficient data on the books recorded: usually she gives the author, title, publisher, and date of publication; but on many occasions, either through whim, oversight, lack of knowledge, or what to me has frequently seemed perverse delight, foregoes any or all but one of the above. Thus we find such books as Mencken's *The American Language* with no further data, the laconic entry "Bible" with no publication information, or a curious entry, "Homer, Burt," which I have deciphered (through the National Union Catalogue) as Pope's *Iliad*, published by A. L. Burt (New York) in 1902. With such lacunae in my major source, it should not be surprising that on a number of entries I am unsure about date of publication, publisher, or even the actual volume in question.

A major supplement to Spink's listing is a list made by Lovecraft himself of "Weird &c. Items in Library of H. P. Lovecraft." This records a few hundred titles, but gives only author and title. Comparing entries from this list with Spink's, I have been able to identify a number of actual editions of the weird items in his library; but for a large number this is clearly impossible.

A few minor sources for this listing can be cited here. In a Fall 1951 catalogue (probably from Dana's bookstore) there appears a list of "Unusual Collection of Books from the Library of Howard Phillips Lovecraft, Formerly in the Possession of Robert Barlow." These are obviously many of the books taken away by Barlow after Lovecraft's death which remained in his possession upon his own death in early 1951. The list fills in many gaps in Lovecraft's and Spink's lists and also supplies a few new titles. Stuart David Schiff issued an undated catalogue containing a list of "Books from Library of Howard Phillips Lovecraft"; I have abbreviated this source as "Schiff" in my listing. L. W. Currey's catalogues have occasionally listed hitherto unknown titles from Lovecraft's library, as have other book dealers and individuals, including the Grill-Binkin catalogue of Lovecraftiana (Mirage Press, 1975); these have been incorporated into the listing. Several individuals owning books from Lovecraft's library have contacted me since the first edition of this listing, and their information has helped me to fill more lacunae.

A final source is Lovecraft's published and unpublished letters. In these letters Lovecraft not only frequently refers to books he has read, but at times records purchases of books. We have taken the liberty of inserting into the listing certain titles mentioned in these letters that appear neither in Lovecraft's nor in Spink's listings, assuming that their absence is due either to oversight, loss, or some other cause. We have been cautious in this procedure, listing only titles that Lovecraft specifically admits to acquiring. Recent consultation of hitherto unavailable letters has much augmented the current list, especially in terms of the books and pamphlets by Lovecraft himself that he clearly admits to owning (in some cases by virtue of bestowing them as gifts to friends and colleagues).

An entry in the listing followed by the annotation "Not located" indicates that I have not succeeded in finding a volume of its title or, in the case of well-known titles, the publisher indicated by Spink.

As an aid to scholarship we have indicated the instances in Lovecraft's work—fiction, poetry, letters, and essays, especially "Supernatural Horror in Literature"—where he mentions the specific volume in question or any part of its contents. References to the editions we have used are indicated below. It has naturally been impossible to record all the instances where Lovecraft mentions a particular author without referring to any specific title by that author. Some notes have also been supplied on the possible influence of the work or the author upon Lovecraft.

In this fourth edition we have taken care to identify the source(s) for each entry. Most, obviously, derive from Spink's or Lovecraft's lists, but a few come from Barlow's, Lovecraft's letters, or private collectors. The abbreviated list of sources—MS (Mary Spink), HPL (H. P. Lovecraft), and RHB (R. H. Barlow)—indicate specifically the listings cited above. X denotes that we have consulted the actual volume in question or been informed of its contents by the owner of the volume; in several cases we have consulted an online listing of a book dealer selling the item in question. A date in diagonal brackets indicates the original publication date for works that Lovecraft owned in a much later edition; we have supplied such dates only for select titles, so that it cannot be assumed that titles lacking such dates are first editions.

Of the five indices, the index of names includes all authors, co-authors, editors, translators, illustrators, and pseudonyms (persons, whether authors or other figures, who are subjects are listed here rather than in the subject index); the index of titles is very selective, listing only titles that are otherwise difficult to locate; the index of works by Lovecraft includes all Lovecraft works cited in the annotations; the index of publishers is very selective; the index of subjects attempts to be comprehensive, especially in reference to Lovecraft's literary holdings.

My major bibliographic sources for the compilation of this listing are as follows (abbreviations indicated in brackets):

Ashley, Mike, and William G. Contento. *The Supernatural Index.* Westport, CT: Greenwood Press, 1995. [Ashley]

Bibliotheca Americana/American Catalogue 1820–1910. New York, 1852f. 14 vols. [AC]

Bleiler, E. F. *The Checklist of Fantastic Literature.* Chicago: Shasta Publishers, 1948.

The British Library General Catalogue of Printed Books to 1975. London: Clive Bingley; London: G. K. Saur, 1979–87. 359 vols. [BLC] (Supersedes *British Museum General Catalogue of Printed Books to 1955.* London: Trustees of the British Museum, 1965–66. 263 vols.)

Catalogue générale des livres imprimés de la Bibliothèque Nationale. Paris: Imprimerie Nationale, 1897–1975. 223 vols. [BN]

A Checklist of American Imprints 1820–1832. Metuchen, NJ: Scarecrow Press, 1964–77. 14 vols.

Cumulative Book Index 1898–1937. Minneapolis: H. W. Wilson, 1900f. 24 vols. [CBI]

The English Catalogue of Books 1801–1935. London, 1864f. 17 vols.

International Science Fiction Database (www.isfdb.org). [ISFDB]

The National Union Catalogue: Pre-1956 Imprints. London: Mansell, 1968–81. 754 vols. (including Supplement). [NUC]

Sabin, Joseph. *Bibliotheca Americana.* New York: Joseph Sabin, 1868–1936. 29 vols. (Index compiled by John Edgar Molnar. Metuchen, NJ: Scarecrow Press, 1974. 3 vols.)

Shaw, Ralph R., and Richard H. Shoemaker. *American Bibliography 1801–1819.* Metuchen, NJ: Scarecrow Press, 1958–65. 22 vols.

Tuck, Donald H. *The Encyclopedia of Science Fiction and Fantasy through 1968.* Chicago: Advent:Publishers, 1974–82. 3 vols.

The United States Catalogue. Minneapolis: H. W. Wilson, 1900–24. 8 vols.

Watson, George, ed. *The New Cambridge Bibliography of English Literature.* Cambridge: Cambridge University Press, 1969–77. 5 vols.

Several electronic databases and library catalogues also have been of immense help in tracking down stray items. These include RLIN (Research Libraries Information Network), OCLC WorldCat (www.worldcat.org; abbreviated in the text as OCLC), MELVYL (the catalogue of the University of California Libraries), and nypl.org (the online catalogue of the New York Public Library).

This fourth revised edition not only incorporates into the general listing those items that had previously appeared in a section of "Addenda," but substantially augments the citations to the volume as found in Lovecraft's essays and letters, based on recent definitive editions of these bodies of work.

Abbreviations used in the text and annotations are as follows:

AG	*Letters to Alfred Galpin* (Hippocampus Press, 2003)
AT	*The Ancient Track: Complete Poetical Works*, 2nd ed. (Hippocampus Press, 2013)
CB	*Commonplace Book* (in *CE* 5.219–35) [citations by item number]
CE	*Collected Essays* (Hippocampus Press, 2004–06; 5 vols.)
CF	*Collected Fiction: A Variorum Edition* (Hippocampus Press, 2015–17; 4 vols.)
CLM	*Letters to C. L. Moore and Others* (Hippocampus Press, 2017)
DS	*Dawnward Spire, Lonely Hill: The Letters of H. P. Lovecraft and Clark Ashton Smith* (Hippocampus Press, 2017)
ES	*Essential Solitude: The Letters of H. P. Lovecraft and August Derleth* (Hippocampus Press, 2008; 2 vols.)
ET	*Letters to Elizabeth Toldridge and Anne Tillery Renshaw* (Hippocampus Press, 2014)
LFF	*Letters to Family and Family Friends* (Hippocampus Press, 2018)
FLB	*Letters to F. Lee Baldwin, Duane W. Rimel, and Nils H. Frome* (Hippocampus Press, 2016)
FDOC	*H. P. Lovecraft: Four Decades of Criticism*, ed. S. T. Joshi (Athens: Ohio University Press, 1980)
JDR	John D. Rockefeller Library, Brown University
JFM	*Letters to James F. Morton* (Hippocampus Press, 2011)
JHL	John Hay Library, Brown University
Joshi	*H. P. Lovecraft: A Comprehensive Bibliography* (University of Tampa Press, 2009)
Josiah	Brown University online catalogue (http://josiah.brown.edu/)
JVS	*Letters to J. Vernon Shea, Carl F. Strauch, and Lee McBride White* (Hippocampus Press, 2016)
MF	*A Means to Freedom: The Letters of H. P. Lovecraft and Robert E. Howard* (Hippocampus Press, 2009)

MTS	*Mysteries of Time and Spirit: The Letters of H. P. Lovecraft and Donald Wandrei* (Night Shade, 2002)
MWM	Maurice Winter Moe
MWM	*Letters to Maurice W. Moe and Others* (Hippocampus Press, 2017)
OFF	*O Fortunate Floridian: H. P. Lovecraft's Letters to R. H. Barlow* (University of Tampa Press, 2007)
RB	*Letters to Robert Bloch and Others* (Hippocampus Press, 2015)
RK	*Letters to Rheinhart Kleiner* (Hippocampus Press, 2005)
SHL	*The Annotated Supernatural Horror in Literature* (Hippocampus Press, rev. ed. 2012)
WHS	August Derleth Papers, State Historical Society of Wisconsin (Madison, WI)
SL	*Selected Letters* (Arkham House, 1965–76; 5 vols.)

This listing is not only incomplete but may also be inaccurate in parts or inadequate in the information listed. The compiler would appreciate any addenda or corrigenda from bibliophiles or owners of books from Lovecraft's library whom I have not contacted, so that such data may be incorporated in future editions.

Among those who assisted in the compilation of this listing are George T. Banister, Henry L. P. Beckwith, R. Boerem, Peter Cannon, Virginia Doris, Ruth and the late Muriel E. Eddy, Steve Eng, Kenneth W. Faig, Jr., Carsten Flaake, William Fulwiler, Frank M. Halpern, Robert C. Harrall, T. E. D. Klein, Donovan K. Loucks, Daniel F. Lorraine, David McClintock, Richard H. Minter, the late Ethel Phillips Morrish, Dirk W. Mosig, Karnig Nalbandian, Kennett Neily, Juha-Matti Rajala, John D. Squires, the late Roy A. Squires, Horace Smith, Chet Williamson, and John H. Stanley and Richard Noble of the John Hay Library.

—S. T. J.

Lovecraft's Library

1. Abbott, Jacob (1803–1879). *Xerxes*. <1878> New York: Harper & Brothers, 1904. 302 pp. [Grill-Binkin/NUC 1:420]

2. Abbott, Lyman (1835–1922). *The Evolution of Christianity*. Boston: Houghton Mifflin, 1892. vi, 258 pp. [MS/NUC 1:454]

3. Abney, Captain W[illiam] De W[iveleslie] (1843–1920). *How to Become a Photographer*. New York: Frank Tousey, [1891]. 61 pp. [X—JHL/NUC 2:30]

4. Adams, John (1750?–1814), ed. *The Flowers of Modern Travels: Being Elegant, Entertaining and Instructive Extracts, Selected from the Works of the Most Celebrated Travellers*. <1797> Boston: Printed for the Subscribers, 1816. 2 vols. [MS/NUC 3:482]
HPL had only Vol. 1. The author is not the second president of the United States, but rather a Scottish clergyman and editor.

5. Addison, Joseph (1672–1719). *The Miscellaneous Works, in Verse and Prose, of the Right Honourable Joseph Addison*. With Some Account of the Life and Writings of the Author, by Mr. [Thomas] Tickell. Dublin: Printed for T. Walker, 1773. 3 vols. [MS/NUC 4:40]

6. ———. *Remarks on Several Parts of Italy, &c., in the Years 1701, 1702, 1703*. <1705> Dublin: Printed for T. Walker, 1773. 303 pp. [MS/NUC 4:43]

7. ———. *Selections from Addison's Papers Contributed to* The Spectator. <1711–14> Edited with an Introduction and Notes by Thomas Arnold. Oxford: Clarendon Press, 1891. xxx, 528 pp. [MS/NUC 4:44]

8. ———. *The Tatler and The Guardian*. <1709–11; 1713> Edited, with Critical and Explanatory Notes, by George Washington Greene. Philadelphia: J. B. Lippincott, 1876 or 1878. 520 pp. [MS/NUC 4:49; 687:29]
Addison's contributions only. MS gives date as 1882. *SL* 5.234 *ES* 379

9. ———; John Gay (1685–1732); and William Somerville (1675–1742). *The Poetical Works of Joseph Addison; Gay's Fables; and Somerville's Chase*. With memoirs and critical dissertations by the Rev. George Gilfillan. The text edited by Charles Cowden Clarke. Edinburgh: J. Nichol, 1859, 1863. *or* Edinburgh: W. P. Nimmo, 1869. *or* London: Cassell, 1875. xxxiii, 386 pp. [NUC 4:42]
HPL acknowledges receipt of the book (a gift from Rheinhart Kleiner) in the poem "To Mr. Kleiner, on Receiving from Him the Poetical Works of Addison, Gay, and Somerville" (1918). Gay's *Fables* were published in two

volumes in 1727 and 1938; Somerville's *The Chase* (originally *The Chace*) was published in 1735.

10. ———, and Sir Richard Steele (1672–1729). *Days with Sir Roger de Coverley.* Illustrated by Hugh Thomson (1860–1920). London: Macmillan & Co., 1886. 82 pp. [HPL to Marian F. Bonner, 9 April 1936 (HPL, "Letters to Marian F. Bonner," *Lovecraft Annual* No. 9 [2015]: 18)/NUC 4:34]

11. ———, Sir Richard Steele, et al. *The Spectator.* <1711–14> With Sketches of the Lives of the Authors. Edinburgh: A. Lawrie, 1804. 8 vols. [MS/NUC 561:78]
CE 1.120n1; 4.270 *AG* 81 *RK* 150n2, 164n2 *ES* 379

12. ———. *The Spectator.* London: J. M. Dent; New York: E. P. Dutton (Everyman's Library), [1930–34]. 4 vols. [MS/NUC 4:49]

13. Aesop (d. 564 B.C.E.). *Aesop's Fables.* A New Version, Chiefly from Original Sources, by the Rev. Thomas James (1809–1863). With More Than One Hundred Illustrations by John Tenniel. London: John Murray, 1848. xxv, 232 pp. [MS/NUC 4:524]
CE 2.186 *SL* 3.77–78

14. ———. *The Fables of Aesop.* Selected, Told Anew and Their History Traced by Joseph Jacobs <1894>. Done into Pictures by Richard Heighway. New York: F. M. Lupton, [1900?]. 228 pp. [MS/OCLC]

15. Agassiz, Louis (1807–1873). *Methods of Study in Natural History.* <1863> 9th ed. Boston: J. R. Osgood, 1874. viii, 319 pp. [MS/NUC 5:105]

16. Ahlhauser, William C. *Ex-Presidents of the National Amateur Press Association: Sketches.* Athol, MA: W. Paul Cook, 1919. 93 pp. [X/NUC 5:456]
Inscribed: "To Howard P. Lovecraft with the compliments of W. Paul Cook."

17. Aikin, John (1747–1822), ed. *Select Works of the British Poets, in a Chronological Series from Ben Jonson to Beattie.* Philadelphia: T. Wardle, 1848. vii, 807 pp. [MS/NUC 687:356]

18. Airne, C[lement] W[allace] (1889–?). *Britain's Story Told in Pictures.* Manchester: Sankey, Hudson, & Co., [1935]. 64 pp. [MS/NUC 6:66]

19. ———. *The Story of Hanoverian and Modern Britain Told in Pictures.* Manchester: Sankey, Hudson & Co., 1935. 63 pp. [HPL to Elizabeth Toldridge, 29 December 1934 (*ET* 286)/NUC 6:66]

20. ———. *The Story of Mediaeval Britain Told in Pictures*. Manchester: Sankey, Hudson & Co., 1935. 63 pp. [HPL to Elizabeth Toldridge, 29 December 1934 (*ET* 286)/NUC 6:66]

21. ———. *The Story of Prehistoric & Roman Britain Told in Pictures*. Manchester: Sankey, Hudson & Co., [1935]. 63 pp. [HPL to Elizabeth Toldridge, 29 December 1934 (*ET* 286)/NUC 6:66]

22. ———. *Story of Saxon and Norman Britain Told in Pictures*. Manchester: Sankey, Hudson & Co. [1935]. 68 pp. [HPL to Elizabeth Toldridge, 29 December 1934 (*ET* 286)/NUC 6:66]

23. ———. *The Story of Tudor and Stuart Britain Told in Pictures*. Manchester: Sankey, & Hudson & Co., 1935. 64 pp. [HPL to Elizabeth Toldridge, 29 December 1934 (*ET* 286)/NUC 6:67]

24. Alcott, Louisa May (1832–1888). *Little Women*. <1868> Boston: Roberts Brothers, 1895. xvi, 532 pp. [X/eBay (no record of 1895 printing in NUC or OCLC)]

    Inscribed to HPL as from his mother (though not signed) for Christmas 1895.

25. Alden, Abner (1758?–1820). *The Reader: Containing the Art of Delivery, Articulation, Accent, Pronunciation*, [etc.]. <1802> 3rd ed. Boston: Printed by J. T. Buckingham for Thomas & Andrews, 1808. 228 pp. [X—MS/NUC 7:604]

    HPL notes that he read this volume around 1897 "for my guidance in correct composition. . . . This was so utterly and absolutely the thing I had been looking for, that I attacked it with almost savage violence. It was in the 'long ſ', and reflected in all its completeness the Georgian rhetorical tradition of Addison, Pope, and Johnson" (*MWM* 430). HPL is in error in dating this book to 1797. *ES* 379 *ET* 23n9 *JVS* 110 *CLM* 354n

26. *All-Story Weekly*.
    24 November 1917. *Contains:* "Through the Dragon Glass" by A. Merritt. [HPL]
    22 June 1918. *Contains:* "The Moon Pool" by A. Merritt. [HPL]

    HPL ranked the original novelette version of "The Moon Pool" among his ten favourite weird tales. But HPL felt that Merritt had later sold himself out to the popular market. *MTS* 341 *AG* 198 *OFF* 24, 29, 31, 32, 99, 207, 406 *ES* 181–82, 83, 138, 179, 460, 545, 620 *MF* 144–45, 727 *ET* 260 *RB* 110, 126 *JVS* 31, 53, 66–67, 90, 96, 117, 215, 353 *FLB* 22, 35, 104–5, 111, 295

27. Allen, Hervey (1889–1949). *Israfel: The Life and Times of Edgar Allan Poe.* <1926> New York: George H. Doran Co., 1927. 2 vols. [MS/NUC 9:320]

 Called by HPL "the best study of Poe I have ever seen" (*ES* 114; cf. 111, 263). HPL also read Allen's well-known historical novel *Anthony Adverse* (*SL* 4.390). This copy inscribed "Providence, RI, Oct. 1929." HPL notes that he "picked [it] up as a remainder for $2.98" (*ES* 228). *ES* 230, 262

28. Allen, John. *How to Make a Magic-Lantern.* New York: Frank Tousey, [1891]. 62 pp. [X—JHL/NUC 9:361]

29. Allen, T[homas] P[rentiss] (1822–1868), and William F[rancis] Allen (1830–1889). *Handbook of Classical Geography, Chronology, Mythology, and Antiquities.* Prepared for the Use of Schools. Boston: Swan, Brewer & Tileston, 1861. xii, 123 pp. [X/HPL to Fritz Leiber, 19 December 1936 (*CLM* 304)/NUC 9:463]

 The book bears HPL's signature on the front endpaper and also an earlier inscription: "Franklin C. Clark / Feb. 25th 1865 / Providence RI / Brown University / Class of '69." Clark (1847–1915) was HPL's uncle. HPL has written the date "May 6, 1904," presumably the date when Clark gave this book to HPL.

30. Allen, William F[rancis] (1830–1889), and Joseph H[enry] Allen (1820–1898). *Latin Lessons Adapted to the Manual Latin Grammar.* Boston: Ginn Brothers, 1871. x, 134 pp. [X/NUC 9:485]

31. ———. *Manual Latin Grammar.* <1868> Boston: Ginn Brothers, 1872. xvi, 145 pp. [X/NUC 9:485]

32. *Amazing Stories.* Edited by Hugo Gernsback. [HPL]
 1926–27. *Contains:* HPL's "The Colour out of Space" (2, No. 6 [September 1927]): 557–67.

 The issues also contain reprints of H. G. Wells's *The Island of Dr. Moreau* (October–November 1926), *The Time Machine* (May 1927), and *The War of the Worlds* (August 1927), along with *Station X* (July–September 1926) by G. MacLeod Winsor (1856–1939).

33. *The Americans' Guide: Comprising the Declaration of Independence, the Articles of Confederation, the Constitution of the United States, and the Constitutions of Several States Composing the Union.* Philadelphia: Hogan & Thompson, [1844]. 419 pp. [MS/OCLC]

 On spine: *American Constitutions* (MS gives this as title of book).

34. *American Poetry Circle Anthology.* New York: Leacy N. Green-Leach, 1928. 154 pp. [HPL to Elizabeth Toldridge, 20 November 1928 (*ET* 22, 23n1)/NUC 13:477]

   Presumably given to HPL by Elizabeth Toldridge. See also below. *ET* 53, 117, 135, 152, 166, 170, 229

35. *American Poetry Circle Anthology.* New York: Leacy N. Green-Leach, 1929. 114 pp. [X—JHL/NUC 13:477]

   Presentation copy from Elizabeth Toldridge "to Judge H. P. Lovecraft." Toldridge refers to HPL's being a judge for a poetry contest sponsored by the League of American Penwomen, in which Toldridge was involved.

36. *The American Poetry Circle Anthology.* New York: Leacy N. Green-Leach, 1930. [HPL to Elizabeth Toldridge, [20 December 1930] (*ET* 170)/NUC 13:477]

37. *American Poetry Circle Anthology.* New York: Leacy Naylor Green-Leach, 1932. 120 pp. [X—JHL]

   Presentation copy from Elizabeth Toldridge "to Judge H. P. Lovecraft."

38. Anderson, Jessie Macmillan. *A Study of English Words.* New York: American Book Co., 1897. 118 pp. [MS/NUC 15:522]

39. Andrews, Ethan Allan (1787–1858). *A Copious and Critical Latin-English Lexicon.* Founded on the Larger Latin-German Lexicon of Dr. W. Freund. New York: Harper & Brothers, 1854. xxv, 1663 pp. [MS/NUC 16:377]

   This dictionary was superseded by Lewis and Short's *Latin Dictionary* (1879)—the standard dictionary until the recent publication of the *Oxford Latin Dictionary*; but HPL seems never to have acquired Lewis and Short. HPL discusses this volume at length in a letter to Ben Abramson (15 February 1937; ms., WHS).

40. Andreyev, Leonid Nikolaevich (1871–1919). *The Seven That Were Hanged.* <1908> Introduction by Thomas Seltzer. New York: Boni & Liveright (Modern Library), [1918] or [1925]. 194 pp. [HPL/NUC 15:245]

   Also includes *The Red Laugh*. The translator is unidentified. Andreyev was a Russian novelist and playwright. *The Seven That Were Hanged* deals with the reflections of leftist revolutionaries as they prepare for their execution by hanging. Some scholars believe the book inspired the assassination of Archduke Ferdinand in 1914, leading to the outbreak of World War I. *CE* 2.190

41. Angell, James Burrill (1829–1916). *The Reminiscences of James Burrill Angell.* New York: Longmans, Green, 1912. vii, 258 pp. [MS/NUC 16:637]

    Angell was a Rhode Island journalist and president of Brown University (1868–77). *CE* 5.161

42. Ansted, David Thomas (1814–1880). *The World We Live In; or, First Lessons in Physical Geography.* Philadelphia: J. B. Lippincott; London: W. H. Allen, 1868. 156 pp. [MS/NUC 17:557]

43. *Anthology of Magazine Verse.* Edited by William Stanley Braithwaite (1878–1962). New York: Schulte Publishing Co., 1913f. [MS/NUC 17:654]

    HPL had the volume for 1921. In 1930 HPL corresponded with Braithwaite, who was on the staff of the *Boston Transcript* and a prominent African-American poet and critic. *CE* 1.299

44. *Anthology of Magazine Verse.* Edited by W[ilhelm] C[rawford] King. New York: Paebar Co., [1932–35]. 4 vols. [MS/NUC 17:654]

    HPL had either the volume for 1934 or the volume for 1933 published in 1934.

45. Anthon, Charles (1797–1867). *A Classical Dictionary, Containing an Account of the Principal Names Mentioned in Ancient Authors.* New York: Harper & Brothers, 1852. 1451 pp. [MS/NUC 17:656]

46. ———. *A System of Ancient and Mediaeval Geography for the Use of Schools and Colleges.* New-York: Harper & Brothers, 1850. viii, 769 pp. [MS/NUC 17:661]

    CLM 304

47. Appleton, John Howard (1844–1930). *The Young Chemist: A Book of Laboratory Work for Beginners.* Providence, RI: J. A. & R. A. Reid, 1876. vi, 54 pp. [HPL to Rheinhart Kleiner, 16 November 1916 (*RK* 71)/OCLC]

    No ed. cited by HPL. HPL notes receiving this book from the author (professor of chemistry at Brown University) in 1899. *SL* 2.109 *AG* 38, 39

48. Apuleius, Lucius (123?–180?). *The Golden Asse of Lucius Apuleius.* Translated out of Latin by William Adlington, anno 1566. Ornamented by Martin Travers. London: Chapman & Dodd, [1898]. xiii, 234 pp. [RHB/NUC 18:690]

    Purchased by HPL from Samuel Loveman (cf. HPL to Lillian D. Clark, 10 May 1928; *LFF*). *CE* 2.30 *SHL* 31

49. *The Arabian Nights Entertainments.* Selected and Edited by Andrew Lang. New York: Longmans, Green, 1898. xvi, 424 pp. [X/HPL/MS/NUC 19:55]

Contains an inscription: "[To] Howard Phillips Lovecraft / From your Mother *Christmas 1898.*" HPL often noted that this was one of the key volumes that turned his attention to weird fiction in youth. HPL first read the *Arabian Nights* (in a different edition) at the age of five (*SL* 1.122). Perhaps observing his fondness for the work, his mother decided to give him this copy.
CF 1.421; 4.63 *CE* 2.186, 224, 225; 5.145, 208, 288 *SHL* 43 *SL* 1.299; 2.107, 116, 165; 4.162 *MTS* 19, 86 *RK* 153, 165n2 *ES* 299, 378, 681, 778 *MF* 40, 55, 101, 265, 580 *RB* 303, 369, 372 *JVS* 223, 365, 366 *FLB* 37 *CLM* 324 *MWM* 299

50. Arbuthnot, John (1667–1735). *The Miscellaneous Works of Dr. Arbuthnot.* 2nd ed. Glasgow: Printed for James Carlile, 1751. 2 vols. [MS/NUC 19:334]

Political and literary essays by a friend of Alexander Pope. HPL had only Vol. 2.

51. *The Argosy.*
23 January 1932f. *Contains: The Dwellers in the Mirage* by A. Merritt. [HPL]
8 September 1934f. *Contains: Creep, Shadow!* by A. Merritt. [HPL]

HPL notes that his copy of the latter serialisation was in "bound instalments" [HPL]. It was bound for him by Duane W. Rimel and F. Lee Baldwin (*FLB* 122).

Dwellers was given to HPL by August Derleth (*OFF* 24). HPL parodied the title of *The Dwellers in the Mirage* in "The Battle That Ended the Century" (1934) as "The Millers in the Garage." Will Murray believes that the novel is a tribute to HPL, as it features a creature called Khalk'ru who is somewhat reminiscent of Cthulhu. *ES* 460n1, 623n2, 664, 691–92 *OFF* 25, 26, 58n5, 99, 183n6, 219, 251 *RB* 138 *JVS* 94n2, 254, 263, 267 *FLB* 105, 127, 205239, 246, 254, 255, 260, 267, 271, 281 *CLM* 211

52. Arlen, Michael (1895–1936). *Ghost Stories.* London: Collins, [1927]. 181 pp. [HPL/MS/NUC 21:239/Tuck 1:18]

Contents: The Prince of the Jews; The Gentleman from America; To Lamoir; The Ghoul of Golders Green; The Ancient Sin; The Loquacious Lady of Lansdowne Passage; The Smell in the Library.
Cf. *SL* 2.186: "I have also waded through—or skimmed through—Michael Arlen's *Ghost Stories*—which are unbelievably lacking in every possible element of the truly weird." *ES* 112, 119

53. Arnold, Sir Edwin (1832–1904). *The Light of Asia; or, The Great Renunciation (Mahabhinishkramana): Being the Life and Teaching of Gautama, Prince of India and Founder of Buddhism (as Told in Verse by an Indian Buddhist).* New York: H. M. Caldwell Co., 1879. 279 pp. [MS/NUC 22:106]

54. Asbury, Herbert (1891–1963), ed. *Not at Night!* New York: Macy-Masius (The Vanguard Press), 1928. 386 pp. [HPL/MS/NUC 23:217/Ashley 723]

Contents: The Purple Cincture, by H. Thompson Rich; The Horror at Red Hook, by H. P. Lovecraft; A Hand from the Deep, by Romeo Poole; The Tortoise-Shell Cat, by Greye La Spina; The House of Horror, by Seabury Quinn; The Coffin of Lissa, by August Derleth; Swamp Horror, by Will Smith and R. J. Robbins; The Parasitic Hand, by R. Anthony; The Death Crescents of Koti, by Romeo Poole; The Beast, by Paul Benton; His Wife, by Zita I. Ponder; Laocoon, by Bassett Morgan; The Life Serum, by Paul S. Powers; The Girdle, by Joseph McCord; Bat's Belfry, by August Derleth; The Sea-Thing, by Frank Belknap Long; The Horror on the Links, by Seabury Quinn; The Experiment of Erich Weigert, by S. Fowler Wright; The Hooded Death, by Joel Martin Nichols, Jr; The Man Who Was Saved, by B. W. Sliney; The Plant-Thing, by R. G. Macready; Death Waters, by Frank Belknap Long; Monsters of the Pit, by Paul S. Powers; Four Wooden Stakes, by Victor Rowan; The Devil Bed, by Gerald Dean.

All stories from *Weird Tales*. This volume appears to have been suspected of plagiarism from several volumes edited by Christine Campbell Thomson (see items 958f.); facing threatened litigation, it was withdrawn from circulation. *SL* 2.260–61 *ES* 159, 160, 170, 180, 184, 208 *JVS* 302

55. Asquith, Lady Cynthia (1887–1960) [et al.]. *My Grimmest Nightmare*. [Edited by Cecil Madden.] London: George Allen & Unwin, 1935. 210 pp. [HPL/MS/NUC 23:688/Ashley 714]

Contents: The Follower, by Cynthia Asquith; To Be Let Furnished, by Gabrielle Vallings; Thunderbolt, by Miranda Stuart; By Water, by Algernon Blackwood; Not Long for This World, by Inez Holden; Jungle Nights, by R. A. Monson; The Anonymous Gift, by L. Vorley; "There Is One S.O.S.", by S. E. Reynolds; In the Jotunheim Mountains, by J. B. Morton; Dead Man's Room, by Ernest Betts; Incubus, by Marjorie Bowen; Into the Enemy's Camp, by Herbert Jay; The Mask, by Henry de Vere Stacpoole; Behind the Wall, by Noel Streatfield; The Mad Hatter, by Edgar Middleton; Six Months Ago, by James Laver; Rendezvous with Fate, by Cecil Madden; Serenade for Baboons, by Noel Langley; The Surprise Item, by Charles Spencer; Split Second, by Ann Knox; The Blackmailers, by Algernon Blackwood; Room 2000 Calling, by Theodora Benson.

Given to HPL by August Derleth (*ES* 725n1). *OFF* 318 *JVS* 286

56. Astor, John Jacob (1864–1912). *A Journey in Other Worlds: A Romance of the Future*. New York: D. Appleton & Co., 1894. 476 pp. [HPL/MS/NUC 24:485]

A proto–science fiction novel about a spacecraft that travels from Earth to Jupiter and Saturn.

57. Austen, Jane (1775–1817). *Emma*. <1816> Philadelphia: Porter & Coates, [1876]. 450 pp. [MS/NUC 26:433]

58. ———. *Mansfield Park*. <1814> Philadelphia: Porter & Coates, [1887]. 431 pp. [MS/NUC 26:437]

59. ———. *Pride and Prejudice*. <1813> London: George Routledge & Sons, [186-?]–[189-?]. 290 pp. [MS/NUC 26:445]

    No date cited by MS; there are at least 3 Routledge eds. *CE* 2.188 *JVS* 165

60. ———. *Sense and Sensibility*. <1811> London: George Routledge & Sons, [1850]–1874. 286 pp. [1883]–[189-?]. 379 pp. [MS/NUC 26:453]

    No date cited by MS; there are at least 6 Routledge eds.

61. Austin, F[rederick] Britten (1885–1941). *On the Borderland*. Garden City, NY: Doubleday, Page & Co., 1923. 279 pp. [HPL/NUC 26:486]

    Contents: Buried Treasure; A Problem in Reprisals; Secret Service; The Strange Case of Mr. Tormorden; Through the Gate of Horn; The White Dog; A Point of Ethics; The Lovers; Held in Bondage; She Who Came Back; From the Depths; Yellow Magic.

    HPL notes that this volume was given to him by August Derleth in 1930: "... one of the items is that mediocre F. Britten Austin collection which we read five years agone" (*SL* 3.187).

62. Austin, George Lowell (1849–1893). *Henry Wadsworth Longfellow: His Life, His Works, His Friendships*. Boston: Lee & Shepard, 1883. x, 419 pp. [MS/NUC 26:487]

63. Austin, John Osborne (1849–1918). *The Journal of William Jefferay, Gentleman.... A Diary That Might Have Been*. Edited [i.e., written] by John Osborne Austin. [Providence: Press of E. L. Freeman & Sons,] 1899. x, 189 pp. [MS/NUC 26:506]

    Historical fiction. The author presented this copy to HPL's uncle Franklin Chase Clark.

64. ———. *More Seven Club Tales*. [Newport, RI: Press of Newport Daily News, 1900.] 101 pp. [MS/NUC 26:507]

    Tales of strange happenings in Rhode Island. One wonders whether this volume could have had a hand in inspiring HPL's projected novel-idea, *The Club of the Seven Dreamers* (see *RK* 183).

65. ———. *Philip and Philippa: A Genealogical Romance of Today*. [Newport, RI: Newport Daily News], 1901. 183 pp. [MS/NUC 26:507]

66. Avebury, John Lubbock, baron (1834–1913). *Chapters in Popular Natural History*. By John Lubbock, bart. London: National Society's Depositor, [1883] *or* New York: T. Whittaker, 1884. viii, 223 pp. [MS/NUC 27:408]

Lubbock is one of the anthropological authorities mentioned by Akeley in "The Whisperer in Darkness" (*CF* 2.476).

67. Bacon, Dolores [pseud. of Mary Schell Hoke Bacon (1870–1934)]. *Old New England Churches and Their Children*. New York: Doubleday, Page & Co., 1906. xxxiv, 442 pp. [MS/NUC 29:512]

SL 1.356. Inscribed: "H. P. Lovecraft, gent., / Providence, in New-England / 1924."

68. Bacon, Edgar Mayhew (1855–1935). *Narragansett Bay: Its Historic and Romantic Associations and Picturesque Setting*. New York: G. P. Putnam's Sons, 1904. xii, 377 pp. [MS/NUC 29:408]

69. Baird, James S[kerret] S[hore]. *The Classical Manual: An Epitome of Ancient Geography, Greek and Roman Mythology, Antiquities, and Chronology*. <1852> New York: Sheldon & Co, 1877. 200 pp. [MS/NUC 31:144/OCLC]

CLM 304

70. Baker, La Fayette Charles (1826–1868). *History of the United States Secret Service*. Philadelphia: King & Baird, 1868. 704 pp. [MS/NUC 31:392]

71. Baldwin, James (1841–1925). *A Guide to Systematic Readings in . . . the* Encyclopaedia Britannica. Chicago: Werner Co., 1895. 316 pp. [MS/NUC 32:105]

72. Bancroft, George (1800–1891). *History of the United States of America from the Discovery of the Continent*. <1834–74> New York: D. Appleton & Co., 1887. 6 vols. [MS/NUC 33:447]

Extends to 1789.

73. Banks, Louis Albert (1855–1933), ed. *Capital Stories about Famous Americans: A Budget of Tales of Love, Heroism and Adventure on Land and Sea*. New York: Christian Herald, [1905]. 542 pp. [MS/NUC 34:48]

74. Barbey d'Aurevilly, Jules (1808–1889). *The Story without a Name*. Translated by Edgar Saltus (1855–1921). <1891> New York: Brentano's, 1919. 233 pp. [X—MS/NUC 34:629]

Translation of *Une Histoire sans nom* (1882). Given to HPL by George Kirk (HPL to Annie E. P. Gamwell, 10 February 1925).

75. Baring-Gould, S[abine] (1834–1924). *Curious Myths of the Middle Ages.* London: Rivingtons, 1866. [HPL]

Contents: The Wandering Jew; Prestor John; The Divining Rod; The Seven Sleepers of Ephesus; William Tell; The Dog Gellert; Tailed Men; Antichrist and Pope Joan; The Man in the Moon; The Mountain of Venus; S. Patrick's Purgatory; The Terrestrial Paradise; S. George; S. Ursula and the Eleven Thousand Virgins; The Legend of the Cross; Schamir; The Piper of Hameln; Bishop Hatto; Melusina; The Fortunate Isles; Swan-Maidens; The Knight of the Swan; The Sangreal; Theophilus.

No ed. cited by HPL. See *SHL* 30–31: "The shade which appears and demands the burial of its bones, the daemon lover who comes to bear away his still living bride, the death-fiend or psychopomp riding the night-wind, the man-wolf, the sealed chamber, the deathless sorcerer—all these may be found in that curious body of mediaeval lore which the late Mr. Baring-Gould so effectively assembled in book form." HPL himself certainly used the themes of the psychopomp and the deathless sorcerer in his own fiction. See Steven J. Mariconda, "Baring-Gould and the Ghouls," in *H. P. Lovecraft: Art, Artifact, and Reality* (New York: Hippocampus Press, 2013), on the influence of the book on HPL's "The Rats in the Walls." *CE* 2.193

76. Bartlett, John (1820–1905). *Familiar Quotations.* 6th ed. Boston: Little, Brown, 1873. xii, 778 pp. [MS/NUC 37:548]

The 15th ed. (1980) contains a quotation from HPL. *CE* 2.191

77. Bartlett, John Russell (1805–1886). *Dictionary of Americanisms: A Glossary of Words and Phrases Usually Regarded as Peculiar to the United States.* 4th ed. Boston: Little, Brown, 1877. xlviii, 813 pp. [X—JHL/NUC 37:555]

Author's inscribed copy to Dr. Franklin Chase Clark, 17 December 1877.

78. Baudelaire, Charles Pierre (1821–1867). *Baudelaire: His Prose and Poetry.* Ed. T. R. Smith. New York: Boni & Liveright (Modern Library), [1919]. x, 248 pp. [HPL/MS/NUC 39:367]

HPL derived the epigraph to "Hypnos" (1922; *CF* 1.325) from p. 214 of this volume (cf. *CB* 23). The citation is in a section titled "Rockets" (tr. Joseph T. Shipley), including notes discovered among Baudelaire's papers after his death. *SL* 3.78 *ET* 38, 135

79. ———. *Lettres 1841–1866.* Paris: Société de Mercure de France, 1907. 556 pp. [MS/NUC 39:381]

A gift from Adolphe de Castro (HPL to E. Hoffmann Price, 4 May [1935]).

80. Bayne, Samuel G[amble] (1844–1924). *The Pith of Astronomy (without Mathematics): The Latest Facts and Figures as Developed by the Giant Telescopes.* <1896> New York: Harper & Brothers, 1903. xii, 122 pp. [HPL to Duane W. Rimel, 30 October 1934 (*FLB* 231)/NUC 40:663]

81. Beardsley, Aubrey (1872–1898). *The Art of Aubrey Beardsley.* Introduction by Arthur Symons. New York: Boni & Liveright (Modern Library), [1918] *or* New York: Modern Library, [1925]. 35 pp., 63 plates. [MS/NUC 41:368]

    Cf. "The Horror at Red Hook": "Daily life had for him [Thomas Malone] come to be a phantasmagoria of macabre shadow-studies . . . glittering and leering with concealed rottenness as in Beardsley's best manner" (*CF* 1.483). *CF* 4.257

82. Beaumont, Francis (1584–1616), and John Fletcher (1579–1625). *Select Plays.* London: J. M. Dent; New York: E. P. Dutton (Everyman's Library), [1911]. xix, 475 pp. [MS/NUC 41:603]

    Contents: The Knight of the Burning Pestle; The Maid's Tragedy; A King and No King; The Faithful Shepherdess; The Wild Goose Chase; Bonduca; Glossary.
    Note that HPL signed his one-act play *Alfredo* (1918) as by "Francis Beaumont, II., and John Fletcher, Jun." (*AT* 449).

83. Beckford, William (1759–1844). *The Episodes of Vathek.* <1912> Translated from the Original French by Sir Frank T. Marzials. Boston: Small, Maynard & Co., [1922?] or [1924?]. xxiii, 226 pp. [HPL/RHB/NUC 42:479]

    Originally lent to HPL by W. Paul Cook (HPL to Winifred V. Jackson, 7 October 1921); this copy obtained in November 1924. Clark Ashton Smith in 1932 completed Beckford's unfinished "Third Episode of Vathek." *SHL* 43–44 *SL* 1.356 *RK* 209, 213 *OFF* 43, 44, 49, 54 *JFM* 49, 90 *JVS* 323

84. ———. *The History of the Caliph Vathek.* <1786> Printed Verbatim from the First Edition, with the Original Prefaces and Notes by [Samuel] Henley. New York: W. L. Allinson, [1868?] or [188-?]. 199 pp. [HPL/MS/NUC 42:480]

    Given to HPL to Rheinhart Kleiner (*RK* 213). HPL's "novel" *Azathoth* (1922), of which fewer than 500 words were ever written, was to have been "Vathek-like" (*SL* 1.185). Peter Cannon (*FDOC* 153f.) notes that *The Dream-Quest of Unknown Kadath* (1926–27) was surely influenced by *Vathek* in many particulars, not least of which is that HPL's novel "is written continuously like *Vathek* without any subdivisions into chapters" (*ES* 53). HPL also made use of Samuel Henley's notes, as his Arabic title (*Al Azif*) for his mythical book, the *Necronomicon*, is taken from these notes; in "History of the 'Necronomicon'" (1927) HPL defines *Azif* as "being the word used by the Arabs to designate that nocturnal sound (made by insects) supposed to be the howling of daemons" (*CF* 2.405). *CE* 2.225 *CF* 4.63 *SHL* 43–44 *SL* 1.195; 4.162 *RK* 209 *ES* 339 *OFF* 43 *JFM* 90 *RB* 54, 395 *JVS* 319, 329 *CLM* 56, 140, 293, 325 *CAS* 49, 149–50

85. ———. *Vathek*. With an Introduction by Ben Ray Redman. Illustrated by Mahlon Blaine. New York: John Day Co., 1928. xx, 229 pp. [MS/NUC 42:484]

    Given to HPL by William Lumley (*SL* 4.271 [CAS]). Of this copy HPL remarks: "I also have the edition of 'Vathek' illustrated by Blaine—the only trouble with which (if indeed it is a serious trouble) is that it doesn't contain all of Henley's learned notes. For this reason I shall keep my older and unillustrated copy" (HPL to R. H. Barlow, 25 November 1932 [*OFF* 43]).

86. Beerbohm, Max (1872–1956). *The Happy Hypocrite: A Fairy Tale for Tired Men*. New York: John Lane, 1906. 53 pp. [HPL to Richard Ely Morse, 28 July 1932/OCLC]

    No ed. cited by HPL.

87. ———. *A Survey*. New York: Doubleday, Page & Co., 1921. viii pp., 52 plates. [MS/NUC 43:185]

88. Beers, D. G., & Co. *Atlas of the State of Rhode Island and Providence Plantations: From Actual Surveys and Official Records*. Philadelphia: D. G. Beers & Co., 1870. 135 pp. [HPL to Lillian D. Clark, 5 March 1926; *LFF*/NUC 43:196]

    HPL states in his letter to Clark that this book, along with the *Atlas Designed to Illustrate Burritt's* Geography of the Heavens (item 150), were lost during HPL's move from Providence to Brooklyn in 1924.

89. Beeton, Samuel Orchart (1831–1877). *Beeton's Dictionary of Universal Biography*. London: Ward, Lock, & Tyler, 1870. iv, 1116 pp. [MS]

    This may not be the volume in question; MS writes only: "Beeton's Dictionary—London." But Beeton compiled many dictionaries; e.g., of geography, gardening, religion, etc. This catalogue previously conjectured that the book was *Beeton's Dictionary of Universal Information* (London: S. O. Beeton, 1859–61), but this book is in 3 volumes, and presumably MS would have noted that fact.

90. Benson, E[dward] F[rederic] (1867–1940). *Visible and Invisible*. New York: George H. Doran, 1923 or 1924. 298 pp. [HPL/MS/NUC 27:233]

Contents: "And the Dead Spake"; The Outcast; The Horror-Horn; Machaon; *Negotium Perambulans* . . .; At the Farmhouse; Inscrutable Decrees; The Gardener; Mr. Tilly's Séance; Mrs. Amworth; In the Tube; Roderick's Story.

HPL was especially fond of "The Horror-Horn" and *"Negotium Perambulans* . . ."* from this volume. In *SHL* HPL also makes note of "The Face" from *Spook Stories* (1928). *SHL* 76 *ES* 265, 472 *JVS* 119 *CLM* 279

91. ———, and Brander Matthews (1852–1929). *Two Masterly Ghost Stories.* Girard, KS: Haldeman-Julius, 1926. 64 pp. [HPL to August Derleth, 14 April [1932] (*ES* 472–73)/OCLC]

    Contents: The Man Who Went too Far, by E. F. Benson [*SHL* 76]; The Rival Ghosts, by Brander Matthews.

92. Béraud, Henri (1885–1958). *Lazarus.* Translated by Eric Sutton. New York: Macmillan Co., 1925. 187 pp. [HPL/MS/NUC 47:574]

    Concerns a man who suffers an anomalous loss of memory; a clear influence on "The Shadow out of Time" (1934–35). Given to HPL by Frank Belknap Long (*ES* 135). *MTS* 205

93. Besant, Sir Walter (1836–1901). *Gaspard de Coligny (Marquis de Chatillon) Admiral of France; Colonel of French Infantry; Governor of Picardy, Ile de France, Paris, and Havre.* New York: G. P. Putnam's Sons, 1881. 232 pp. [MS/NUC 51:26]

94. ———, and James Rice (1843–1882). *Sir Richard Whittington, Lord Mayor of London.* New York: G. P. Putnam's Sons, 1881. 222 pp. [MS/NUC 51:37]

95. Bible. *The Apocryphal New Testament: Being All the Gospels, Epistles, and Other Pieces Now Extant.* Translated from the Original Tongues, and Now First Collected into One Volume. New York: Worthington & Co., 1890. xvi, 184 pp. [MS/NUC 56:662]

96. ———. *The Holy Bible: Containing the Old and New Testaments.* Translated out of the Original Tongues, and with the Former Translations Diligently Compared and Revised, by His Majesty's Special Command. Edinburgh: M. & C. Kerr, 1795. n.p. [MS/NUC 53:171]

    Also includes the Apocrypha. Gift of H. Warner Munn (see HPL to Lillian D. Clark, 1 July [1928]; *LFF*). *CF* 1.211, 2.278 *SL* 1.299; 3.147, 266

97. ———. *The Bible.* [MS]

    MS gives no further data.

98. Bierce, Ambrose (1842–1914?). *Can Such Things Be?* <1893> New York: Boni & Liveright (Modern Library), 1918. 427 pp. [HPL/RHB/NUC 57:175]

Contents: The Death of Halpin Frayser; The Secret of Macarger's Gulch; One Summer Night; The Moonlit Road; A Diagnosis of Death; Moxon's Master; A Tough Tussle; One of Twins; The Haunted Valley; A Jug of Sirup; Staley Fleming's Hallucination; A Resumed Identity; A Baby Tramp; The Night-Doings at "Deadman's"; Beyond the Wall; A Psychological Shipwreck; The Middle Toe of the Right Foot; John Mortonson's Funeral; The Realm of the Unreal; John Bartine's Watch; The Damned Thing; Haïta the Shepherd; An Inhabitant of Carcosa; The Stranger; [The Ways of Ghosts:] Present at a Hanging; A Cold Greeting; A Wireless Message; An Arrest; [Soldier-Folk:] A Man with Two Lives; Three and One Are One; A Baffled Ambuscade; Two Military Executions; [Some Haunted Houses:] The Isle of Pines; A Fruitless Assignment; A Vine on a House; At Old Man Eckert's; The Spook House; The Other Lodgers; The Thing at Nolan; The Difficulty of Crossing a Field; An Unfinished Race; Charles Ashmore's Trail.

Reissue of Volume III of Bierce's *Collected Works* (1909–12), where the contents differ significantly from the original edition of 1893. This copy obtained in New York in 1922 (HPL to Annie E. P. Gamwell, 9–11 September 1922). HPL first read Bierce in 1919, and one wonders whether the title of the story "Beyond the Wall" influenced HPL's own "Beyond the Wall of Sleep" (1919). Bierce also refers (in "Haïta the Shepherd" and "An Inhabitant of Carcosa") to Hastur and Hali, mentioned by HPL in "The Whisperer in Darkness" (*CF* 2.483); but in Bierce Hali is a person ("Pondering the words of Hali (whom God rest)"), although HPL refers to a "Lake of Hali." In Bierce Hastur is a god of the shepherds, but HPL may in this case, as with that of Hali, be following Robert W. Chambers's interpretation, who regards Hastur as a place (see #183). HPL also once refers to "old Morryster's wild *Marvells of Science*" (*CF* 1.410), taken from Bierce's "The Man and the Snake." *CE* 5.49 *SHL* 65–68 *ES* 77, 80, 113, 123, 129 *JVS* 58 *FLB* 149, 234

99. ———. *In the Midst of Life: Tales of Soldiers and Civilians.* <1891> Introduction by George Sterling. New York: Modern Library, [1927]. 403 pp. [HPL/MS/NUC 57:178]

Contents: A Horseman in the Sky; An Occurrence at Owl Creek Bridge; Chickamauga; A Son of the Gods; One of the Missing; Killed at Resaca; The Affair at Coulter's Notch; The Coup de Grâce; Parker Adderson, Philosopher; An Affair of Outposts; A Story of a Conscience; One Kind of Officer; One Officer, One Man; George Thurston; The Mocking-Bird; The Man out of the Nose; An Adventure at Brownville; The Famous Gilson Bequest; The Applicant; A Watcher by the Dead; The Man and the Snake; A Holy Terror; The Suitable Surroundings; The Boarded Window; A Lady from Red Horse; The Eyes of the Panther.

Reissue of Volume II of Bierce's *Collected Works* (1909–12), where the contents differ significantly from the original edition of 1891. This copy obtained in November 1927 (*ES* 113). *SHL* 65–68 *SL* 5.120 Cf. *CB* 56 *ES* 77, 80, 129 *OFF* 238 *FLB* 149 *MWM* 133

100. ———. *The Monk and the Hangman's Daughter; Fantastic Fables;* [etc.]. <1911> New York: Albert & Charles Boni, 1925. 383 pp. [HPL/RHB/NUC 57:179]

    Contents: The Monk and the Hangman's Daughter [with Adolphe Danziger (de Castro) (1859–1959)]; Fantastic Fables; Fables from *Fun*; Aesopus Emendatus; Old Saws with New Teeth.

    Reissue of Volume VI of Bierce's *Collected Works* (1909–12). Given to HPL by Adolphe de Castro. The novel is a translation by de Castro of Richard Voss's *Der Mönch von Berchtesgarten* (1890), revised for publication (1891) by Bierce. Although HPL was fond of *The Monk*, he ultimately declared that "It is not a weird tale" (*SL* 5.69). See also *SL* 2.204–7 *MTS* 195, 205–6, 207, 209, 215, 216, 217, 222 *AG* 229 *ES* 77, 122, 129, 131, 134, 135, 157 *OFF* 415n11 *JFM* 161 *RB* 175 *FLB* 107, 112, 252, 321 *MWM* 530

101. ———. *Twenty One Letters of Ambrose Bierce.* Edited with a Note by Samuel Loveman. Cleveland: George Kirk, 1922. 33 pp. [MS/NUC 57:181]

    HPL was a close friend of both Samuel Loveman and George Kirk. *SHL* 66 *JFM* 87

102. Bierstadt, Edward Hale (1891–1970). *Dunsany the Dramatist.* New and rev. ed. Boston: Little, Brown, 1919. xxvi, 244 pp. [MS/NUC 57:218]

    First book-length study of Dunsany's plays. *CE* 2.62 *AG* 83

103. Bingham, Caleb (1757–1817), ed. *The Columbian Orator: Containing a Variety of Original and Select Pieces . . . Calculated to Improve Youth and Others in the Ornamental and Useful Art of Eloquence.* 7th Troy Ed. Troy, NY: Parker, 1821. 300 pp. [MS/NUC 58:43]

    OFF 237

104. Birch, A[lbert] G. *The Moon Terror.* And Stories by Anthony M. Rud, Vincent Starrett, and Farnsworth Wright. Indianapolis: Popular Fiction Publishing Co., [1927]. 192 pp. [HPL/MS/NUC 58:283/Tuck 1:46]

    Contents: The Moon Terror, by A. G. Birch; Ooze, by Anthony M. Rud; Penelope, by Vincent Starrett; An Adventure in the Fourth Dimension, by Farnsworth Wright.

    Reprints of stories from *Weird Tales*. Of Starrett's tale HPL declared, when it appeared in *Weird Tales* (May 1923): "'Penelope' is clever—but Holy Pete! If the illustrious Starrett's ignorance of astronomy is an artfully concealed attribute of his character's whimsical narrative, I'll say he's right there with the verisimilitude!" (*H. P. Lovecraft in "The Eyrie,"* 16.) See also *SL* 1.253–54. For a glancing reference to "Ooze" see *H. P. Lovecraft in "The Eyrie,"* 20. "Ooze" may have influenced "The Dunwich Horror." *ES* 119, 123, 155

105. Birkhead, Edith (1889–1951). *The Tale of Terror.* New York: E. P. Dutton, 1921. x, 241 pp. [HPL/MS/NUC 58:452]

HPL derived much of his information on the Gothic novel (for the first five chapters of *SHL*) from this volume. *CE* 5.172 *SHL* 42 *MTS* 2, 3 *ES* 34 *RB* 24 *JVS* 92 *CLM* 30 *MWM* 525

106. Blackwood, Algernon (1869–1951). *Jimbo: A Fantasy.* New York: Macmillan, 1909. viii, 225 pp. [HPL/NUC 59:685]

SHL 89 *ES* 759 *JVS* 269 *FLB* 321

107. ———. *John Silence—Physician Extraordinary.* London: Eveleigh Nash, 1908. 390 pp. [HPL/MS/NUC 59:685]

Contents: A Psychical Invasion; Ancient Sorceries; The Nemesis of Fire; Secret Worship; The Camp of the Dog.

"I find in the 'Incredible Adventures' & 'John Silence' material a serious & sympathetic understanding of the human illusion-weaving process which makes Blackwood rate far higher as a creative artist than many another craftsman of mountainously superior word-mastery & general technical ability" (*SL* 2.211 [Starrett]). *CE* 5.264 *SHL* 88 *MTS* 13 *ES* 29, 41, 57, 101, 139, 182, 187, 188, 206, 244, 246, 280, 664, 759 *OFF* 281 *RB* 130, 418 *JVS* 35 *FLB* 47, 172 *CLM* 276

108. ———. *John Silence—Physician Extraordinary.* New York: E. P. Dutton, [1920] or [1929]. v, 345 pp. [MS/NUC 59:685]

Given to HPL by August Derleth (*ES* 280).

109. ———. *Julius LeVallon: An Episode.* New York: E. P. Dutton, 1916. 354 pp. [HPL/RHB/NUC 59:685]

Obtained in September 1933 (HPL to J. Vernon Shea, 25 September 1933 [JVS 167]]). *ES* 759

110. ———. *The Lost Valley and Other Stories.* London: Eveleigh Nash, 1910. 328 pp. [HPL/RHB/NUC 59:685]

Contents: The Lost Valley; The Wendigo; Old Clothes; Perspective; The Terror of the Twins; The Man from the "Gods"; The Man Who Played upon the Leaf; The Price of Wiggin's Orgy; Carlton's Drive; The Eccentricity of Simon Parnacute.

Given to HPL in 1936 by August Derleth (*ES* 759). HPL read these stories much earlier than 1936, as he cites them in *SHL* (88). "The Wendigo" probably influenced "The Dunwich Horror" (1928), since both make use of an invisible monster whose trail can be followed by the huge footprints it leaves. *ES* 60, 75, 188, 736

111. ———. *Shocks.* <1935> New York: E. P. Dutton, [1936]. 300 pp. [HPL/MS/NUC 59:687]

Contents: The Stranger; Elsewhere and Otherwise; Full Circle; Dr. Feldman; A Threefold Cord; Chemical; Shocks; The Survivors; The Adventure of Tornado Smith; Hands of Death; The Land of Green Ginger; The Colonel's Ring; Revenge; The Man Who Lived Backwards; Adventures of Miss De Fontenay.

Given to HPL by August Derleth (HPL to August Derleth, [24 November 1936]; *ES* 759; cf. 763). HPL cited "Chemical" (first published in Cynthia Asquith's *Ghost Book* [1927]) in the list of works to mention in the revised ed. of *SHL* (cf. *CB* p. 14), but never in fact discussed the tale in *SHL*. Annie E. P. Gamwell told Derleth (13 April 1937; JHL) that HPL had taken this book with him when he entered Jane Brown Memorial Hospital during his terminal illness in March 1937. *OFF* 395

112. Blackwood's Edinburgh Magazine. *Tales from* Blackwood. [Second Series.] Selected by H. Chalmers Roberts. New York: Doubleday, Page & Co., 1903. 6 vols. [MS/NUC 59:697]

113. Blair, Hugh (1718–1800). *Lectures on Rhetoric and Belles Lettres.* <1783> With a Memoir of the Author's Life. To Which Are Added, Copious Questions, and an Analysis of Each Lecture, by Abraham Mills. Philadelphia: J. Kay, Jun., and Brother; Pittsburgh: J. I. Kay & Co., 1829. 557 pp. [MS/NUC 60:96; 699:233]

A landmark work of criticism by a Scottish reverend and professor. "For real, honest training you can't beat Blair's 'Rhetorick' . . . , Alden's 'Reader' (1797), or Parker's 'Aid to Composition' (1845)" (*JVS* 110). It was from Blair's *A Critical Dissertation on the Poems of Ossian* (1763) that HPL derived information on Olaus Wormius (Ole Wurm, 1588–1654), whom he identified as the Latin translator of the *Necronomicon;* but HPL misinterpreted a passage in Blair's book and dated Wormius to the 13th century. *ES* 379

114. Blaisdell, Albert F[ranklin] (1847–1927). *A Practical Physiology: A Text-book for Higher Schools.* Boston: Ginn & Co., 1897. vi, 448 pp. [MS/OCLC]

No ed. cited by MS; but the above is the only edition.

115. Blake, William (1757–1827). *Poems of William Blake.* Edited by William Butler Yeats <1893>. New York: Modern Library, [192-]. 278 pp. [RHB/NUC 60:234]

116. Blakeborough, Richard (1850–1918). *The Hand of Glory and Further Grandfather's Tales and Legends of Highwaymen and Others.* Collected by the Late R.

Blakeborough. Edited by J. Fairfax Blakeborough. London: Grant Richards, [1924]. 268 pp. [HPL/MS/NUC 60:251]

Contents: The Hand of Glory: A Thrilling Legend of Stage-coach Days; The Wrath of Little Smeaton Hall; The Mystery of Anngrove Hall; Abbas: The Cross-roads Spectre; The Highwayman of Leeming Lane; The Wicked Giant of Penhill; The Maid of the Golden Shoon; Elphi the Dwarf and Siba the Good; The Giant's Lapstone; T' Hunt o' Yatton Brig; Auld Nan of Sexhow; The Coach Ghost; Bonny Bona; "Swift Nick" the Highwayman; The Story of Dick Turpin; Pennock's Curse.

117. Bloomfield, Robert (1766–1823). *The Farmer's Boy: A Rural Poem.* <1800> Ornamented with Elegant Wood Engravings by A. Anderson. The 5th American, from the 6th London ed. New York: Printed by Hopkins & Seymour, and Sold by G. F. Hopkins, 1803. xxxii, 128 pp. [Schiff/NUC 61:594]

Obtained in New York in September 1922 (HPL to Lillian D. Clark, 29 September 1922; *LFF*). *SL* 3.317–18 *ES* 391 *JVS* 191

118. Bond, Mary Bligh (1895–?). *Avernus.* Oxford: Basil Blackwell, 1924. 320 pp. [HPL/NUC 65:429]

A novel of the occult, derived from the author's own purportedly psychic experiences regarding "automatic drawing." *CE* 5.154

119. *The Book of Facts.* American ed. 1832. [MS]

Not located.

120. *The Book of History: A History of All Nations from the Earliest Times to the Present, with Over 9,000 Illustrations.* With an Introduction by Viscount Bryce. New York: Grolier Society; London: Educational Book Co., [1915?–21]. 18 vols. [MS/NUC 66:328]

HPL owned only Vols. XII (*Europe in the Nineteenth Century*) and XV (*United States, Canada, Newfoundland, The West Indies*).

121. *The Book of the Dead.* An English Translation of the Chapters, Hymns, etc. of the Theban Recension, with Introduction, Notes, etc., by Sir E[rnest] A[lfred] Wallis Budge (1857–1934). 2nd ed., rev. & enl. London: Kegan Paul, Trench, Trübner & Co.; New York: E. P. Dutton, 1923. 3 vols. in 1. [HPL/MS/NUC 66:359]

Given to HPL by William Lumley (*SL* 5.208). *OFF* 303 *JVS* 166 *FLB* 298

122. Borrow, George (1803–1881). *Lavengro: The Scholar—the Gypsy—the Priest.* 6th Thousand. New-York: G. P. Putnam, 1851. x, 550 pp. [MS/NUC 67:437]

123. Boston Museum of Fine Arts. *Handbook of the Museum of Fine Arts.* Boston: [Metcalf Press,] 1910. viii, 347 pp. [MS/NUC 68:255]

124. Boswell, James (1740–1795). *Journal of a Tour to the Hebrides with Samuel Johnson, LL.D.* <1785> London & New York: J. M. Dent & Co./E. P. Dutton (Everyman's Library), 1910f. [HPL to R. H. Barlow, 30 November 1936 (*OFF* 370)/NUC 68:483f.]
    No ed. cited by HPL; he merely states that he had "the usual edition."

125. ———. *The Life of Samuel Johnson, LL.D.* <1791> London: J. M. Dent; New York: E. P. Dutton (Everyman's Library), December 1910. 2 vols. [X/NUC 68:494]
    Many of the details in HPL's story "A Reminiscence of Dr. Samuel Johnson" (*CF* 1.59–64) were taken from this celebrated biography. *CE* 2.33n19, 188, 193

126. Botta, Anne Charlotte (Lynch) (1815–1891). *The Rhode-Island Book: Selections in Prose and Verse from the Writings of Rhode-Island Citizens.* [Edited] by Anne C. Lynch. Providence: H. Fuller; Boston: Weeks, Jordan & Co., 1841. viii, 352 pp. [MS/NUC 68:620]

127. Brady, Cyrus Townsend (1861–1920). *The True Andrew Jackson.* Philadelphia: J. B. Lippincott, 1906. 504 pp. [MS/NUC 71:635]

128. Brandow, John Henry. *The Story of Old Saratoga: The Burgoyne Campaign; to Which Is Added New York's Share in the Revolution.* <1900> 2nd ed. Albany: Brandow Printing Co., 1919. xxiii, 528 pp. [MS/NUC 72:481]

129. Bregenzer, Don (1888–1931), and Samuel Loveman (1887–1976), ed. *A Round-Table in Poictesme: A Symposium.* Cleveland: Privately Printed by Members of the Colophon Club, 1924. xi, 126 pp. [MS/NUC 74:76]
    Contents: The Author of *The Eagle's Shadow,* by James Branch Cabell; Cabell versus Cabell and Others, by Ernest Boyd; A Practitioner in Perfection, by Don Bregenzer; The Book of Life, by Samuel Loveman; Some Impressions of Cabell's Satire, by Frank L. Minarik; Bülg the Forgotten, by Ben Ray Redman; Some Rogueries of James Branch Cabell, by M. P. Mooney; A Cabellian Comment, by Christopher Morley; A Note on the Poetry of James Branch Cabell, by Edwin Meade Robinson; James Branch Cabell and Wil-

liam Jennings Bryan, by Howard Wolf; The Style of Cabell, by H. L. Mencken; A Letter concerning *Jurgen*, by Burton Rascoe; "From the Hidden Way," by Carr Liggett.
>Essays on James Branch Cabell. HPL owned #299 of 774 numbered copies. *OFF* 23, 130 *JFM* 87

130. Brett, Reginald Baliol (1852–1930). *Footprints of Statesmen during the Eighteenth Century.* London: Macmillan & Co., 1892. 197 pp. [MS/NUC 162:20]

131. *The British Essayists.* With Prefaces, Historical and Biographical, by Alexander Chalmers. <1802–03> Boston: Little, Brown, 1855–57. 38 vols. [MS/NUC 76:358]
>Landmark collection of the 18th-century periodical essayists. HPL had only Vols. 22–24 (*The World*) and 35–37 (*The Looker-On*), both published in 1856. *ES* 380

132. *British Museum Manuscripts: Famous Manuscripts Reproduced by Photo-Engraving and Printed on Bond Paper. First Series.* Grand Rapids, MI: Bookery Press, 1934. [18] pp. [MS/NUC 76:540]

133. Brocklesby, John (1811–1889). *Elements of Meteorology.* <1848> 3d rev. ed. New York: Pratt, Woodford & Co., 1849. 240 pp. [MS/NUC 77:239]

134. Brontë, Charlotte (1816–1855). *Jane Eyre.* <1847> New York: Harper & Brothers, 1848–1902. 483 pp. [MS/NUC 77:582f]
>MS gives no date; there are at least 12 Harper eds. *CE* 2.188

135. [Brougham and Vaux, Henry Brougham, baron (1778–1868).] *Albert Lunel; or, The Château of Languedoc.* London: Charles Knight, 1844. 3 vols. [MS/NUC 78:426]
>A novel.

136. Browning, Robert (1812–1889). *Selections from the Poetical Works of Robert Browning.* Chicago: Donohue, Henneberry, [189-]. 373 pp. [MS/NUC 80:8]
>*SHL* 27, 79

137. Brucker, Johann Jakob (1696–1770). *Historia Critica Philosophiae a Mvndi Incvnabvlis ad Nostram vsqve Aetatem Dedvcta.* 2nd ed. Lipsiae [i.e., Leipzig]: Weidemanni et Reichii, 1766–77. 6 vols. [MS/NUC 80:202]
>HPL had only Vol. 4, parts 1 and 2. Given to HPL in November 1925 by Samuel Loveman (HPL to Clark Ashton Smith, 4 November 1925 [*DS* 86]).

138. Bryant, William Cullen (1794–1878). *Poems.* Collected and Arranged by the Author. New York: D. Appleton & Co., 1855. 2 vols. [MS/NUC 81:413]

HPL had only Vol. 2.

139. ———. *Thanatopsis, Sella, and Other Poems.* Edited and with an Introduction by J. H. Castleman. New York: Macmillan, 1906. xxv, 238 pp. [MS/NUC 81:423]

140. Bryce, James, Viscount (1838–1922). *The American Commonwealth.* 2d rev. ed. London: Macmillan Co., 1889. 2 vols. [MS/NUC 81:443]

141. Buchan, John (1875–1940). *The Runagates Club.* Boston: Houghton Mifflin, 1928. viii, 306 pp. [HPL/MS/NUC 81:603]

Contents: The Green Wildebeest; The Frying-Pan and the Fire; Dr. Lartius; The Wind in the Portico; "Divus" Johnson; The Loathly Opposite; Sing a Song of Sixpence; Ship to Tarshish; Skule Skerry; "Tendebant Manus"; The Last Crusade; Full Circle.

Given to HPL by August Derleth (*SL* 3.187). Aside from the three stories—"Skule Skerry," "The Wind in the Portico," and "The Green Wildebeest"—mentioned in the revised ed. of *SHL* (75), HPL also quotes the epigraph to "Sing a Song of Sixpence" in *CB* 222. *CE* 5.234 *MTS* 229 *ES* 152, 159, 160, 179 *JVS* 120

142. Bulfinch, Thomas (1796–1867). *The Age of Fable; or, Beauties of Mythology.* <1855> Edited by J[ohn] Loughran Scott (1846–1919). Rev. ed. Philadelphia: David McKay, [1898]. xxiii, 501 pp. [HPL/MS/NUC 83:503]

One of the volumes that awakened HPL's early interest in classical antiquity. *CE* 2.186, 193; 3.11; 5.145, 272n1, 288 *SL* 1.300 *RK* 69 *ES* 378 7 *MWM* 45

143. Bullen, John Ravenor (1886–1927). *White Fire.* Athol, MA: The Recluse Press, 1927. 86 pp. [X—JHL/NUC 83:660]

Contains a "Preface" by HPL (pp. 7–13; *CE* 2.135–40), who edited the volume. The book, a posthumous collection of poems by a British amateur journalist, was dedicated to HPL. HPL's copy bears an inscription by W. Paul Cook, the publisher: "This is one of 25 specially bound copies. See Orton, *Private Presses,* etc." A second edition (1929) was printed but never bound (cf. HPL to Lillian D. Clark, 26 April 1929; *LFF*). *CE* 2.9, 222 *SL* 2.243 *MTS* 139 *OFF* 228 *ES* 103n2, 122, 123 *JFM* 144n1, 164 *FLB* 19n1

144. Bulwer-Lytton, Edward (1803–1873). *The Coming Race; or, The New Utopia.* Edinburgh: William Blackwood, 1871. 292 pp. [HPL/OCLC]

No ed. cited by HPL. Acquired summer 1933; cf. HPL to Carl F. Strauch, 8 July 1933 (*JVS* 349).

145. ———. *A Strange Story; The Haunted House* [*sic*]*; Zanoni*. <1862; 1859; 1842> Boston: Desmond Publishing Co., [18—?]. 418, 25, 354 pp. [HPL/NUC 347:694]

The second work in the volume is the story "The Haunted and the Haunters; or, The House and the Brain." Acquired in May 1925. *CE* 2.226 *SHL* 47–48 *SL* 2.7–8 *MTS* 207, 209, 211, 213

146. Bunyan, John (1628–1688). *The Pilgrim's Progress from This World to That Which Is to Come: Delivered under the Similitude of a Dream*. <1678> With Copious Notes, &c., by the Rev. J[ohn] Newton (1725–1807), Dr. [Robert] Hawker (1753–1827), and Others. Boston: Published by Isaiah Thomas, Jun., E. Merriam & Co., Printers, 1817. 300 pp. [MS/NUC 84:312]
CF 1.211 *CE* 2.187 *JVS* 166

147. Burnett, Frances Hodgson (1849–1924). *Little Lord Fauntleroy*. <1885–86> New York: Charles Scribner's Sons, 1895. ix, 290 pp. [MS/NUC 85:681]

148. Burney, Frances (1752–1840). *Evelina; or, The History of a Young Lady's Entrance Into the World*. <1778> By Fanny Burney. With an Introduction and Notes by Annie Raine Ellis. London: George Bell & Sons, 1907. lxiii, 427 pp. [MS/NUC 19:301]

149. Burns, Robert (1759–1796). *The Poetical Works of Robert Burns*. New York: Houghton Mifflin, 1882–98. 3 vols. in 1. [MS/NUC 86:159–62]

No date cited by MS. *SHL* 33

150. Burritt, Elijah Hinsdale (1794–1838). *Atlas Designed to Illustrated Burritt's Geography of the Heavens*. A New Edition, Revised and Corrected by Hiram Mattison. New York: Mason Brothers, 1856. 10 plates. [MS/NUC 86:307/OCLC]

In a letter to Lillian D. Clark (see item 87), HPL states that he lost his copy of the book when moving from Providence to Brooklyn in 1924. He must have obtained another copy later.

151. ———. *The Geography of the Heavens, and Classbook of Astronomy: Accompanied by a Celestial Atlas*. A New Edition, Revised and Illustrated by Hiram Mattison. New York: F. J. Huntington, 1853. 324 pp. [MS/NUC 86:309]

HPL's maternal grandmother Robie Alzada Place's "copy of Burritt's *Geography of the Heavens* is today the most prized volume in my library" *CE* 3.89, 132 *SL* 2.39 *FLB* 157 *MWM* 45

152. Burton, Warren (1800–1866). *The District School as It Was*. By One Who Went to It. Edited by Clifton Johnson. Boston: Lee & Shepard, 1897. xii, 171 pp. [MS/NUC 86:550]

    Given to Whipple Phillips by Annie E. Phillips Gamwell on Christmas 1897 and subsequently given to HPL (HPL to Lillian D. Clark, 16 February 1925; *LFF*).

153. Bush, David Van (1882–1959). *Grit and Gumption*. [St. Louis: David Van Bush, 1921.] 128 pp. [NUC 87:31]

154. ———. *Inspirational Poems*. St. Louis: Hicks Almanac & Publishing Co., [1921]. 208 pp. [NUC 87/31]

155. ———. *Poems of Mastery and Love Verse*. [St. Louis: David Van Bush, 1922.] 206 pp. [NUC 87:31]

    See HPL to James F. Morton, 22 April 1923 (*JFM* 37): "Bush has just shot me three of his new books of pomes, containing work by you & me." The above three books are probably the items in question.

156. Busson, Paul (1873–1924). *The Man Who Was Born Again*. Translated by Prince Mirski and Thomas Moult. New York: John Day Co., 1927. 343 pp. [HPL/MS/NUC 87:211]

    Given to HPL by August Derleth (*ES* 256, 280). A translation of *Die Wiedergeburt des Melchior Dronte* (1921). An historical Gothic novel set in 18th-century Austria, Germany, and France. *ES* 195

157. Butler, Joseph (1692–1752). *The Analogy of Religion, Natural and Revealed, to the Constitution and Course of Nature*. <1736> To Which Is Prefixed a Life of the Author by Dr. Kippis; with a Preface, Giving Some Account of His Character and Writings, by Samuel Halifax. New-Haven: A. H. Maltby, 1822. xli, 299 pp. [MS/NUC 87:392]

    A celebrated theological work that seeks to defend traditional Christianity against the attacks of contemporary Deists.

158. Butler, Samuel (1613–1680). *Hudibras*. <1663–78> With Notes and a Literary Memoir by the Rev. T. R. Nash. New-York: D. Appleton & Co., 1864. 598 pp. [MS/NUC 87:458]

    HPL comments on this celebrated satirical poem in "The Allowable Rhyme" (1915; *CE* 2.14). *CE* 1.193; 2.187

159. Byrd, Mary Emma (1849–1934). *A Laboratory Manual in Astronomy*. Boston: Ginn & Co., 1899. ix, 273 pp. [MS/NUC 88:115]

160. Cabell, James Branch (1879–1958). *The Line of Love: Dizain des Mariages*. <1905> With an Introduction by H. L. Mencken. New York: Robert M. McBride & Co., 1921. xv, 261 pp.

    Given to HPL by George Kirk (HPL to Annie E. P. Gamwell, 10 February 1925). *ES* 109

161. Caesar, C[aius] Julius (102–44 B.C.E.). *Commentaries on the Civil War*. Literally Translated with Explanatory Notes. New York: Hinds & Noble, [189-]. 138 pp. [MS/NUC 705:150]

162. ———. *Caesar's Commentaries*. With an Analytical and Interlinear Translation . . . by James Hamilton . . . [and] Thomas Clark. Philadelphia: David McKay, [19—]. 435 pp. [MS/NUC 89:14]
    CE 2.186

163. ———. *Commentaries of Caesar on the Gallic War*. The Original Text Reduced to the Natural English Order with a Literal Interlinear Translation. New York: Hinds & Co., [1893?]. 312 pp. [MS/NUC 89:55]

164. Calvert, George H[enry] (1803–1889). *The Gentleman*. <1863> 3rd ed. Boston: Ticknor & Fields, 1863. 159 pp. [MS/NUC 91:230]
    On self-conduct.

165. Campbell, Thomas (1777–1844). *The Complete Poetical Works of Thomas Campbell*. New York: J. W. Lovell Co., [1885]. 386 pp. [MS/NUC 92:303]

166. Canby, Henry Seidel (1878–1961), Frederick Erastus Pierce, and Willard Higley Durham. *Facts, Thought, and Imagination: A Book on Writing*. New York: Macmillan Co., 1917. xi, 318 pp. [MS/NUC 93:565]
    It is interesting that this book was published in the year HPL recommended writing fiction after a nine-year hiatus. See also #320.

167. Carleton, Will (1845–1912). *Farm Ballads*. New York: Harper & Brothers, 1882. 159 pp. [MS/NUC 95:420]

168. Carlyle, Thomas (1795–1881). *The French Revolution: A History*. <1837> New York: A. L. Burt, [190-?] or [1916?]. 2 vols. in 1. [MS/NUC 95:588–89]
    CE 2.188

169. ———. *Sartor Resartus.* <1833–34> [MS]
No ed. cited by MS. *CE* 2.188 *JVS* 365

170. Carrel, Alexis (1873–1944). *Man, the Unknown.* New York: Harper & Brothers, 1935. xv, 346 pp. [MS/NUC 96:517]
On human psychology. *CLM* 194

171. Carroll, Ellen M. *Lonely Shores.* Atlanta: Bonner Press, Emory University, 1934. 66 pp. [NUC 96:676]
A book of poems. Gift of Elizabeth Toldridge (*ET* 282n2; cf. 285, 289).

172. Carroll, Lewis [pseud. of Charles Lutwidge Dodgson (1832–1898)]. *Alice's Adventures in Wonderland, and Through the Looking-Glass.* <1865/1871> With Ninety-two Illustrations by John Tenniel. New York: A. L. Burt, [19—]. viii, 346 pp. [NUC 145:566]
CF 4.306 *ES* 2.188 *ES* 66 *ET* 234, 240 *CLM* 96

173. *Cassell's Latin Dictionary (Latin-English and English-Latin).* Revised by J. R. V. Marchant and Joseph F. Charles. London: Cassell & Co.; New York: A. L. Burt, [191-]. xiv, 927 pp. [X—JHL/MS/NUC 98:138]

174. *The Century.*
94, No. 6 (October 1917). *Contains:* "The Coming of the Terror" by Arthur Machen, pp. 801–25. [HPL]
An abridged version of the novel *The Terror.* Machen remarked that the anonymous editor had done a skilful job in the abridgment. HPL also read the complete version (*SHL* 87).

175. Chalmers, Alexander (1759–1834), ed. *The Works of the English Poets from Chaucer to Cowper.* Including the Series Edited with Prefaces, Biographical and Critical, by Dr. Samuel Johnson. . . . The Additional Lives by Alexander Chalmers. London: J. Johnson, 1810. 21 vols. [MS/NUC 102:365]
An updating of Johnson's *Lives of the English Poets* (1779–81; #516). HPL had only Vol. 13 (poems of Isaac Watts, Ambrose Philips, Gilbert West, William Collins, John Dyer, William Shenstone, and Edward Young).

176. Chamberlain, Arthur Bensley. *Thomas Gainsborough.* London: Duckworth; New York: E. P. Dutton, [1903]. xii, 228 pp. [MS/NUC 102:497]

177. Chambers, George F[rederick] (1841–1915). *The Story of Eclipses.* New York: D. Appleton & Co., 1912. 208 pp. [MS/NUC 102:612]

178. ———. *The Story of the Solar System.* New York: McClure, Phillips & Co., 1904. 188 pp. [MS/NUC 102:612]

179. ———. *The Story of the Stars, Simply Told for General Readers.* New York: D. Appleton & Co., 1895. 156 pp. [MS/NUC 102:612]

180. ———. *The Story of the Weather, Simply Told for General Readers.* London: George Newnes, 1897. 232 pp. [MS/NUC 102:613]
No ed. cited by MS.

181. Chambers, Robert (1802–1871). *Vestiges of the Natural History of Creation.* <1844> From the 3d London ed., Greatly Amended by the Author. New York: Wiley & Putnam, 1845. xxviii, 280 pp. *or* vi, 353 pp. [MS/NUC 102:640]

HPL owned two copies. There are two Wiley & Putnam eds. (the 2d and the 3rd) in 1845. A celebrated work of natural philosophy that presents an early but crude and outmoded theory of evolution.

182. Chambers, Robert (1802–1871), ed. *Cyclopaedia of English Literature: A Selection of the Choicest Productions of English Authors, from the Earliest to the Present Time, Connected by a Critical and Biographical History.* <1843> 14th thousand. Boston: Gould & Lincoln, 1853. 2 vols. [MS/NUC 102:632]
CE 2.202

183. Chambers, Robert W[illiam] (1865–1933). *In Search of the Unknown.* New York: Harper & Brothers, 1904. 285 pp. [HPL/RHB/NUC 102:645]

Given to HPL by August Derleth (*SL* 3.187). The first five chapters of this episodic novel make up the story "The Harbor-Master" (1897), much appreciated by HPL and possibly an influence on "The Shadow over Innsmouth" (1931). *SHL* 70 *SL* 2.252 *MTS* 98, 109 *ES* 88, 129, 222, 256, 280

184. ———. *The King in Yellow.* New York: F. Tennyson Neely, 1895. [HPL]

Contents: The Repairer of Reputations; The Mask; In the Court of the Dragon; The Yellow Sign; The Demoiselle D'Ys; The Prophet's Paradise; The Street of the Four Winds; The Street of the First Shell; The Street of Our Lady of the Fields; Rue Barrée.

Only the first five stories are fantastic; "The Prophet's Paradise" is a series of prose-poems and the remaining tales deal with the Franco-Prussian War. In several stories Chambers adapts some names (e.g., Hastur, Hali, Carcosa) from Ambrose Bierce (see #87), but has somewhat altered their connotation; HPL's use of these terms seems to follow Chambers more than Bierce. HPL listed "The Yellow Sign" among his ten favourite weird tales. No ed. cited by HPL.

This copy given to HPL by H. Warner Munn (HPL to Lillian D. Clark, 25 June 1928; *LFF*), but in 1927 HPL had read a copy lent to him by W. Paul Cook.

SHL 69–70 *CF* 2.408 *SL* 2.252; 3.226; 5.[120], 348 *MTS* 79, 92–93, 98, 102, 109–10, 111, 131 *ES* 87, 88, 123, 129, 220, 222, 776, 779 *JVS* 297 *FLB* 286 *CLM* 209, 349 *CAS* 145

185. *Chambers's Encyclopædia: A Dictionary of Universal Knowledge*. London: W. & R. Chambers, 1860–68. 10 vols. Philadelphia: J. B. Lippincott Co., 1860–69. [Rev eds. up to 1935.] [HPL to R. H. Barlow, 23 July 1936 (*OFF* 356)/NUC 102:671f.]

Gift of Alice Sheppard (HPL's downstairs neighbour at 66 College Street). See also #505 and #569. *CE* 2.191, 202

186. Chase, Thomas (1827–1892). *Hellas: Her Monuments and Scenery*. Cambridge, MA: Sever & Francis, 1863. vi, 220 pp. [MS/NUC 104:397]

187. Chatterton, Thomas (1752–1770). *The Poetical Works of Thomas Chatterton*. With a Memoir. Boston: Houghton Mifflin, [1855]. 2 vols. in 1. [MS/NUC 104:583]

188. Chaucer, Geoffrey (1343?–1400). *The Prologue, The Knight's Tale, The Nonne Prestes Tale, from the Canterbury Tales*. A Revised Text Edited by Rev. Richard Morris. Oxford: Clarendon Press, 1882. lv, 221 pp. [MS/NUC 104:620]

CE 2.186

189. Chesnutt, Charles W[addell] (1858–1932). *The Conjure Woman*. Boston: Houghton Mifflin, 1900. 229 pp. [MS/NUC 105:575]

Fiction about African Americans by an important early African-American novelist.

190. Chesterfield, Philip Dormer Stanhope, earl of (1694–1773). *The Works of Lord Chesterfield, Including His Letters to His Son, &c.* <1774> 1st Complete American Ed. New York: Harper & Brothers, 1860. lxxviii, 647 pp. [X—JHL/MS/NUC 105:620]

Gift of James Ferdinand Morton; signed by HPL, 23 July 1931. *CF* 1.45

191. Church, Alfred J[ohn] (1829–1912). *Stories from Livy*. With Illustrations from Designs by [Bartolommeo] Pinelli. New York: Dodd, Mead, 1883. vi, 277 pp. [MS/NUC 108:685]

192. Cicero, M[arcus] Tullius (106–43 B.C.E.). *Select Orations*. The Four Orations against Catiline, with an Interlinear Translation on the Hamiltonian System, by William Underwood. The Seven Remaining Orations, with an

Interlinear Translation on the System of Locke, by Thomas Clark. Philadelphia: C. DeSilver, 1861 or 1870; *or* Philadelphia: David McKay, [1915?]. 508 pp. [MS/NUC 710:443]

No publisher or date cited by MS; probably HPL had one of the DeSilver eds. *RK* 68

193. Clarke, James Freeman (1810–1888). *How to Find the Stars: With Indications of the Most Interesting Objects in the Starry Heavens, and an Account of the Astronomical Lantern and Its Use.* <1878> Boston: D. C. Heath & Co., 1907. 47 pp. [MS/NUC 111:281/OCLC]

194. Clarke, Mary Cowden (1809–1898). *The Complete Concordance to Shakspere.* Boston: C. C. Little & J. Brown, [184-]. vii, 860 pp. [MS/NUC 111:331]

195. Cleveland, Charles Dexter (1802–1869), ed. *A Compendium of English Literature, Chronologically Arranged from Sir John Mandeville to William Cowper.* Philadelphia: E. C. & J. Biddle, 1848. 776 pp. [MS/NUC 112:411]

196. ———, ed. *English Literature of the Nineteenth Century.* Philadelphia: E. C. & J. Biddle; Boston: Philips, Samson & Co., 1853. 785 pp. [MS/NUC 112:413]

197. Clifford, Lucy (Lane) (1846–1929). *Miss Fingal.* By Mrs. W. K. Clifford. London: Blackwood, 1919 *or* New York: Charles Scribner's Sons, 1919. 312 pp. [MS/NUC 112:561]

A sentimental novel that hints of the transmigration of souls.

198. Cline, Leonard (1893–1929). *The Dark Chamber.* New York: Viking, 1927. 282 pp. [HPL/RHB/NUC 112:606]

A powerful weird novel about hereditary memory. Given to HPL c. February 1931 by Henry S. Whitehead (*ES* 322). August Derleth's "posthumous collaboration," "The Ancestor," is an unwitting plagiarism of this novel; see Schultz, *CB* 67. *CE* 2.167; 5.234 *SHL* 71 *MTS* 205, 214 *ES* 135, 136, 137, 138, 141, 148

199. Clodd, Edward (1840–1930). *The Story of "Primitive" Man.* New York: D. Appleton & Co., 1895. 190 pp. [MS/NUC 112:667]

200. Coates, Walter John (1880–1941). *Diapason: Nuances in Verse.* North Montpelier, VT: Driftwind Press, January 1937. 44 pp. [X—JHL/NUC 113:241]

Author's presentation copy to HPL, dated 20 January 1937. Coates was the editor of *Driftwind* (see #202) and publisher of the Driftwind Press.

201. ———. *Hubbardton Battle: A Ballad. Written for the Vermont Sesqui-Centennial Commission and Read at the 150th Anniversary Celebration at Hubbardton July seventh, 1927*. [North Montpelier, VT: Driftwind Press,] 1927. [17 pp.] [X—Univ. of Wisconsin at Madison/OCLC]

Author's presentation copy to HPL, dated 7 September 1927.

202. ———. *Sonnets of an Editor*. North Montpelier, VT: Driftwind Press, December 1934. 45 pp. [X—JHL/NUC 113:241]

Author's presentation copy to HPL, dated 19 December 1934.

203. ———, ed. *Harvest: A Sheaf of Poems from* Driftwind. North Montpelier, VT: Driftwind Press, May 1933. 57 pp. [X—JHL/NUC 113:241]

Contains: HPL's "The Canal," p. 33, and a biographical note on HPL, p. 55. *ET* 245

204. Colange, L[eo de] (1819–?), ed. *Twentieth Century Encyclopedia: A Summary of Universal Knowledge, with Pronunciation of Every Subject Title. For Teachers, Pupils and Families. 1000 Illustrations*. New York: Twentieth Century Encyclopedia Co., 1902. 991 pp. [X/Not in NUC or OCLC]

205. Coleridge, Samuel Taylor (1772–1834) [et al.]. *The Poetical Works of Coleridge, Shelley, and Keats. Complete in One Volume*. Philadelphia: Crissy & Markley, 1849. 607 pp. [MS/NUC 115:101]

HPL reports reading Coleridge's *Ancient Mariner* with Doré's illustrations at the age of six (HPL to J. Vernon Shea, 25 September 1933 [*JVS* 199–200]). *SHL* 33

206. Collar, William C[oe] (1833–1916). *Practical Latin Composition*. Boston: Ginn & Co., 1889. ix, 268 pp. [X/NUC 115:236]

207. ———, and Clarence W. Gleason (1866–1942). *Via Latina: An Easy Latin Reader*. Boston: Ginn & Co., 1897. vi, 203 pp. [X/NUC 115:236]

208. Collins, Arthur (1682?–1760). *The Peerage of England: Containing a Genealogical and Historical Account of All the Peers of That Kingdom*. <1735> 5th ed. London: Printed for W. Strahan, J. F. & C. Rivington, [et al.], 1779–84. 9 vols. [MS/NUC 115:615]

HPL had vols. 3, 5, and 7.

209. Collins, William Lucas (1817–1887). *Thucydides*. New York: J. B. Alden, 1883. 156 pp. [MS/NUC 116:38]

210. Collins, William (1789–1853), Sons &. Co. *Collins' Illustrated Guide to London and Neighbourhood*. London: William Collins, Sons & Co., 1880. 200 pp. [MS/NUC 116:28]

211. *The Colonnade*. Volume XIV: 1919–22. New York, 1922. 555 pp.
    Part I: Contributions to scholarship and belles-lettres.
    Part II: The Poetical Works of John Trumbull, reprinted from the original edition of 1820. [MS/NUC 116:435]

    Obtained in February 1925 (HPL to Lillian D. Clark, 16 February 1925; *LFF*). Trumbull (1750–1831) was an early American satirical poet. *ES* 380

212. Comstock, George Cary (1855–1934). *A Text-Book of Astronomy*. New York: D. Appleton & Co, 1903. viii, 391 pp. [MS/NUC 118:315]

213. Conder, Claude Reignier (1848–1910). *Judas Maccabaeus and the Jewish War of Independence*. New York: G. P. Putnam's Sons, 1881. 218 pp. [MS/NUC 118:498/OCLC]

214. Cornell, Sarah S. *Cornell's High School Geography*. New York: D. Appleton & Co., [1863?]. 405 pp. [MS/NUC 123:132]

215. Corte, Matteo della (1875–1962). *Pompeii: The New Excavations (Houses and Inhabitants)*. Valle de Pompeii: Tip. di F. Sicignano, 1927. 102 pp. [MS/NUC 123:622]

216. Corvo, Frederick, Baron [pseud. of Frederick William Rolfe (1860–1913)]. *Hadrian the Seventh*. <1904> New York: Alfred A. Knopf, 1925. 350 pp. [MS/NUC 501:697]

    A novel about an Englishman who becomes Pope Hadrian VII.

217. Cowan, Frank (1844–1905). *Revi-Lona: A Romance of Love in a Marvellous Land*. [Greensburg, PA: Tribune Press Publishing Co., 188-?]. 247 pp. [HPL/MS/NUC 125:418]

    Given to HPL by Samuel Loveman (HPL to Lillian D. Clark, 29 April 1928; *LFF*).

218. Cowper, William (1731–1800). *New Poems*. London: Oxford University Press, 1931. iii, 17 pp. [RHB/NUC 125:565]

219. ———, and James Thomson (1700–1748). *The Works of Cowper and Thomson*. Philadelphia: J. Grigg, 1831. x, 404, xxxvi, 133 pp. [MS/NUC 125:580]

220. Crabb, George (1778–1851). *Crabb's English Synonyms*. <1816> Revised and enlarged ... by John H. Finlay. New York: Harper & Brothers, 1917. 769 pp. [NUC 126:90/MS]

    CE 2.191, 202

221. Crabbe, George (1754–1832). *George Crabbe's Poetical Works; Preface to the Tales*. Life by A. C. Cunningham. Boston: Crosby, Nichols, Lee, 1860. xvi, 523 pp. [MS/NUC 126:97]

222. Creasy, Sir Edward Shepherd (1812–1878). *The Fifteen Decisive Battles of the World, from Marathon to Waterloo*. New York: Harper & Brothers, 1908. xviii, 518 pp. [MS/NUC 126:668]

    Contents: Marathon, 490 B.C.; Syracuse, 413 B.C.; Arbela, 331 B.C.; Metaurus, 207 B.C.; Arminius, A.D. 9; Chalons, 451; Tours, 732; Hastings, 1066; Orleans, 1429; The Spanish Armada, 1588; Blenheim, 1704; Pultowa, 1709; Saratoga, 1777; Valing, 1792; Waterloo, 1815.

    CE 4.152, 165

223. *Creeps: A Collection of Uneasy Tales*. [Edited by Charles Lloyd Birkin (1907–1985).] London: Philip Allan, 1932. 248 pp. [MS/Ashley 706]

    Contents: Silent, White and Beautiful, by Tod Robbins; The Red Lodge, by H. Russell Wakefield; The Ghost Tale, by Elliott O'Donnell; Spurs, by Tod Robbins; "He Cometh and He Passeth By," by H. Russell Wakefield; The Charnel House, by Philip Murray; A Wager and a Ghost, by Elliott O'Donnell; The Last Night, by Charles Lloyd [pseud. of Charles Lloyd Birkin]; Cockcrow Inn, by Tod Robbins.

    RB 315

224. Creighton, M[andell] (1843–1901). *History of Rome*. <1875> New York: American Book Co., [19—]. 127 pp. [MS/NUC 127:44]

225. Cumberland, Richard (1732–1811). *Memoirs of Richard Cumberland*. <1806> Illustrative Notes by Henry Flanders. Philadelphia: Parry & McMillan, 1856. viii, 397 pp. [MS/NUC 129:257]

226. [Cunningham, Peter (1816–1869).] *Modern London; or, London as It Is*. London: John Murray, 1851. lxiv, 327 pp. [MS/NUC 129:479]

Darwin, Erasmus   53

227. Curtis, George William (1824–1892). *Prue and I and The Public Duty of Educated Men.* <1856/1878> Edited by Vincent B. Brecht. New York: Macmillan Co., 1919. xxiv, 224 pp. [MS/NUC 130:80]
The first work is fiction, the second nonfiction.

228. *Cyclopaedia of Arts and Sciences.* By a Society of Gentlemen. London: W. Owen, 1764. [MS]
Not located; HPL owned Vols. 1, 2, and 4. *ES* 379

229. Dalton, John Call (1825–1889). *A Treatise on Physiology and Hygiene.* New York: Harper & Brothers; London: Sampson Low, Son & Marston, 1869. 399 pp. [MS/NUC 131:665]

230. Dampier, Captain William (1652–1715).
MS lists title as *The Travels of Captain William Dampier* and cites no ed., but there is no such title. There is a volume called *The Voyages and Adventures of Capt. William Dampier* (London, 1776), and another, *The Voyages and Discoveries of Captain William Dampier* (Glasgow, 1801).

231. Dana, James D[wight] (1813–1895). *A Text-Book of Geology.* <1863> 2nd ed. New York: Ivison, Blakeman, Taylor & Co., [1874]. vii, 358 pp. [MS/NUC 132:190]

232. Dante Alighieri (1265–1321). *Dante's Inferno.* Translated by the Rev. Henry Francis Cary <1805–06> ... and Illustrated with the Designs of M. Gustave Doré. New York: P. F. Collier, 1892. xxiv, 183 pp. [MS/NUC 132:686]

233. ———. *The Vision; or, Hell, Purgatory and Paradise.* Translated by the Rev. H. F. Cary. Boston: Thomas Y. Crowell Co., 1881. x, 452 pp. [MS/NUC 132:661]
CF 2.518; 4.23, 25 *CE* 2.186

234. Dark, Sidney (1874–1947). *London.* London: Macmillan & Co., 1924. xi, 176 pp. [MS/NUC 133:212]

235. ———. *London Town.* New York: Farrar & Rinehart, [1934]. 303 pp. [MS/NUC 133:213]

236. Darwin, Erasmus (1731–1802). *Beauties of The Botanic Garden.* New York: D. Longworth, 1805. 216 pp. [MS/NUC 133:429]
RK 69 *ES* 380 *MWM* 45. *The Botanic Garden* (1791) is a lengthy poetical work that attempted to popularise the study of botany by anthromorphising plant

life. Darwin presented a rudimentary version of evolution that his grandson, Charles Darwin, developed with greater scientific rigour.

237. Davis, Owen (1874-1956). *Icebound: A Play.* Boston: Little, Brown, 1923. 116 pp. [HPL to Lillian D. Clark (30 March 1924); LFF/OCLC]
HPL describes this work as "the celebrated new play of New England life."

238. Davis, Mrs. Sarah Matilda Henry. *The Life and Times of Sir Philip Sidney.* 3rd ed. Boston: Ticknor & Fields, 1859. 281 pp. [MS/NUC 135:106]

239. Davis, William Morris (1850–1934). *Elemental Physical Geography.* Boston: Ginn & Co., 1902. xviii, 401 pp. [MS/NUC 135:138]

240. Davis, William Stearns (1877–1930). *A Friend of Caesar: A Tale of the Fall of the Roman Republic, 50–47 B.C.* New York: Macmillan Co., 1900. xii, 501 pp. [MS/NUC 135:147]
CE 2.186 *ES* 98 *ET* 41 *CLM* 305

241. Defoe, Daniel (1660–1731). *History of the Plague in London.* <1722> New York: American Book Co., [1894]. 253 pp. [MS/NUC 136:559]
Originally published as *A Journal of the Plague Year.*

242. ———. *The Life and Surprising Adventures of Robinson Crusoe, of York, Mariner, as Related by Himself.* <1719> With One Hundred and Twenty Original Illustrations by Walter Paget. New York: McLoughlin Brothers, [1895?]. viii, 416 pp. [MS/NUC 136:606]
CE 2.187 *MTS* 270

243. de la Mare, Walter (1873–1956). *The Connoisseur and Other Stories.* New York: Alfred A. Knopf, 1926. 309 pp. [HPL/RHB/NUC 137:364]
Contents: Mr. Kempe; Missing; The Connoisseur; Disillusioned; The Nap; Pretty Poll; All Hallows; The Wharf; The Lost Track.
SHL 75–76 *ES* 74, 174, 216 *ES* 74, 111, 174 *OFF* 262

244. ———. *The Riddle and Other Tales.* <1923> New York: Alfred A. Knopf, 1930. 290 pp. [HPL/RHB/NUC 137:373]
Contents: The Almond Tree; The Count's Courtship; The Looking Glass; Miss Duveen; Selina's Parable; Seaton's Aunt; The Bird of Travel; The Bowl; The Three Friends; Lispet, Lispet and Vaine; The Tree; Out of the Deep; The Creatures; The Riddle; The Vats.
Given to HPL by Wilfred B. Talman (HPL to Lillian D. Clark, 16 July 1931; LFF). *SHL* 75–76 *SL* 2.57 *ES* 74, 111 *OFF* 262

245. De Mille, James (1837–1880). *A Strange Manuscript Found in a Copper Cylinder.* <1888> New York: Harper & Brothers, 1900. viii, 291 pp. [HPL/MS/NUC 138:519]

A weird novel that may have influenced "The Mound" and *At the Mountains of Madness.* See Joshi, *Lovecraft and a World in Transition* (New York: Hippocampus Press, 2014), 388–92. *MTS* 37, 69, 73

246. Dennie, John. *Rome of To-day and Yesterday: The Pagan City.* <1894> 5th ed. New York: G. P. Putnam's Sons, 1914. 392 pp. [MS/NUC 139:368] *SL* 1.356 *CLM* 304

247. De Quincey, Thomas (1785–1859). *Confessions of an English Opium-Eater and Selected Essays.* Edited with Notes by David Masson. New York: A. L. Burt, n.d. 369 pp. [MS/NUC 139:670]

Contents: The Confessions; The English Mail-Coach; Revolt of the Tartars; Murder as One of the Fine Arts.

No date cited by MS; there are at least 3 Burt printings. Presumably derived from Masson's edition of De Quincey's *Complete Writings* (1889–90).

248. Derham, William (1637–1735). *Astro-Theology; or, A Demonstration of the Being and Attributes of God, from a Survey of the Heavens.* <1715> 10th ed. London: Robinson & Roberts, 1767. l, 216 pp. [MS/NUC 140:46]

HPL to Wilfred B. Talman, Thursday [7 February 1928]; ALS, JHL.

249. Derleth, August (1909–1971). *The Man on All Fours: A Judge Peck Mystery Story.* New York: Loring & Mussey, 1934. 244 pp. [MS/NUC 140:71] *AG* 223 *ES* 619, 621, 629, 633, 639, 654, 655, 664–66, 667, 669, 678, 684 *RB* 128 *JVS* 242 *FLB* 240, 246, 255, 257, 259, 265, 271

250. ———. *Place of Hawks.* Illustrated with Wood Engravings by George Barford. New York: Loring & Mussey, 1935. 250 pp. [MS/NUC 140:72]

Contents: Five Alone; Farway House; Nine Strands in a Web; Place of Hawks.

HPL read all four novelettes in ms. and made extensive comments (principally grammatical), but Derleth does not seem to have followed his recommendations. *SL* 4.90, 110; 5.124 *AG* 223, 229 *ES* 555, 563, 591, 616, 621, 623, 624, 644, 646, 660, 669, 672, 673, 678, 681, 691, 693, 696, 702, 703, 705, 707, 715, 723 *OFF* 256, 275, 318 *RB* 321 *JVS* 242, 275, 285, 286 *FLB* 126, 259 *CLM* 331

251. ———. *Sign of Fear: A Judge Peck Mystery.* New York: Loring & Mussey, 1935. 283 pp. [MS/NUC 140:72]

AG 223 *ES* 672, 677, 713–14, 718, 720 *OFF* 300 *RB* 159, 321 *JVS* 275, 363 *FLB* 251

252. ———. *Still Is the Summer Night.* New York: Charles Scribner's Sons, 1937. 356 pp. [HPL to August Derleth, [17 February 1937] (*ES* 768)/NUC 140:73]

Author's presentation copy to HPL. *ES* 718, 719, 720, 723, 725, 735, 747, 749, 752, 757, 763, 765 *JFM* 400

253. ———. *Three Who Died: A Judge Peck Mystery.* New York: Loring & Mussey, 1935. 252 pp. [MS/NUC 140:73]

AG 223 *ES* 621, 633, 639, 644, 646, 672, 678, 679, 683, 684–86, 687, 691 *OFF* 219, 227 *JFM* 362 *RB* 231 *JVS* 267 *FLB* 126, 129, 265–66

254. *The Dial.*
November 1922. *Contains: The Waste Land* by T. S. Eliot. [HPL to Alfred Galpin, 24 March 1933 (*AG* 180)]

First American printing of Eliot's poem; it had appeared in the UK in Eliot's journal, the *Criterion,* in October 1922. Cf. HPL's parody, "Waste Paper" (1923?; *AT* 257–61).
CF 2.337 *CE* 1.349n1; 2.64; 5.68n48, 123 *AT* 187 *SL* 1.230, 262; 3.52, 294 *MTS* 320 *AG* 123, 153n5 *ES* 59, 97n3 *JFM* 36n3, 197 *ET* 16, 234 *JVS* 126, 134–35, 372

255. Dick, Thomas (1774–1857). *The Practical Astronomer.* New York: Harper & Brothers, 1846. xiv, 437 pp. [L. W. Currey, *Catalogue 61*/NUC 142:558]

Contains some notes and drawings by HPL in the text.

256. ———. *Works.* Philadelphia: E. C. & J. Biddle, 1849. 10 vols. in 5. [X/MS/NUC 142:552]

CE 3.103–4

257. Dickens, Charles (1812–1870). *American Notes and Pictures from Italy.* <1842; 1846> London: J. M. Dent; New York: E. P. Dutton (Everyman's Library), [1907] or [1926]. xxii, 430 pp. [MS/NUC 142:598]

258. ———. *Barnaby Rudge.* <1841> New York: A. L. Burt, [1902?]. 646 pp. [MS/NUC 142:602]

ES 143

259. ———. *Bleak House.* <1852–53> New York: A. L. Burt, [189-?]. 888 pp. [MS/NUC 142:607]

JVS 197

260. ———. *A Child's History of England.* <1851–53> [MS]

MS cites Dwight Publishing Co. ed., but no data available.

261. ———. *Christmas Books.* <1843–48> London: Chapman & Hall, [1881]. 840 pp. [MS/NUC 142:578]

ES 66

262. ———. *Great Expectations.* <1860–61> New York: A. L. Burt, [1907?] or [1928?]. 456 pp. [MS/NUC 142:655]

263. ———. *The Life and Adventures of Martin Chuzzlewit.* <1843–44> [MS]

MS cites Dwight Publishing Company Co. ed., but no data available.

264. ———. *The Life and Adventures of Nicholas Nickleby.* <1838–39> New York: A. L. Burt, [19—]. 850 pp. [MS/NUC 142:683]

MF 445

265. ———. *Little Dorrit.* <1855–57> London: Chapman & Hall, [1881?]. viii, 423 pp. [MS/NUC 142:666]

266. ———. *The Old Curiosity Shop.* <1840–41> New York: A. L. Burt, [1904?]. 549 pp. [MS/NUC 142:690]

267. ———. *A Tale of Two Cities.* <1859> New York: A. L. Burt, [1904?]. 350 pp. [MS/NUC 143:40]

ES 143

268. Disraeli, Benjamin (1804–1881). *Alroy.* <1833> [HPL]

No ed. cited by HPL. A gift from an unidentified source (HPL to J. Vernon Shea, 24 March 1933 [*JVS* 125]). The novel is in fact not a weird tale but a story of mediaeval adventure based on the 12th-century Jewish prince David Alroy.

269. Dixon, Thomas, Jr. (1864–1946). *The Leopard's Spots: A Romance of the White Man's Burden 1865–1900.* <1902> New York: A. Wessels Co., 1906. 469 pp. [Grill-Binkin/NUC 145:143]

Historical novel by the author of *The Clansman* (1905; cf. *CE* 1.57), which was the basis for the film *The Birth of a Nation*.

270. Dobson, Austin (1840–1921). *Poems on Several Occasions.* <1889> New ed., rev. & enl. New York: Dodd, Mead, 1895. 2 vols. [MS/NUC 145:341]

HPL had only Vol. 2. Dobson was, like HPL, devoted to the eighteenth century, although his poetry is not as slavishly imitative or consciously archaic as HPL's.

271. *Dr. Browder's Family Almanac on a New Plan, for 1847*. Boston: William A. Egery, [1846]. 24 pp. [MS/NUC 145:377]

272. Dodsley, Robert (1703–1764), ed. *A Collection of Poems by Several Hands.* <1748–49> 2nd ed. London: Printed for G. Pearch, 1770. 4 vols. in 2. [MS/NUC 145:600]

   It is not clear whether HPL had both vols.

273. Dowden, Edward (1843–1913). *Shakspere*. New York: D. Appleton & Co., 1880. 167 pp. [X—JHL/NUC 48:100–101]

274. Downing, Andrew Jackson (1815–1852). *Landscape Gardening and Rural Architecture*. New York: G. P. Putnam & Co., 1849. 451 pp. [MS/NUC 148:181]

275. Doyle, Sir Arthur Conan (1859–1930). *The Lost World: Being an Account of the Recent Amazing Adventures of Professor George E. Challenger, Lord John Roxton, Professor Summerlee, and Mr. E. D. Malone of* The Daily Gazette. <1912> London: George Newnes, 1921 or 1925. 126 pp. [HPL/BLC 86:435]

   Read c. 1912 (HPL to Lillian D. Clark, 23 September 1925; *LFF*); this copy must have been obtained at a later date.

276. ———. *The Mystery of Sasassa Valley; A Night among the Nihilists; Our Derby Sweetstakes; Bones*. New York: George Munro's Sons, [1900?]. 90 pp. [MS/NUC 148:262]

277. ———. *Tales of Long Ago*. London: John Murray, [1922]. 211 pp. [HPL/MS/NUC 891:144/X—JHL]

   Contents: The Last of the Legions; The Last Galley; Through the Veil; The Coming of the Huns; The Contest; The First Cargo; An Iconoclast; Giant Maximin; The Red Star; The Silver Mirror; The Home-coming; A Point of Contact.

278. ———. *Tales of Twilight and the Unseen*. London: John Murray, 1922. 312 pp. [HPL/MS/BLC 86:440/NUC 148:280]

   Contents: The Brown Hand; The Usher of Lea House School; B.24; The Great Keinplatz Experiment; A Literary Mosaic; Playing with Fire; The Ring of Thoth; The Los Amigos Fiasco; How It Happened; Lot No. 249; De Profundis; The Lift.
   SHL 76–77

279. Drake, Joseph Rodman (1795–1820). *The Culprit Fay*. New York: Rudd & Carleton, 1859. 62 pp. [MS/NUC 148:426]

   Poem.

280. Drake, Samuel Adams (1833–1905). *A Book of New England Legends and Folk Lore in Prose and Poetry*. Boston: Roberts Brothers, 1884. xxviii, 461 pp. [MS/NUC 148:435]

281. ———. *Nooks and Corners of the New England Coast*. New York: Harper & Brothers, 1876. 459 pp. [MS/NUC 148:437]
CE 2.193

282. ———. *On Plymouth Rock*. Boston: Lee & Shepard, 1897. 173 pp. [MS/NUC 148:438]

283. Dryden, John (1631–1700). *The Poetical Works of John Dryden*. London: Frederick Warne, 1893. xxxii, 575 pp. [MS/NUC 149:458]
Much of HPL's "18th-century" verse is more derivative of Dryden than of any actual 18th-century poets.

284. ———. *The Wild Gallant: A Comedy*. <1669> London: Printed by T. Warren for Henry Herringman, 1694. 47 pp. [HPL to Richard F. Searight, 15 October 1933/NUC 149:471]

285. Dumas, Alexandre (1802–1870). *The Three Musketeers; or, The Three Guardsmen*. <1844> New York: R. F. Fenno & Co., 1899. 592 pp. [X/NUC 151:311]
No translator listed. Inscribed: "H. P. Lovecraft / 1903. / From your mother. / We saw the play July 25th 1903." *CE* 2.189

286. Duncan, Robert Kennedy (1868–1914). *The Chemistry of Commerce: A Simple Interpretation of Some New Chemistry and Its Relation to Modern Industry*. New York: Harper & Brothers, 1907. xii, 262 pp. [X/NUC 151:639]
Flyleaf has rubber stamp with HPL's name and address (598 Angell St.), and also a full inscription of same in his hand.

287. Dunsany, Edward John Moreton Drax Plunkett, 18th baron (1878–1957). *The Blessing of Pan*. London: G. P. Putnam's Sons, 1927. vi, 277 pp. [HPL/MS/NUC 152:194]
ES 135, 138, 140 *OFF* 55 *ET* 27 *FLB* 271

288. ———. *The Book of Wonder* [and *Time and the Gods*]. New York: Boni & Liveright (Modern Library), [1918]. v, 234 pp. [HPL/RHB/NUC 152:194]
Contents: [*The Book of Wonder* (1912):] The Bride of the Man-Horse; The Distressing Tale of Thangobrind the Jeweller; The House of the Sphinx; The

Probable Adventure of the Three Literary Men; The Injudicious Prayers of Pombo the Idolater; The Loot of Bombasharna; Miss Cubbidge and the Dragon of Romance; The Quest of the Queen's Tears; The Hoard of the Gibbelins; How Nuth Would Have Practised His Art upon the Gnoles; How One Came, as Was Foretold, to the City of Never; The Coronation of Mr. Thomas Shap; Chu-Bu and Sheemish; The Wonderful Window; [*Time and the Gods* (1906):] Time and the Gods; The Coming of the Sea; A Legend of the Dawn; The Vengeance of Men; When the Gods Slept; The King That Was Not; The Cave of Kai; The Sorrow of Search; The Men of Yarnith; For the Honour of the Gods; Night and Morning; Usury; Mlideen; In the Land of Time; The Relenting of Sardinac; The Jest of the Gods; The Dreams of the Prophet; The Journey of the King.

CF 1.237, 2.263 *CE* 2.57; 5.264 *SHL* 90 *RK* 174 *OFF* 55, 204 *ET* 27 *RB* 251, 407 *JVS* 24, 49 *CLM* 244, 277 *DS* 143

289. ———. *Don Rodriguez: Chronicles of Shadow Valley*. New York: G. P. Putnam's Sons, 1922. x, 318 pp. [HPL/NUC 152:195]

Originally published (London: G. P. Putnam's Sons, 1922) as *The Chronicles of Rodriguez*. *CE* 2.59 *OFF* 55 *ET* 27 *JVS* 35 *CLM* 277 *DS* 44

290. ———. *A Dreamer's Tales and Other Stories*. Introduction by Padraic Colum. New York: Boni & Liveright (Modern Library), [1917], [1919], or [1921]. xviii, 212 pp. [HPL/NUC 152:195]

Contents: [*A Dreamer's Tales* (1910):] Poltarnees, Beholder of Ocean; Bladgaross; The Madness of Andelsprutz; Where the Tides Ebb and Flow; Bethmoora; Idle Days on the Yann; The Sword and the Idol; The Idle City; The Hashish Man; Poor Old Bill; The Beggars; Carcassonne; In Zaccarath; The Field; The Day of the Poll; The Unhappy Body; [*The Sword of Welleran* (1908):] The Sword of Welleran; The Fall of Babbulkund; The Kith of the Elf-Folk; The Highwayman; In the Twilight; The Ghosts; The Whirlpool; The Hurricane; The Fortress Unvanquishable Save for Sacnoth; The Lord of Cities; The Doom of La Traviata; On the Dry Land.

CF 2.483 *CE* 5.264 *SHL* 90 *CB* 6); *AG* 83 *ES* 30, 46, 64, 329 *OFF* 55, 90, 223 *ET* 27 *RB* 251, 407 *JVS* 24, 49, 75, 245, 366 *JVS* 24 *FLB* 148, 172 *CLM* 244, 276 *DS* 44, 172 *MWM* 471

291. ———. *Fifty-one Tales*. London: Elkin Mathews, 1915. [HPL]

Contents: The Assignation; Charon; The Death of Pan; The Sphinx at Gizeh; The Hen; Wind and Fog; The Raft-Builders; The Workman; The Guest; Death and Odysseus; Death and the Orange; The Prayer of the Flowers; Time and the Tradesman; The Little City; The Unpasturable Fields; The Worm and the Angel; The Songless Country; The Latest Thing; The Demagogue and the Demi-monde; The Giant Poppy; Roses; The Man with the Golden Ear-rings; The Dream of King Karna-Vootra; The Storm; A Mistaken Identity; The True History of the Hare and the Tortoise; Alone the Immortals; A Moral Little Tale; The Return of Song; Spring in Town; How the Enemy Came to Thlūnrana; A Losing Game; Taking Up Piccadilly; After the Fire; The City; The Food of Death; The Lonely Idol; The Sphinx in Thebes (Massachusetts); The Reward; The Trouble in Leafy Green Street; The Mist; Furrow-Maker; Lobster Salad; The Return of the Exiles; Nature and Time; The Song of the Blackbird; The Messengers; The Three Tall Sons; Compromise; What We Have Come To; The Tomb of Pan.

No ed. cited by HPL (he probably had one of the Little, Brown eds. [Boston, 1917, 1919, 1920]). *SL* 1.356 *CLM* 281

292. ———. *Five Plays: The Gods of the Mountain; The Golden Doom; King Argimēnēs and the Unknown Warrior; The Glittering Gate; The Lost Silk Hat.* <1914> Boston: Little, Brown, 1923. xii, 116 pp. [HPL/MS/NUC 152:196]

CE 2.58, 59; 5.48 *SHL* 90–91 *SL* 1.356; 4.72 *MTS* 387 *OFF* 55 *JFM* 31 *RB* 204 *JVS* 240

293. ———. *The Gods of Pegāna.* London: Elkin Mathews, 1905. [HPL]

Contents: Preface; The Gods of Pegāna; Of Skarl the Drummer; Of the Making of the Worlds; Of the Game of the Gods; The Chaunt of the Gods; The Sayings of Kib; Concerning Sish; The Sayings of Slid; The Deeds of Mung; The Chaunt of the Priests; The Sayings of Limpang-Tung; Of Yoharneth-Lahai; Of Roon, the God of Going; The Revolt of the Home Gods; Of Dorozhand; The Eye in the Waste; Of the Thing That Is Neither God Nor Beast; Yonath the Prophet; Yug the Prophet; Alhireth-Hotep the Prophet; Kabok the Prophet; Of the Calamity That Befel Yun-Ilara by the Sea, and of the Building of the Tower of the Ending of Days; Of How the Gods Whelmed Sidith; Of How Imbaun Became High Prophet in Aradoc of All the Gods Save One; Of How Imbaun Met Zodrak; Pegāna; The Sayings of Imbaun; Of How Imbaun Spake of Death to the King; Of Ood; The River; The Bird of Doom and the End.

No ed. cited by HPL. *CE* 2.57 *AG* 83 *RK* 172 *OFF* 55 *MF* 40 *ET* 27 *RB* 251 *MWM* 430

294. ———. *The King of Elfland's Daughter.* London: G. P. Putnam's Sons, 1924. 301 pp. [HPL/NUC 152:198]

SL 1.356 *CLM* 39, 51, 96, 277

295. ———. *The Last Book of Wonder.* With Illustrations by S. H. Sime. Boston: John W. Luce, [1916]. 213 pp. [HPL/NUC 152:198]

Contents: A Tale of London; Thirteen at Table; The City on Mallington Moor; Why the Milkman Shudders When He Perceives the Dawn; The Bad

Old Woman in Black; The Bird of the Difficult Eye; The Long Porter's Tale; The Loot of Loma; The Secret of the Sea; How Ali Came to the Black Country; The Bureau d'Echange de Maux; A Story of Land and Sea; A Tale of the Equator; A Narrow Escape; The Watch-Tower; How Plash-Goo Came to the Land of None's Desire; The Three Sailors' Gambit; The Exiles' Club; The Three Infernal Jokes.
CE 2.58 *RK* 171 *CLM* 277

296. ———. *Plays of Gods and Men.* Boston: John W. Luce, [1917]. 207 pp. [HPL/RHB/NUC 152:200]

Contents: The Tents of the Arabs; The Laughter of the Gods; The Queen's Enemies; A Night at an Inn.
CE 2.58, 59, 122, 190 *SHL* 91 *SL* 4.154 *RK* 171 *MTS* 387 *RK* 169, 171 *RB* 204

297. ———. *Plays of Near and Far: The Compromise of the King of the Golden Isles; The Flight of the Queen; Cheezo; A Good Bargain; If Shakespeare Lived To-day; Fame and the Poet.* New York: G. P. Putnam's Sons, 1923. vii, 245 pp. [HPL/MS/NUC 152:200]
RK 172

298. ———. *Tales of Three Hemispheres.* Boston: John W. Luce, 1919. [HPL]

Contents: The Last Dream of Bwona Khubla; The Postman of Otford; The Prayer of Boob Aheera; East and West; A Pretty Quarrel; How the Gods Avenged Meoul Ki Ning; The Gifts of the Gods; The Sack of Emeralds; The Old Brown Coat; An Archive of the Older Mysteries; A City of Wonder; Idle Days on the Yann; A Shop in Go-By Street; The Avenger of Perdóndaris.

No ed. cited by HPL. *CE* 2.59 *CB* 24; cf. 6. A reprint of this book (Owlswick Press, 1976) contains HPL's essay "Lord Dunsany and His Work" (1922) as the foreword.

299. ———. *The Travel Tales of Mr. Joseph Jorkens.* London: G. P. Putnam's Sons, [1931]. vii, 304 pp. [HPL/NUC 152:202]

Contents: The Tale of the Abu Laheeb; The King of Sarahb; How Jembu Played for Cambridge; The Charm against Thirst; Our Distant Cousins; A Large Diamond; A Queer Island; The Electric King; A Drink at a Running Stream; A Daughter of Rameses; The Showman; Mrs. Jorkens; The Witch of the Willows.

Humorous stories about a London clubman; HPL called them "tripe" (*CLM* 277).

300. ———. *Unhappy Far-off Things.* Boston: Little, Brown, 1919. 104 pp. [MS/NUC 152:202]

Vignettes of World War I battlefields in France. *CE* 2.59 *RK* 173

301. Durant, Will (1885–1981). *The Story of Philosophy: The Lives and Opinions of the Greater Philosophers.* Garden City, NY: Garden City Publishing Co. (A Star Book), 1927. 592 pp. [MS/NUC 152:579f.]

No ed. cited by MS. "You ought emphatically to read 'The Story of Philosophy' by Dr. Will Durant. . . . This is a simple layman's introduction to the subject, and reads as easily, straightforwardly, and fascinatingly as a novel" (*ET* 146). This work is no longer highly regarded. *CE* 2.198 *RB* 258

302. Durfee, Job (1790–1847). *What Cheer; or, Roger Williams in Banishment: A Poem.* <1832> Rev. ed. by Thomas Durfee. Providence: Preston & Rounds, 1896. viii, 225 pp. [MS/NUC 152:651]

303. Durfee, Thomas (1826–1901). *The Village Picnic and Other Poems.* Providence: George H. Whitney, 1872. v, 214 pp. [MS/NUC 152:652]

304. Dutt, R[ajani] Palme (1896–1974). *Fascism and Social Revolution.* London: M. Lawrence, 1934. *or* New York: International Publishers, 1934 (xi, 296 pp.); rev. ed. 1935 (318 pp.). [HPL to R. H. Barlow, 3 January 1937 (*OFF* 392)/NUC 153:272]

Given to HPL by Kenneth Sterling, Christmas 1936 (probably the revised edition of 1935). *JFM* 402

305. Dyer, Walter Alden (1878–1943). *Early American Craftsmen.* New York: Century Co., 1920. xv, 387 pp. [MS/NUC 153:604]

CE 2.193 *SL* 1.356

306. Earle, Alice (Morse) (1851–1911). *Home Life in Colonial Days.* New York: Macmillan Co., 1898. xvi, 470 pp. [MS/NUC 154:107]

307. ———. *In Old Narragansett: Romances and Realities.* New York: Charles Scribner's Sons, 1898. vii, 196 pp. [MS/NUC 154:108]

308. Eberlein, Harold Donaldson (1875–1964). *The Architecture of Colonial America.* Boston: Little, Brown, 1921. xiv, 289 pp. [MS/NUC 154:518]

CE 2.193, 200; 4.55 *SL* 1.356 *ET* 67

309. Eddison, E[ric] R[ücker] (1882–1945). *The Worm Ouroboros: A Romance.* Illustrated by Keith Henderson. New York: Albert & Charles Boni, 1926. xiii, 445 pp. [HPL/RHB/NUC 155:326]

SL 2.171, 177; 4.156–57 *MTS* 11, 164, 165–66, 215 *ES* 106, 107, 108, 110, 238, 537 *OFF* 50, 53, 56, 131n1, 158, 160, 162, 201, 207 *MF* 527 *JVS* 121, 125, 333, 359 *CLM* 277, 293, 307–8 *DS* 144–45

310. Eggleston, George Cary (1839–1911). *Life in the Eighteenth Century*. New York: A. S. Barnes & Co., 1905. xiv, 264 pp. [MS/NUC 156:451]

Life in Colonial America. *CE* 2.193

311. Ellet, Elizabeth Fries (Lummis) (1818–1877). *The Women of the American Revolution*. <1848> 3rd ed. New York: Baker & Scribner, 1849. 2 vols. [MS/NUC 157:280]

HPL had only Vol. 1.

312. Ellis, Edward S[ylvester] (1840–1916), and Charles F[rancis] Horne, ed. *The Story of the Greatest Nations, from the Dawn of History to the Twentieth Century*. New York: F. R. Niglutsch, [1901–03]. 9 vols. [MS/NUC 157:460]

HPL apparently had two sets of this series.

313. Emerson, Ralph Waldo (1803–1882). *Culture*. New York: Barse & Hopkins, 1910. 30 pp. [OCLC]

See *RK* 148: "[Alfred] Galpin sent me an exquisite little gift book de luxe for a birthday present last Tuesday—Emerson's Essay on Culture." It is not certain that the above title is the edition in question. *AG* 33n2, 41

314. ———. *Emerson's Earlier Poems*. Edited, with an Introduction and Notes, by Oscar Charles Gallagher. New York: Macmillan Co., 1908. xxxv, 161 pp. [MS/NUC 159:314]

315. ———. *Essays: First Series*. <1841> Boston: Houghton Mifflin, 1889. 343 pp. [MS/NUC 159:320]

Contents: History; Self-Reliance; Compensation; Spiritual Laws; Love; Friendship; Prudence; Heroism; The Over-Soul; Circles; Intellect; Art.

316. ———. *Essays: Second Series*. <1844> Boston: Houghton Mifflin, 1889. 270 pp. [MS/NUC 159:322]

Contents: The Poet; Experience; Character; Manners; Gifts; Nature; Politics; Nominalist and Realist; New England Reformers.

317. ———. *Representative Men: Seven Lectures*. <1850> Boston: Houghton Mifflin, 1887. 276 pp. [MS/NUC 159:340]

Contents: Uses of Great Men; Plato or the Philosopher; Plato: New Readings; Swedenborg or the Mystic; Montaigne or the Skeptic; Shakespeare or the Poet; Napoleon or the Man of the World; Goethe or the Writer.

318. *The Encyclopaedia Britannica: A Dictionary of Arts, Sciences, and General Literature* . . . With . . . Revisions and Additions by W. H. De Puy. 9th ed. Chicago: Werner Co., 1896. 24 vols. [MS/NUC 159:596]

HPL used this reference work in various ways in his fiction: the incantations in "The Horror at Red Hook," the list of cryptographic authorities in "The Dunwich Horror," information on Australia in "The Shadow out of Time," etc. *CE* 1.364; 2.191, 202; 5.220, 222 *CB* 22, 47 *MTS* 202 *OFF* 324 *ET* 377 *RB* 415 *FLB* 294 *DS* 84. *MWM* 527 See also #71.

319. Eschenburg, Johann Joachim (1743–1820). *Manual of Classical Literature*. From the German of J. J. Eschenburg . . . with Additions . . . by N. W. Fiske. <1836> 4th Ed. Philadelphia: E. C. Biddle, 1843. xxviii, 690 pp. [MS/NUC 162:55]

Translation of *Handbuch der klassischen Literatur* (1783). *CLM* 304

320. Esenwein, Joseph Berg (1867–1946). *Writing the Short-Story: A Practical Handbook on the Rise, Structure, Writing, and Sale of the Modern Short-Story*. New York: Hinds, Hayden & Eldredge, 1918. xvi, 445 pp. [MS/NUC 162:193]

Like #166, a book published (and perhaps purchased by HPL) shortly after his recommencement of fiction writing in 1917.

321. Evelyn, John (1620–1709). *The Diary of John Evelyn (Reign of Charles II)*. With an Introduction by Austin Dobson. London: Cassell, 1909. 224 pp. [MS/NUC 164:144]

322. Everett, Mrs. H[enrietta] D. (1851–1923). *The Death-Mask and Other Ghosts*. London: Philip Allan, 1920. 321 pp. [HPL to Robert Bloch, 1 June 1933 (*RB* 43n2)/OCLC]

MTS 229

323. *Evolution in Modern Thought*. New York: Boni & Liveright (Modern Library), [1917]. 289 pp. [MS/NUC 164:324]

Contents: Darwin's Predecessors, by J. Arthur Thomson; The Selection Theory, by August Weismann; Heredity and Variation in Modern Lights, by W. Bateson; *The Descent of Man*, by G. Schwalbe; Charles Darwin as an Anthropologist, by Ernst Haeckel; Mental Factors in Evolution, by C. Lloyd Morgan; The Influence of the Conception of Evolution on Modern Philosophy, by H. Höffding; The Influence of Darwin upon Religious Thought, by P. H. Waggett; Darwinism and History, by J. B. Bury; Darwinism and Sociology, by C. Bouglé.

324. Falconer, William (1732–1769). *The Shipwreck.* <1762> New-York: Solomon King, 1825. 107 pp. [MS/NUC 166:168]
Poem.

325. *The Fantasy Fan.* Edited by Charles D. Hornig. [HPL]
HPL had a complete set of all 18 issues (September 1933–February 1935). The magazine contained many contributions by him, including an uncompleted serialisation of the revised version of *SHL.* Many references to this periodical in HPL's letters.

326. *Fantasy Magazine.* Edited by Julius Schwartz. [HPL]
HPL's holdings began with the January 1934 issue. Many references to this periodical in HPL's letters.

327. Farington, Joseph (1747–1821). *The Farington Diary.* Edited by James Greig. New York: George H. Doran, 1923–28. 8 vols. [MS/NUC 166:639]
HPL had only Vol. 1 (1923), covering diary entries from 13 July 1793 to 24 August 1802. Farington was a British landscape painter.

328. *The Farmer's, Mechanic's, and Gentleman's Almanack, for the Year of Our Lord 1840.* By Nathan Wild. Keene, NH: J. & J. W. Prentiss, 1839. [MS/NUC 167:95]

329. Farrar, Frederic William (1831–1903). *The Life of Christ.* <1874> New York: E. P. Dutton, [1874] or [189-]. 2 vols. [MS/NUC 167:245f.]
Long a standard work, from which HPL probably derived many of his views of Christ and Christianity.

330. Fénelon, François de Salignac de la Mothe (1651–1715). *Lives of the Ancient Philosophers.* Translated from the French of Fénelon, with Notes and a Life of the Author, by the Rev. John Cormack. 1st American ed. Philadelphia: J. Grigg; Richmond: Collins & Co., 1824. 300 pp. [MS/NUC 169:389]
Translation of *Abrégé de la vie des plus illustres philosophes de l'antiquité* (1726).

331. *Fessenden's New England Farmer's Almanac for the Year of Our Lord . . .* Boston: John B. Russell; Boston: Carter, Hendee & Co. [MS/NUC 171:45]
Written by Thomas G. Fessenden (1771–1837). HPL had the issues for 1829, 1830, 1831, and 1833.

332. Field, Edward (1858–1928), ed. *State of Rhode Island and Providence Plantations at the End of the Century.* Boston: Mason Publishing Co., 1902. 3 vols. [MS/NUC 171:546]

333. *50 Years of Ghost Stories.* London: Hutchinson, [1935]. xiii, 702 pp. [HPL/MS/NUC 172:113/Ashley 709]

Contents: The Familiar, by J. Sheridan LeFanu; Green Tea, by J. Sheridan LeFanu; The Saint and the Vicar, by Cecil Binney; The Tapestried Chamber, by Sir Walter Scott; Gibbet Lane, by Anthony Gittins; The Old Nurse's Story, by Mrs. [Elizabeth] Gaskell; The Residence at Whitminster, by M. R. James; A Warning to the Curious, by M. R. James; The Haunted and the Haunters, by Sir Edward Bulwer-Lytton; The Green Room, by Walter de la Mare; Eveline's Visitant, by Miss [Mary] Braddon; Afterward, by Edith Wharton; The Middle Toe of the Right Foot, by Ambrose Bierce; Man Overboard!, by F. Marion Crawford; In a Glass Dimly, by Shane Leslie; The Lord-in-Waiting, by Shane Leslie; Dracula's Guest, by Bram Stoker; Expiation, by E. F. Benson; Pirates, by E. F. Benson; The Woman's Ghost Story, by Algernon Blackwood; Thurnley Abbey, by Perceval Landon; The Rosewood Door, by Oliver Onions; The Virgin of the Seven Daggers, by Vernon Lee; The Library Window, by Mrs. [Margaret] Oliphant; The Song in the House, by Ann Bridge; The Operation, by Violet Hunt; The Sweeper, by Ex-Private X [pseud. of A. M. Burrage]; The Running Tide, by Ex-Private X; Perez, by W. L. George.

334. Figuier, Louis (1819–1894). *Primitive Man.* Rev. trans. New York: D. Appleton & Co., 1870. xix, 348 pp. [MS/NUC 172:194]

Translation of *L'Homme primitif* (1870). Contains a preface by E. B. Tylor.

335. Finger, Charles J[oseph] (1869–1941). *Hints on Writing Short Stories.* Girard, KS: Haldeman-Julius Co., 1922. 64 pp. [HPL to Zealia Bishop, 13 July 1927/OCLC]

HPL notes in his letter to Bishop: "I am enclosing a little Haldeman-Julius booklet which I frequently send to fictional aspirants without charge."

336. Fiske, John (1842–1901). *American Political Ideals Viewed from the Standpoint of Universal History.* New York: Harper & Brothers, 1885. 158 pp. [MS/NUC 174:115]

Contents: Preface; The Town-Meeting; The Federal Union; "Manifest Destiny."

337. ———. *The Beginning of New England; or, The Puritan Theocracy in Its Relation to Civil and Religious Liberty.* Boston: Houghton Mifflin, 1889. xvii, 296 pp. [MS/NUC 174:116]

338. ———. *Myths and Myth-Makers: Old Tales and Superstitions Interpreted by Comparative Mythology.* <1872> Boston: Houghton Mifflin, 1900. 251 pp. [HPL/RHB/NUC 174:127]

Contents: The Origins of Folklore; The Descent of Fire; Werewolves and Swan-Maidens; Light and Darkness; Myths of the Barbaric World; Juventus Mundi; The Primeval Ghost-World.

The probable source for much of HPL's knowledge of the origin of religion. The chapter on "Werewolves and Swan-Maidens" contains a section on Jacques Roulet of Caude which HPL used almost verbatim in "The Shunned House" (1924). *CE* 2.193; 3.318, 321; 5.8, 44

339. FitzGerald, Edward (1809–1893). *More Letters of Edward FitzGerald.* [Edited by William Aldis Wright.] London: Macmillan & Co., 1901. 295 pp. [MS/NUC 174:260]

340. Flammarion, Camille (1842–1925). *Haunted Houses.* London: T. Fisher Unwin, [1924]. 328 pp. [HPL/MS/NUC 174:509]

Translation by Edmund Edward Fournier d'Albe of *Les Maisons hantées* (1923). *CB* 180 *SL* 3.193, 233, 444, 446–47; 4.44; 5.140, 171

341. Flaubert, Gustave (1821–1880). *Salammbô: A Romance of Ancient Carthage.* <1862> [HPL/MS]

MS only states: "(Paper ed.)" HPL surely had an English translation; the first was in 1862 by J. W. Matthews, and there are others by M. French Sheldon (1885f.) and J. S. Chartres (1886f.). Obtained by HPL in New York in September 1922 (HPL to Lillian D. Clark, 13–16 September 1922; *LFF*). *CE* 2.189 *FLB* 104, 112, 115–16, 126, 246, 266, 267, 271, 321

342. ———. *The Temptation of St. Anthony.* <1874> Translated by Lafcadio Hearn <1910>. New York: Boni & Liveright (Modern Library), [1920]. 280 pp. [HPL/RHB/NUC 174:610]

Given to HPL by Frank Belknap Long. This copy bears an inscription by Long on the title page: "Christmas Greetings to Howard P. Lovecraft from his Petit Grandson Frank Belknap." *CE* 2.189, 226 *SHL* 52, 73 *MTS* 39 *ES* 74

343. Forbes, Esther (1891–1967). *A Mirror for Witches in Which Is Reflected the Life, Machinations, and Death of Famous Doll Bilby.* With woodcuts by Robert Gibbings. Boston: Houghton Mifflin, 1928. 213 pp. [HPL/MS/NUC 177:423]

A novel about the Salem witch trials. A copy of this book was lent to HPL by H. Warner Munn (HPL to Lillian D. Clark, 2 July 1928; *LFF*); in September 1932 W. Paul Cook gave him a copy. *ES* 148

344. Forest, J. *Plan de Paris*. [Paris:] A. Tirade, [1900]. Map: 59 × 80 cm. [MS]

This may not be the item in question: MS lists only "Plan de Paris," and there are many such titles. Suffice it to say that HPL had a map of Paris. Perhaps he used it in writing "The Music of Erich Zann" (1921).

345. Forster, John (1812–1876). *The Life of Oliver Goldsmith.* <1854> Abridged and Newly Edited with Notes, etc. New York: Frederick A. Stokes, 1903. 460 pp. [MS/NUC 178:346]

346. Foster, Sir Michael (1836–1907). *Physiology. Hygiene* by R. S. Tracy. New York: American Book Co., [189-]. x, 170 pp., 18 plates. [X/NUC 179:58]

347. Foulke, William Dudley (1848–1935). *Slav or Saxon: A Study of the Growth and Tendencies of Russian Civilization.* New York: G. P. Putnam's Sons, 1887. v, 148 pp. [MS/NUC 179:253]

348. Fowler, William Chauncey (1793–1881). *English Grammar: The English Language in Its Elements and Forms.* <1850> Abridged from the octavo ed. New York: Harper & Brothers, 1866. xiv, 381, iv, 181 pp. [MS/NUC 179:518]

349. *Francis's New Guide the Cities of New-York and Brooklyn, and the Vicinity.* New-York: C. S. Francis & Co., 1856. vii, 148 pp. [MS/NUC 182:359]

350. Frank, Waldo (1889–1967). *City Block.* Darien, CT: Waldo Frank, 1922. 320 pp. [NUC 182:644]

An experimental novel of social realism. Given to HPL by George Kirk (HPL to Annie E. P. Gamwell, 10 February 1925). *JVS* 92

351. Fraser, Maxwell. *Somerset.* London: Great Western Railway Co., 1934. x, 186 pp. [MS/NUC 183:431]

352. Freeman, Edward Augustus (1823–1892). *William the Conqueror.* London: Macmillan & Co., 1888. viii, 200 pp. [MS/NUC 183:63]

353. Freeman, Mary Eleanor (Wilkins) (1852–1930). *Giles Corey, Yeoman: A Play.* By Mary E. Wilkins. New York: Harper & Brothers, 1893. 108 pp. [MS/NUC 183:101]

"I toured the literary emporia [at Union Square, New York] independently; picking up several ten-cent bargains, the most striking of which was a play of the Salem witchcraft by Mary E. Wilkins" (*SL* 1.360).

354. ———. *The Wind in the Rose-Bush and Other Stories of the Supernatural.* By Mary E. Wilkins. New York: Doubleday, Page & Co., 1903. 237 pp. [HPL/MS/NUC 184:104]

Contents: The Wind in the Rose-Bush; The Shadows on the Wall; Ruella Mather; The Southwest Chamber; The Vacant Lot; The Lost Ghost.

Given to HPL by Samuel Loveman (HPL to R. H. Barlow, 5 September 1935 [*OFF* 291]). *SHL* 70 *ES* 137, 138, 139, 183, 190, 472 *MWM* 456

355. French, Joseph Lewis (1858–1936), ed. *The Best Psychic Stories.* Introduction by Dorothy Scarborough. New York: Boni & Liveright (Modern Library), [1920]. xv, 299 pp. [HPL/MS/NUC 184:562]

Contents: When the World Was Young, by Jack London; The Return, by Algernon Blackwood; The Second Generation, by Algernon Blackwood; Joseph—A Story, by Katherine Rickford; The Clavecin Bruges, by George Wharton Edwards; Ligeia, by Edgar Allan Poe; The Sylph and the Father, by Elsa Barker; A Ghost, by Lafcadio Hearn; The Eyes of the Panther, by Ambrose Bierce; Photographing Invisible Beings, by William T. Stead; The Sin-Eater, by Fiona Macleod [pseud. of William Sharp]; Ghosts in Solid Form, by Gambier Bolton; The Phantom Armies Seen in France, by Hereward Carrington; The Portal of the Unknown, by Andrew Jackson Davis; The Supernormal: Experiences, by St John D. Seymour; Nature-Spirits, or Elements, by Nizida; A Witches' Den, by Helena Blavatsky; Some Remarkable Experiences of Famous Persons, by Walter F. Prince.

It was from this volume that HPL read Fiona Macleod's "Sin-Eater" (*SL* 1.258; *CLM* 47), cribbing from it the Celtic oaths at the end of "The Rats in the Walls" (1923).

356. ———, ed. *Masterpieces of Mystery.* Garden City, NY: Doubleday, Page & Co., 1920f. 4 vols. [HPL/MS/NUC 184:564]

Contents: Riddle Stories: The Mysterious Card, by Cleveland Moffett; The Great Valdez Sapphire, by Anonymous; The Oblong Box, by Edgar Allan Poe; The Birth-Mark, by Nathaniel Hawthorne; A Terribly Strange Bed, by Wilkie Collins; The Torture by Hope, by Villiers de l'Isle-Adam [*SHL* 53]; The Box with the Iron Clamps, by Florence Marryat; My Fascinating Friend, by William Archer; The Lost Room, by Fitz-James O'Brien.

Mystic-Humorous Stories: May-Day Eve, by Algernon Blackwood; The Diamond Lens, by Fitz-James O'Brien [*SHL* 65]; The Mummy's Foot, by Théophile Gautier [*SHL* 51]; Mr. Bloke's Item, by Mark Twain; A Ghost, by Lafcadio Hearn; The Man Who Went Too Far, by E. F. Benson [*SHL* 76]; Chan Tow the Highrob, by Chester Bailey Fernald; The Inmost Light, by Arthur Machen; The Secret of Goresthorpe Grange, by A. Conan Doyle; The Man with the Pale Eyes, by Guy de Maupassant; The Rival Ghosts, by Brander Matthews.

Detective Stories: The Purloined Letter, by Edgar Allan Poe; The Black Hand, by Arthur B. Reeve; The Biter Bit, by Wilkie Collins; Missing: Page Thirteen, by

Anna Katherine Green; A Scandal in Bohemia, by A. Conan Doyle; The Rope of Fear, by Mary E. and Thomas W. Hanshew; The Safety Match, by Anton Chekhov; Some Scotland Yard Stories, by Sir Robert Anderson.

Ghost Stories: The Listener, by Algernon Blackwood [*SHL* 88]; Number 13, by M. R. James; Joseph: A Story, by Katherine Rickford; The Horla, by Guy de Maupassant [*SHL* 52, 65]; The Beast with Five Fingers, by William F. Harvey; Sister Maddelena, by Ralph Adams Cram; Thrawn Janet, by Robert Louis Stevenson; The Yellow Cat, by Wilbur Daniel Steele; Letter to Sura, by Pliny the Younger [*SHL* 31].

MS lists Collier ed., but there is no such edition. HPL had only 3 vols. (perhaps he did not have the volume of *Detective Stories*, as stories from all three other volumes are cited in *SHL*).

357. French, Nora May (1881–1907). *Poems.* San Francisco: Strange Co., 1910. 91 pp. [RHB/NUC 184:571]

French was a friend of George Sterling.

358. Fricker, Karl (1865–?). *The Antarctic Regions.* [Translated by A. Sonnenschein.] London: S. Sonnenschein & Co.; New York: Macmillan Co., 1900. xii, 292 pp. [MS/NUC 185:349]

Translation of *Antarktis* (1898).

359. Froissart, Jean (1338?–1410?). *The Chronicles of England, France, Spain, etc.* <1400?> [HPL to Lillian D. Clark, 29–30 September 1924; LFF/NUC 186:456f.]

HPL states only that he obtained an "abridged edition."

360. Frost, John (1800–1859). *Select Works of the British Poets, in a Chronological Series from Falconer to Sir Walter Scott.* <1838> Designed as a Continuation of Dr. Aikin's British Poets. Philadelphia: Thomas Wardle, 1840. vii, 807 pp. [MS/NUC 5:616; 687:356/OCLC]

361. Gall, James (1808–1895). *An Easy Guide to the Constellations with a Miniature Atlas of the Stars.* <1861> New & enl. ed. New York: G. P. Putnam's Sons, 1903. viii, 73 pp. [MS/NUC 189:401]

362. Galt, John (1779–1839). *Works of John Galt.* Edited by D. Storrar Meldrum. Boston: Roberts Brothers, 1895–96. 8 vols. [MS/NUC 190:21]

Scottish fiction. HPL had only 4 vols.

363. Garrett, Edmund Henry (1853–1929). *Romance and Reality of the Puritan Coast.* Boston: Little, Brown, 1897. 221 pp. [MS/NUC 191:606]

364. [Garth, Sir Samuel (1661–1719).] *The Dispensary: A Poem in Six Canto's.* <1699> 6th ed. London: J. Nutt, 1706. xv, 120 pp. [MS/NUC 192:39]

ES 380. Cf. "The Bookstall" (1916): "Go smell the drugs in Garth's Dispensary!" (*AT* 111).

365. Gautier, Théophile (1811–1872). *Clarimonde.* <1836> New York: Brentano's, 1899. 81 pp. *or Clarimonde and Other Stories.* London: T. C. & E. C. Jack, 1908. xxii, 150 pp. [HPL/NUC 192:679]

Contents of *Clarimonde and Other Stories:* Clarimonde; The Mummy's Foot; King Candaules.
    No ed. cited by HPL. Both volumes are translated by Lafcadio Hearn. *SHL* 51

366. ———. *Mademoiselle de Maupin.* <1835> New York: Boni & Liveright (Modern Library), [1918]; *or* New York: Modern Library, 1925. 294 pp. [Schiff/NUC 192:690]

No date cited. No translator listed. *ES* 71

367. ———. *One of Cleopatra's Nights and Other Fantastic Romances.* Translated by Lafcadio Hearn. New York: R. Worthington, 1882. ix, 321 pp. [HPL/NUC 192:695]

Contents: One of Cleopatra's Nights; Clarimonde; Arria Marcella; The Mummy's Foot; Omphale; A Rococo Story; King Candaules.
    No ed. cited by HPL. *SHL* 51–52

368. ———, and Prosper Mérimée (1803–1870). *Tales Before Supper.* Told in English by Myndart Verelst [i.e., Edgar Saltus] and Delayed with a Poem by Edgar Saltus. New York: Brentano's, 1887. 224 pp. [HPL/RHB/NUC 193:6]

Includes Gautier's "Avatar" and Mérimée's "The Venus of Ille." *SHL* 33, 51, 52; cf. HPL to Lillian D. Clark, 4–6 November 1924, *LFF.*

369. Gawsworth, John [pseud. of Terence Ian Fytton Armstrong (1912–1970)], ed. *Strange Assembly.* London: Unicorn Press, 1932. 334 pp. [HPL/MS/NUC 21:492/Ashley 782]

Contents: Prologue, by John Gawsworth; The Flying Cat, by M. P. Shiel; The Vivisector Vivisected, by Sir Ronald Ross; The Black Lad, by Frederick Carter; The Franc-Tireur's Escape, by Herbert E. Palmer; The Gift of Tongues, by Arthur Machen; A Fellside Tragedy, by Hubert Crackanthorpe; The Mask, by Francis Marsden; Ilya Vilka, by Stephen Graham; The Journey, by Rhys Davies; A Fragment, by Stephen Hudson; Londoners, by Wilfrid Ewart; The Captain, by Francis Marsden; Three Days, by Wilfrid Ewart;

The Harrying of the Dead, by Frederick Carter; A Night in Venice, by M. P. Shiel; The Rose Garden, by Arthur Machen.
Given to HPL by August Derleth (HPL to R. H. Barlow, [24 July 1934] [*OFF* 155]). *ES* 651, 652, 655, 656 *RB* 108 *FLB* 93

370. Geikie, Sir Archibald (1835–1924). *Geology.* New York: American Book Co., [1890?] or 1896. 137 pp., 52 plates. [X/NUC 193:615]
CE 2.194

371. *The Gentleman's Magazine.* London, 1731–1907. [HPL to MWM, 18 May 1922 *MWM* 83)/OCLC]
HPL states that in a trip to Boston in January 1922 he picked up "a volume of the old *Gentleman's Magazine* so dear to Mr. Pope and Mr. Johnson." Presumably the volume is from the 18th century.

372. The Gentleman's Magazine (London). *A Selection of Curious Articles from The Gentleman's Magazine.* London: Longmans, Hurst, Rees & Orme, 1809–11. 4 vols. [MS/NUC 195:6]
HPL had only Vol. 2 (1809).

373. Gibbon, Edward (1738–1794). *The Autobiography of Edward Gibbon.* <1796> London: J. M. Dent; New York: E. P. Dutton (Everyman's Library), [1911]–[1932]. xi, 202 pp. [MS/NUC 198:449]
No date cited by MS; there are at least 3 Everyman printings.

374. ———. *The History of the Decline and Fall of the Roman Empire.* <1776–88> With Notes by the Rev. H. H. Milman. New York: A. L. Burt, [1845]. 5 vols. [MS/NUC 198:458]
RK 43. Cf. *MF* 746, in which HPL quotes Milman's comment, "Who can refute a sneer?" in regard to Gibbon's criticism of the early Christian church.

375. ———. *The Student's Gibbon: The History of the Decline and Fall of the Roman Empire.* Abridged, Incorporating the Researches of Recent Commentators, by William Smith. New York: Harper & Brothers, 1864. xxviii, 677 pp. [MS/NUC 198:469]
Acquired summer 1933 (*JVS* 349). *CE* 2.192

376. Gibson, Frank Markey (1857–1929). *The Amateur Telescopist's Handbook.* New York: Longmans, Green & Co., 1894. xi, 163 pp. [MS/NUC 198:652]

377. Gilman, Arthur (1837–1909). *The Story of Rome, from the Earliest Times to the End of the Republic.* New York: G. P. Putnam's Sons, 1885. xvi, 355 pp. [MS/NUC 200:283]

378. Gladstone, William Ewart (1809–1898). *Homer.* New York: D. Appleton & Co., 1879. 153 pp. [X/NUC 201:559]

379. Gleeson, Alice Collins (d. 1938). *Colonial Rhode Island.* Pawtucket, RI: Automobile Journal Publishing Co., 1926. 260 pp. [MS/NUC 202:192]
SL 2.73

380. Godfrey, Hollis (1874–1936). *Elementary Chemistry.* New York: Longmans, Green, and Co., 1909. xiv, 456 pp. [X/NUC 203:183]

Rear endpaper inscribed: "A very commendable volume—superior in simplicity and comprehensibility to any work since Steele. Especially clear on recent discoveries. Better adapted for popular perusal than for academic instruction. A more rigid adherence to the periodic order in discussing the elements would render it doubly desirable. / H. P. Lovecraft—1910." *CE* 2.194

381. *Godfrey's Almanack.* By Albert Godfrey. Keene, NH: J. W. Prentiss & Co. [MS/NUC 203:194]

HPL had the issues for 1845 and 1848.

382. Goethe, Johann Wolfgang von (1749–1832). *Goethe's Faust* [Part I]. <1808> Translated by Anne Swanwick. New York: W. L. Allison Co., [1890?]. 261 pp. [MS/NUC 203:633]
CE 2.188, 189 *SHL* 33, 40 *OFF* 186, 204

383. ———. *Faust.* <1808–32> Translated into English, in the Original Metres, by Bayard Taylor <1870>. With Illustrations by Harry Clarke. New York: J. J. Little & Ives, n.d. 251 pp. [MS/OCLC]

OCLC gives date as 1856, but Clarke's illustrations were first published only in 1925.

384. ———. *The Poems of Goethe.* Translated in the Original Metres by E. A. Bowring, W. E. Aytoun, Theodore Martin, [et al.]. Boston: Estes & Lauriat, 1883. [MS/NUC 203:565]
CF 4.24, 25 *SHL* 33

385. Goldsmith, Oliver (1730?–1774). *The Grecian History from the Earliest State to the Death of Alexander the Great.* <1774> Revised and Corrected by William Grimshaw. Philadelphia: J. Grigg, 1826. 322 pp. [MS/NUC 205:6]

386. ———. *The Miscellaneous Works of Oliver Goldsmith.* Edited by Washington Irving. Philadelphia: J. Cressy & J. Grigg, 1830. 527 pp. [X—American Antiquarian Society/MS/NUC 205:20]

Contents: The Vicar of Wakefeld; An Inquiry into the Present State of Polite Learning; Miscellaneous Poems; The Good-Natured Man; She Stoops to Conquer; An Oratorio; Prefaces and Criticisms; Letters from a Citizen of the World to His Friends in the East; The Bee; Essays.
  CE 2.187 *AT* 278 *ET* 24, 298

387. Gonzales, Manoel [pseud.]. *London in 1731.* <1745> London: Cassell, 1888. 192 pp. [HPL to Lillian D. Clark, 29–30 September 1924; *LFF*/NUC 205:592]

  The work is conjectured to be by Daniel Defoe (1661?–1731).

388. Goodrich, Charles A[ugustus] (1790–1862). *A History of the United States of America, on a Plan Adapted to the Capacity of Youths.* <1823> A new stereotype ed., rev. & enl. from the 44th ed. Boston: Russell, Shattuck & Co., 1836. 352 pp. [MS/NUC 206:391]

389. [Goodrich, Samuel Griswold (1793–1860).] *Peter Parley's Arithmetic.* Boston: Charles J. Hendee, 1837. 144 pp. [MS/NUC 206:424]

390. ———. *A Pictorial History of England.* Philadelphia: Sorin & Ball, 1847. 444 pp. [MS/NUC 206:454]

391. ———. *A Pictorial History of France.* Philadelphia: Sorin & Ball & S. Agnew, 1846. 347 pp. [MS/NUC 206:454]

392. ———. *A Pictorial History of Greece: Ancient and Modern.* Philadelphia: Sorin & Ball & S. Agnew, 1847. 371 pp. [MS/NUC 206:455]

393. Goodyear, W[illiam] H[enry] (1846–1923). *Roman and Medieval Art.* Meadville, PA: Flood & Vincent, 1897. 307 pp. [MS/NUC 206:600]
  CE 2.201 *SL* 2.186) *CLM* 305

394. Gourmont, Remy de (1858–1915). *A Night at the Luxembourg.* Translated by Arthur Ransome <1912>. Girard, KS: Haldeman-Julius, [19—]. 124 pp. [HPL to Frank Belknap Long, 4 September 1923 (*SL* 1.250)/OCLC]

  A translation of *Une Nuit au Luxembourg* (1906), a philosophical dialogue. *CE* 2.63n10, 190 *SL* 1.250 *ES* 71

395. Grattan, C[linton] Hartley (1902–1980). *Bitter Bierce: A Mystery of American Letters.* Garden City, NY: Doubleday, Doran, 1929. xi, 291 pp. [MS/NUC 210:636]

396. Gray, Asa (1810–1888). *Gray's Lessons in Botany and Vegetable Physiology.* New York: Ivison, Blakeman, Taylor & Co., [1868]. xii, 236. [MS/NUC 211:196]

397. Gray, Thomas (1716–1771). *An Elegy Written in a Country Churchyard.* <1751> The Artists' Edition. Philadelphia: J. B. Lippincott, 1885. 47 pp. [MS/NUC 211:343]

"I have written . . . decasyllabic quatrains, as in Gray's *Elegy*" (*MWM* 38). The first stanza of "Sunset" (1917) bears some resemblances to the first stanza of Gray's *Elegy*. *CE* 2.18, 188

398. Grayson, David [pseud. of Ray Stannard Baker (1870–1946)]. *Adventures in Contentment.* Illustrated by Thomas Fogarty. <1907> [HPL to August Derleth, 2 February [1932] (*ES* 447)/NUC 31:424f.]

No ed. cited by HPL.

399. Great Western Railway Co. (Great Britain). *Handbook for Travellers from Overseas.* [London: Morton Burt & Sons,] 1924. 72 pp. [MS/NUC 216:212]

400. Green, John Richard (1837–1883). *History of the English People.* New York: Harper & Brothers, [1878]–1903. [MS/NUC 216:497f.]

No date cited by MS; there are 7 Harper printings. A landmark history of England, regarded as authoritative for many years. *CE* 2.192

401. Greene, Albert Gorton (1802–1868). *Old Grimes.* Providence: S. S. Rider & Brother, 1867. 12 pp. [MS/NUC 216:656]

A poem. Given to HPL by Lillian D. Clark while HPL was living in New York (HPL to Marian F. Bonner, 9 April 1936).

402. [Greene, Charles S. (1825–?).] *Thrilling Stories of the Great Rebellion.* By a Disabled Officer. Philadelphia: J. E. Potter, [1865?]. 494 pp. [MS/NUC 216:667]

403. Greene, Welcome Arnold (1795–1870). *The Providence Plantations for Two Hundred and Fifty Years.* Providence: J. A. & R. A. Reid, 1886. 468 pp. [MS/NUC 217:74]

404. Grieve, Robert. *Picturesque Boston: An Illustrated Guide to the City as It Appears To-day.* Providence: J. A. & R. A. Reid, 1889. 120 pp. [MS/NUC 218:393]

This may not be the volume in question: MS lists only "(Illustrated Guide to Boston)."

405. Grimm, Jakob Ludwig Karl (1785–1863), and Wilhelm Grimm (1786–1859). *Fairy Tales.* <1812–15> [HPL]

No ed. cited by HPL. *CE* 2.193; 5.288 *SL* 1.136, 299; *RK* 67 *ET* 147 *FLB* 37 *MWM* 45, 299, 429

406. Griswold, Rufus Wilmot (1815–1857), ed. *The Poets and Poetry of America. With an Historical Introduction.* Philadelphia: Carey & Hart, 1842. xxiv, 468 pp. [MS/NUC 219:355]

A celebrated anthology by the editor of Edgar Allan Poe's works. *ET* 172

407. Gudeman, Alfred (1862–1942), ed. *Latin Literature of the Empire.* New York: Harper & Brothers, 1898–99. 2 vols. [X/MS/NUC 221:430]

Vol. 1: Prose (ix, 579 pp.); Vol. 2: Poetry (ix, 493 pp.).

408. Guizot, François Pierre Guillaume (1787–1874). *General History of Civilization in Europe, from the Fall of the Roman Empire to the French Revolution.* <1839> 9th American ed. from the 2nd English ed. With Occasional Notes by C. S. Henry. New York: D. Appleton & Co, 1873. 316 pp. [MS/NUC 223:133]

Translation of *Histoire de la civilisation en Europe depuis la chute de l'Empire romain jusqu'à la révolution française* (1838). A notable historical work by a renowned French historian.

409. Guy, Joseph, the elder (1784–1867). *Guy's Elements of Astronomy, and an Abridgment of Keith's New Treatise on the Use of the Globe.* <1831> 30th ed. Philadelphia: C. DeSilver, 1873. viii, 136, 173 pp. [MS/OCLC]

410. Haggard, Audrey. *The Double Axe: A Romance of Ancient Crete.* London: J. M. Dent; New York: E. P. Dutton (Everyman's Library), 1929. ix, 289 pp. [X/NUC 226:35]

CLM 133, 173

411. Haggard, H[enry] Rider (1856–1925). *She: A History of Adventure.* <1887> New York: Gorton & Payne, [19—]. 384 pp. [HPL/MS/OCLC]

SHL 48; see *ES* 47: "I've recently begun reading the work of Sir H. Rider Haggard *for the first time.* 'She' is very good, & if the others are at all commensurate, I have quite a treat ahead." *RK* 182

412. Haklyut, Richard (1552–1616). *Voyagers' Tales: From the Collections of Richard Hakluyt.* New York: Cassell, [1886?]. 192 pp. [MS/NUC 226:478]

413. Haldane, J[ohn] B[urton] S[anderson] (1892–1964). *Daedalus; or, Science and the Future: A Paper Read to the Heretics, Cambridge, on February 4th, 1923.* London: Kegan Paul, Trench, Trübner & Co., 1924 *or* New York: E. P. Dutton, 1924. 93 pp. [NUC 226:539]

    Given to HPL by George Kirk (cf. HPL to Lillian D. Clark, 4–5 November 1924 and to Annie E. P. Gamwell, 10 February 1925; *LFF*). *CLM* 307

414. ———. *The Last Judgment: A Scientist's Vision of the Future of Man.* New York & London: Harper & Brothers, 1927. 41 pp. [HPL to Clark Ashton Smith, [5 December 1932] (*DS* 399)/NUC 226:540]

415. Hale, Edward Everett (1822–1909). *New England History in Ballads.* Boston: Little, Brown, 1903. xv, 182 pp. [MS/NUC 226:598]

416. Hale, Salma (1787–1866). *History of the United States, from Their First Settlement as Colonies to the Close of the War with Great Britain in 1815.* Keene, NH: J. & J. W. Prentiss, 1838. 298, 24 pp. [MS/NUC 226:664]

417. Hale, Susan (1833–1910). *Men and Manners of the Eighteenth Century.* Philadelphia: George W. Jacobs, 1898. 326 pp. [MS/NUC 226:673]

    Contents: Pope and Lady Mary [Wortley Montagu]; Charlotte Lennox; Addison and Gay; Richardson and Harriet Byron; Fielding; Goldsmith; Horace Walpole and Gray; Evelina [Frances Burney] and Dr. Johnson; Beau Nash and Beth; Mrs. Radcliffe and Her Followers.
    RK 198

418. Hall, Frederic Aldin (1854–1925). *Homeric Stories for Young Readers.* New York: American Book Co., [1903]. 200 pp. [MS/NUC 227:252]

419. Hals, Frans. *The Masterpieces of Frans Hals the Elder (1580–1666).* Sixty Reproductions of Photographs from the Original Paintings by F. Hanfstaengl. New York: Frederick A. Stokes Co., 1907. 66 pp. [MS/NUC 228:90]

420. Hamilton, Anne. *How to Revise Your Own Poems: A Primer for Poets.* Los Angeles: Abbey San Encino Press, 1936. 81 pp. [X—JHL/NUC 228:407]

    Given to HPL by Frank Earle Schermerhorn (F. E. Schermerhorn to HPL, 30 September 1936). *CE* 1.405 *RB* 213, 404

421. Hammett, Dashiell (1894–1961), ed. *Creeps by Night: Chills and Thrills.* New York: John Day Co., 1931. 525 pp. [HPL/MS/NUC 229:40]

Contents: A Rose for Emily, by William Faulkner (*ES* 391n1, 399–400, 402, 403–4, 406–7, 408, 414, 416–17, 419, 440); Green Thoughts, by John Collier; The Ghost of Alexander Parks, A.B., by R. D. Frisbie; The House, by André Maurois; The Kill, by Peter Fleming; Ten O'Clock, by Philip MacDonald; The Spider, by Hanns Heinz Ewers (*SHL* 51); Breakdown, by L. A. G. Strong; The Witch's Vengeance, by W. R. Seabrook; The Rat, by S. Fowler Wright; Faith, Hope, and Charity, by Irvin S. Cobb; Mr. Arcularis, by Conrad Aiken; The Music of Erich Zann, by H. P. Lovecraft; The Strange Case of Mrs. Arkwright, by Harold Dearden; The King of the Cats, by Stephen Vincent Benét; The Red Brain, by Donald Wandrei; The Phantom Bus, by W. Elwyn Backus; Beyond the Door, by Paul Suter; Perchance to Dream, by Michael Joyce; A Visitor from Egypt, by Frank Belknap Long.

Ewers's "The Spider" clearly influenced HPL's "The Haunter of the Dark" (1935). For Backus's "The Phantom Bus" see *CB* 208 and Schultz's note ad loc. *MTS* 288–89 *ES* 348n1, 390, 393, 395, 396, 398, 399, 403, 404, 455, 458, 619, 775, 780 *OFF* 6, 7, 11, 12, 13 *MF* 214 *ET* 186, 224 *RB* 19 *JVS* 67, 70, 76, 98–99, 299, 302, 328 *CLM* 362 *MWM* 311

422. ———, ed. *Modern Tales of Horror.* London: Victor Gollancz, 1932. 448 pp. [RHB/NUC 229:42]

Contents: A Rose for Emily, by William Faulkner; The House, by André Maurois; The Spider, by Hanns Heinz Ewers; The Witch's Vengeance, by W. R. Seabrook; Mr. Arcularis, by Conrad Aiken; The Music of Erich Zann, by H. P. Lovecraft; The Strange Case of Mrs. Arkwright, by Harold Dearden; The King of the Cats, by Stephen Vincent Benét; Beyond the Door, by Paul Suter; Perchance to Dream, by Michael Joyce; A Visitor from Egypt, by Frank Belknap Long.

Abridged edition of #419. HPL heard of this volume's appearance in October 1932 (*JVS* 99); presumably the publisher ultimately sent him a copy. *ES* 455n1

423. *The Handy World Atlas and Gazeteer.* New York: Frederick Warne & Co., [1900?]. [MS/BC]

424. Harkness, Albert (1822–1907). *A Latin Grammar for Schools and Colleges.* <1867> Revised Standard Edition of 1881. New York: Appleton & Co., 1889. xvi, 430 pp. [X/NUC 231:211]

Front endpaper inscribed "H. P. Lovecraft., 598 Angell St., Providence, R.I."

425. Harré, T[homas] Everett (1884–1948), ed. *Beware After Dark! The World's Most Stupendous Tales of Mystery, Horror, Thrills and Terror.* New York: Macauley, 1929. 461 pp. [MS/NUC 231:555]

Contents: *Negotium Perambulans* ... , by E. F. Benson; Back There in the Grass, by Gouverneur Morris; The Mollmeit of the Mountain, by Cynthia Stockley; Fishhead, by Irvin S. Cobb; The Fountain of Gold, by Lafcadio Hearn; The Shadowy Third, by Ellen Glasgow; Lukundoo, by Edward Lucas White; Rappaccini's Daughter, by Nathaniel Hawthorne; Lazarus, by Leonid Andreyeff; The Lame Priest, by S. Carleton; The Call of Cthulhu, by H. P. Lovecraft; Novel of the White Powder, by Arthur Machen; The Devils of Po Sung, by Bassett Morgan; The Isle of Voices, by Robert Louis Stevenson; The Sunken Land, by George W. Bayly; Two Spinsters, by E. Phillips Oppenheim; The Monster-God of Mamurth, by Edmond Hamilton; Huguenin's Wife, by M. P. Shiel; The Coconut Pearl, by Beatrice Grimshaw; The Quest of the Tropic Bird, by John Fleming Wilson; The Striding Place, by Gertrude Atherton.

HPL sent Harré a copy of his T.Ms. of "The Call of Cthulhu," hence the text as printed here is far superior to the *Weird Tales* (February 1928) appearance. HPL met Harré in New York in the winter of 1933–34 (*OFF* 99). *SL* 2.251–52 *MTS* 235, 241 *ES* 370, 775, 780 *OFF* 159n5m 251 *ET* 95, 97, 260 *RB* 19 *JVS* 50, 215, 299 *FLB* 22, 134, 152

426. Harrison, Frederic (1831–1923). *Oliver Cromwell.* London: Macmillan & Co., 1888. vi, 288 pp. [MS/NUC 232:274]

427. Harrison, James A[lbert] (1848–1911). *George Washington: Patriot, Soldier, Statesman, First President of the United States.* New York: G. P. Putnam's Sons, 1906. xxiii, 481 pp. [MS/NUC 232:302]

Harrison was also editor of the first critical edition of Edgar Allan Poe (1902; 17 vols.), not owned by HPL.

428. Hawthorne, Julian (1846–1934), ed. *The Lock and Key Library: Classic Mystery and Detective Stories.* New York: Review of Reviews Co., 1909. 10 vols. [HPL/MS/NUC 235:680]

Contents: Volume 1 (*North Europe: Russian, Swedish, Danish, Hungarian*): The Queen of Spades, by Alexander Pushkin; The General's Will, by Vera Jelihovsky; Crime and Punishment (excerpts), by Feodor Dostoyevsky; The Safety Match, by Anton Chekhoff; Knights of Industry, by Vsevolod Vladimirovitch Krestovski; The Amputated Arms, by Jorgen Wilhelm Bergsoe; The Manuscript, by Otto Larssen; The Sealed Room, by Bernhard Severin Ingemann; The Rector of Veilbye, by Steen Steensen Blicher; The Living Death, by Ferencz Molnar; Thirteen at Table, by Maurus Jokai; The Dancing Bear, by Etienne Barsony; The Tower Room, by Arthur Elck.

Volume 2 (*Mediterranean: Italian, Spanish, Oriental, Ancient Latin and Greek*): Shadows, by I. M. Palmarini; The Gray Spot, by Camillo Boito; The Stories of the Castle of Trezza, by Giovanni Gerga; The Imp in the Mirror, by Antonio Fogazzaro; The Deposition, by Luigi Capuana; The Nail, by Pedro de Alarcon; The Moscow Theater Plot, by Alfred Oranio; [Oriental Mystery Stories]; The Thief versus King Rhampsinitus, by Herodotus; The Oracle—Its Test by Croesus, by Herodotus; The Oracle—Behind the Scenes, by Herodotus; The Adventure of the Three Robbers, by Lucius Apuleius [*SHL* 31]; Letter to Sura, by Pliny the Younger [*SHL* 31].

Volume 3 (*German*): The Skeleton in the House, by Friedrich Spielhagen; The Man in the Bottle, by Gustav Meyrink; Christian Lahusen's Baron, by Dietrich Theden; Andrea Delfin, by Paul Heyse; The Singer, by Wilhelm Hauff; The Deserted House, by E. T. A. Hoffmann; The Versegy Case, by Karl Rosner; The Story in the Notebook, by August Groner; Well-Woven Evidence, by Dietrich Theden.

Volume 4 (*Classic French*): Ines de Las Sierras, by Charles Nodier; An Episode of Terror, by Honoré de Balzac; Madame Firmiani, by Honoré de Balzac; Melmoth Reconciled, by Honoré de Balzac [*SHL* 40]; The Conscript, by Honoré de Balzac; Zadig the Babylonian (excerpts), by Voltaire; D'Artagnan, Detective, by Alexandre Dumas.

Volume 5 (*Modern French*): The Crime of the Boulevard, by Jules Claretie; The Necklace, by Guy de Maupassant; The Man with the Pale Eyes, by Guy de Maupassant; An Uncomfortable Bed, by Guy de Maupassant; Ghosts, by Guy de Maupassant; Fear, by Guy de Maupassant; The Confession, by Guy de Maupassant; The Horla, by Guy de Maupassant [*SHL* 52, 65]; The Miracle of Zobéide, by Pierre Mille; The Torture of [*sic*] Hope, by Villiers de l'Isle-Adam [*SHL* 53]; The Owl's Ear, by Erckmann-Chatrian [*SHL* 53]; The Invisible Eye, by Erckmann-Chatrian [*SHL* 53]; The Waters of Death, by Erckmann-Chatrian [*SHL* 53]; The Man-Wolf, by Erckmann-Chatrian [*SHL* 53].

Volume 6 (*French Novels*): Count Kostia, by Victor Cherbuliez; André Cornélis, by Paul Bourget; The Lady of the Costellos, by Anonymous; Lady Betty's Indiscretion, by Anonymous.

Volume 7 (*Old Time English*): The Haunted House, by Charles Dickens; No. 1 Branch Line—The Signalman, by Charles Dickens; The Haunted and the Haunters, or, The House and the Brain, by Edward Bulwer-Lytton [*SHL* 46]; The Incantation, by Edward Bulwer-Lytton; The Avenger, by Thomas De Quincey; Melmoth the Wanderer (abridged), by Charles Robert Maturin [*SHL* 40–42]; A Mystery with a Moral, by Laurence Sterne; On Being Found Out, by William Makepeace Thackeray; The Notch on the Ax, by William Makepeace Thackeray; Bourgonef, by Anonymous; The Closed Cabinet, by Anonymous.

Volume 8 (*Modern English*): My Own True Ghost Story, by Rudyard Kipling; The Sending of Dana Da, by Rudyard Kipling; In the House of Suddhoo, by Rudyard Kipling; His Wedded Wife, by Rudyard Kipling; A Case of Identity, by A. Conan Doyle; A Scandal in Bohemia, by A. Conan Doyle; The Red-Headed League, by A. Conan Doyle; The Baron's Quarry, by Egerton Castle; The Fowl in the Pot, by Stanley J. Weyman; The Pavilion on the Links, by Robert Louis Stevenson; The Dream Woman, by Wilkie Collins; The Lost Duchess, by

Anonymous; The Minor Canon, by Anonymous; The Pipe, by Anonymous; The Puzzle, by Anonymous; The Great Valdez Sapphire, by Anonymous.

Volume 9 (*American*): By the Waters of Paradise, by F. Marion Crawford; The Shadows on the Wall, by Mary E. Wilkins Freeman [*SHL* 70]; The Corpus Delicti, by Melville Davisson Post; An Heiress from Red Horse, by Ambrose Bierce; The Man and the Snake, by Ambrose Bierce; The Oblong Box, by Edgar Allan Poe; The Gold-Bug, by Edgar Allan Poe; Wolfert Webber; or, Golden Dreams, by Washington Irving; Adventure of the Black Fisherman, by Washington Irving; Wieland's Madness [excerpt from *Wieland*], by Charles Brockden Brown [*SHL* 37–38]; The Golden Ingot, by Fitz-James O'Brien; My Wife's Tempter, by Fitz-James O'Brien; The Minister's Black Veil, by Nathaniel Hawthorne [*SHL* 63]; Horror: A True Tale, by Anonymous.

Volume 10 (*Real Life*): A Flight into Texas, by Arthur Train; Adventures in the Secret Service of the Post-Office Department, by P. H. Woodward; Saint-Germain the Deathless, by Andrew Lang; The Man in the Iron Mask, by Andrew Lang; A Conjuror's Confessions, by M. Robert-Houdin; Fraudulent Spritualism Unveiled, David P. Abbott; More Tricks of "Spritualism," by Hereward Carrington; How Spirits Materialize, by Anonymous; Inspector Bucket's Job, by Charles Dickens.

Obtained in New York in 1922 (HPL to Lillian D. Clark, 26 January 1926; *LFF*). HPL derived much of his source-material for *SHL* from this series: he read and commented on only the four Erckmann-Chatrian tales printed here, and confessed (HPL to R. H. Barlow, 1 December 1934 [*OFF* 193]) that he never read the entirety of Brown's *Wieland* but only the excerpt printed here (Volume IX); he made a similar admission concerning Maturin's *Melmoth the Wanderer* (see #644). *CE* 5.174 *MTS* 213 *ES* 137, 691 *OFF* 237, 259

429. Hawthorne, Nathaniel (1804–1864). *Grandfather's Chair: A History for Youth.* <1841> Philadelphia: H. Altemus, 1898. 282 pp. [MS/NUC 236:6]

    CF 4.143 *RB* 129

430. ———. *The House of the Seven Gables, and The Snow-Image and Other Twice-Told Tales.* <1851; 1852> Boston: Houghton Mifflin, 1886. 641 pp. [HPL/MS/NUC 236:10]

    Contents: The House of the Seven Gables; The Snow-Image: A Childish Miracle; The Great Stone Face; Main Street; Ethan Brand; A Bell's Biography; Sylph Etherege; The Canterbury Pilgrims; Old News; The Man of Adamant: An Apologue; The Devil in Manuscript; John Inglefield's Thanksgiving; Old Ticonderoga: A Picture of the Past; The Wives of the Dead; Little Daffydowndilly; My Kinsman, Major Molineux.

    CE 2.228 *SHL* 63–65, 91 *CB* 83 *AG* 137n13 *OFF* 231 *JFM* 25n9 *RB* 176 *JVS* 198

431. ———. *Legends of the Province House.* <1837> New York: Hurst, [190-?]. 255 pp. [MS/NUC 236:16]

Contents: Howe's Masquerade; Edward Randolph's Portrait; Lady Eleanor's Mantle; Old Esther Dudley.
SHL 63 *CB* 210

432. ———. *The Marble Faun; or, The Romance of Monte Beni*. <1860> 15th ed. Boston: Houghton Mifflin, 1887. 527 pp. [MS/NUC 236:19]
CE 5.227 *SHL* 62 *CB* 129

433. ———. *Mosses from an Old Manse*. <1846> New York: Lovell, Coryell & Co., [189-]. 463 pp. [MS/NUC 236:23]
Contents: The Old Manse; The Birth-Mark; A Select Party; Young Goodman Brown; Rappacini's Daughter; Mrs. Bullfrog; Fire-Worship; Buds and Bird-Voices; Monsieur de Miroir; The Hall of Fantasy; The Celestial Railroad; The Procession of Life; The New Adam and Eve; Egotisme; The Christmas Banquet; Drowne's Wooden Image; The Intelligence Office; Roger Malvin's Burial; P.'s Correspondence; Earth's Holocaust; The Old Apple Dealer; The Artist of the Beautiful; A Virtuoso's Collection.
Obtained in New York in September 1924 (HPL to Lillian D. Clark, 29–30 September 1924; *LFF*).

434. ———. *The Scarlet Letter and The Blithedale Romance*. <1850; 1852> 13th ed. Boston: Houghton Mifflin, 1887. 600 pp. [MS/NUC 236:35]
AG 137n12 *JVS* 343

435. ———. *Tanglewood Tales for Girls and Boys: Being a Second Wonder-Book*. <1853> New York: A. L. Burt, [189-?] or [1907]. 317 pp. [MS/ NUC 236:48–49]
Contents: The Wayside (Introductory); The Minotaur; The Pygmies; The Dragon's Teeth; Circe's Palace; The Pomegranate Seeds; The Golden Fleece.
This volume, along with *A Wonder Book* (#436), helped awaken HPL's interest in classical antiquity. *CE* 1.165; 5.143, 145, 288 *SHL* 62 *SL* 1.299 *MWM* 45

436. ———. *Twice-Told Tales*. <1837/1842> Edited for School Use by Robert Herrick and Robert Walter Bruère. Chicago: Scott, Foresman & Co., 1903 (542 pp.) or [1919] (554 pp.). [MS/NUC 236:55–56]
Contents: Biographical Sketch; Hawthorne's Literary Work; The Gray Champion; Sunday at Home; The Wedding Knell; The Minister's Black Veil; The May-Pole of Merry Mount; The Gentle Boy; Mr. Higginbotham's Catastrophe; Little Annie's Ramble; Wakefield; A Rill from the Town Pump; The Great Carbuncle; The Prophetic Pictures; David Swan; Sights from a Steeple; The Hollow of the Three Hills; The Toll-Gatherer's Day; The Vision of the Fountain; Fancy's Show Box; Dr. Heidegger's Experiment; Legends of the

Province House; Edward Randolph's Portrait; Lady Eleanor's Mantle; Old Esther Dudley; The Haunted Mind; The Village Uncle; The Ambitious Guest; The Sister-Years; Snow-Flakes; The Seven Vagabonds; The White Old Maid; Peter Goldthwaite's Treasure; Chippings with a Chisel; The Shaker Bridal; Night Sketches; Endicott and the Red Cross; The Lily's Quest; Footprints on the Seashore; Edward Fane's Rosebud; The Threefold Destiny.

SHL 63 *CB* 210

437. ———. *A Wonder Book for Boys and Girls, Comprising Stories of Classical Fables.* <1852> New York: A. L. Burt, n.d. iv, 290 pp. [MS/NUC 236:57]

Contents: The Gorgon's Head; The Golden Touch; The Paradise of Children; The Three Golden Apples; The Miraculous Pitcher; The Chimaera.
CE 5.143, 145, 288 *SHL* 63 *SL* 1.299 *MWM* 45

438. Hayden, John A. B. *A Compendium of the Fabulous History of Greece: Being the First Part of a Plain Digest of the Classical Fables.* Dublin: William Shaw, 1821. 12, 89, 34 pp. [MS/OCLC]

439. Hayes, Isaac Israel (1832–1881). *The Open Polar Sea: A Narrative of a Voyage of Discovery towards the North Pole.* Philadelphia: David McKay, 1885. xxiv, 454 pp. [MS/NUC 236:431]

440. Hearn, Lafcadio (1850–1904). *Kwaidan: Stories and Studies of Strange Things.* <1904> Boston: Houghton Mifflin, 1930. 240 pp. [HPL/NUC 237:251]

Contents: Kwaidan; The Story of Mimi-nashi-Hoichi; Oshidori; The Story of O-Tei; Ubazakura; Diplomacy; Of a Mirror and a Bell: Jinininki; Mujina; Rokuro-Kubi; A Dead Secret; Yuki-Onna; The Story of Aoyagi; Jiu-roku-zakura; The Dream of Akinosuke; Riki-Bara; Hi-mawari; Horai; Insect Studies: Butterflies; Mosquitoes; Ants.
SHL 73. In *SHL* HPL also speaks highly of Hearn's *Fantastics,* posthumously published in 1914. *ES* 75, 78, 92, 246

441. Heatley, H[enry] R[ichard], and H[erbert] N[apier] Kingdon. *Gradatim: An Easy Latin Translation Book for Beginners.* Revised for American Schools by W[illiam] C[oe] Collar. Boston: Ginn & Co., 1889. vii, 139 pp. [X/NUC 237:389]

442. Heller, Louie Regina (1870–?), ed. *Early American Orations 1760–1824.* <1909> New York: Macmillan Co., 1923. xvii, 199 pp. [MS/NUC 239:433]

443. Hemans, Felicia Dorothea (1793–1835). *The Breaking Waves Dashed High (The Pilgrim Fathers)*. Boston: Lee & Shepard, 1870. 18 leaves. [MS/NUC 240: 33]

No ed. cited by MS. A series of poems about the Pilgrims by Hemans, illustrated by chromolithographs.

444. Herbert, Edward Herbert, baron (1582–1648). *The Life of Edward Lord Herbert of Cherbury*. <1643?> Written by Himself. London: Printed for Hunt & Clarke, 1827. 171 pp. [MS/NUC 241:521]

Herbert was an Anglo-Welsh poet, theologian, and diplomat.

445. Hergesheimer, Joseph (1880–1954). *Balisand*. New York: Alfred A. Knopf, 1924. 371 pp. [HPL to Lillian D. Clark, 29–30 September 1924; *LFF*/NUC 242:81]

Gift of J. C. Henneberger. Hergesheimer was a bestselling American novelist of the period. *JFM* 261

446. Herodotus (fl. 5th c. B.C.E.). *The Ancient History of Herodotus*. Translated from the Original Greek by Rev. William Beloe <1791>. With the Life of Herodotus by Leonhard Schmitz. New ed., rev., & cor. New York: Bangs Brothers, 1855. xv, 489 pp. [MS/NUC 242:480]

Obtained in New York in September 1924 (HPL to Lillian D. Clark, 29–30 September 1924; *LFF*). *SL* 1.352 *CLM* 332

447. Hersey, Harold (1893–1956). *Night*. With Forty-four Full-Page Drawings and Nineteen Decorations by Elliot Dold. New York: Privately printed for subscribers only, 1923. 176 pp. [HPL to Richard Ely Morse, 30 November 1935/NUC 243:183]

Given to HPL by Richard Ely Morse.

448. Hervey, James (1714–1758). *Meditations and Contemplations*. <1746–47> The Sixteenth Edition. London: Printed; New York: Re-printed, by H. Gaine, 1778. 2 vols. in 1. [MS/NUC 243:372]

Contents: Vol. 1: Meditations among the Tombs; Reflections on a Flower Garden; A Descant on Creation; Vol. 2: Contemplations on the Night; Contemplations on the Starry Heavens; A Winter Piece.

Gift of Laurie A. Sawyer (HPL to Sarah S. Lovecraft, 17 March 1921). Hervey was one of the "Graveyard Poets" of the 18th century, a school that featured occasional elements of weirdness in their verse.

449. Hesiod (fl. 700 B.C.E.?). *The Works of Hesiod.* Translated from the Greek by Mr. [Thomas] Cooke. London: Printed by J. Wilson for J. Wood and C. Woodward, 1740. lv, 240 pp. [MS/NUC 243:569]

  SL 3.317 *ES* 379

450. Higgins, Lothrop D[avis] (1876–1935). *Lessons in Physics.* Boston: Ginn & Co., 1903. vii, 403 pp. [L. W. Currey, *Catalogue 74* (Fall 1983)/NUC 245:291]

451. Hill, George Canning (1825–1898). *Benedict Arnold: A Biography.* Philadelphia: Lippincott, 1868. 295 pp. [MS/NUC 246:4]

452. Hinks, Arthur R[obert] (1873–1945). *Astronomy.* New York: Henry Holt & Co., 1911. 256 pp. [MS/NUC 246:652]

453. Hoag, Jonathan E. (1831–1927). *The Poetical Works of Jonathan E. Hoag: With Portrait and Autograph of the Author.* Author's Edition. Biographical and Critical Preface by H. P. Lovecraft. New York: [Privately Printed,] 1923. xi, 72 pp. [X—JHL/NUC 248:489]

  Contains HPL's "Introduction," pp. iii–vii; "Prologue" to "Amid Inspiring Scenes" by J. E. Hoag, p. 41; 6 birthday poems to Hoag, pp. 61–67. The book also contains the poems "Death" and "To the American Flag," which, though long ascribed to HPL, seem unquestionably to be Hoag's (though perhaps revised by HPL); see S. T. Joshi, "Two Spurious Lovecraft Poems," in *Lovecraft and a World in Transition* (New York: Hippocampus Press, 2014), 437–39. HPL edited the volume, with some assistance from James F. Morton and Samuel Loveman. It was funded by Hoag. Author's presentation copy to HPL, with inscription: "To my friend H. P. Lovecraft. Please accept compliments of your friend J. E. Hoag," dated 3 July 1923. *CE* 1.267n5; 2.65–68 *MTS* 197 *RK* 230n1 *JFM* 12, 25n11, 28, 36–37, 39

454. Hogarth, William (1697–1764). *The Complete Works of William Hogarth.* Introductory Essay by James Hannay. London: Printing & Publishing Co., 1890. 2 vols.; 150 plates. [MS/NUC 250:568/ OCLC]

455. [Holbrook, Josiah (1788–1854).] *A Familiar Treatise on the Fine Arts, Painting, Sculpture, and Music.* Boston: Waitt & Dow, 1833. 277 pp. [MS/NUC 251:112]

456. Holliday, Carl (1879–1936). *The Wit and Humor of Colonial Days (1607–1800).* Philadelphia: J. B. Lippincott Co., 1912. 319 pp. [MS/NUC 251:528]

Obtained at Dauber & Pine bookshop in February 1926 (HPL to Lillian D. Clark, 12 February 1926; *LFF*).

457. Holmes, Oliver Wendell (1809–1894). *The Autocrat of the Breakfast-Table: Every Man His Own Boswell.* <1858> Boston: Houghton Mifflin, 1887. ix, 321 pp. or x, 411 pp. [MS/NUC 252:160]

There were 3 printings and 2 eds. in 1887. HPL met Holmes when he was an infant (see *RK* 30). *CE* 2.188

458. ———. *The Poetical Works of Oliver Wendell Holmes.* Boston: Houghton Mifflin, 1887. x, 357 pp. [MS/NUC 252:204]

"I like . . . the verse of O. W. Holmes" (*RK* 148). Holmes "was a devotee of Pope, & has been called 'the modern Pope'" (*RK* 30).

459. Holmes, Prescott. *The Story of Exploration and Adventure in the Frozen Seas.* Philadelphia: H. Altemus, 1896. 256 pp. [MS/NUC 252:227]

460. *Home Brew.* Edited by Mrs. and Mr. G. J. Houtain. 1922–23.

Contains: HPL's "Herbert West—Reanimator" (February–July 1922; as "Grewsome Tales") and "The Lurking Fear" (February–May 1923), the latter illustrated by Clark Ashton Smith. Many references to this periodical in HPL's letters.

461. Homer (fl. 750 B.C.E.?). *The Hymns of Homer; The Batrachonomyomachia; and Two Original Poetical Hymns.* By George Chapman <1616?; 1625?> Chiswick: From the Press of C. Whittingham, 1818. lxiv, 153, 47 pp. [MS/NUC 253:207]

CF 4.25

462. ———. *The Iliad of Homer.* With an Interlinear Translation . . . on the Hamiltonian System, as Improved by Thomas Clark. Philadelphia: C. DeSilver & Sons, [1888]. viii, 367 pp. [MS/NUC 253:113]

AT 19

463. ———. *The Iliad of Homer.* Translated by Alexander Pope <1715–20>. With Notes and Introduction by Theodore Alois Buckley. New York: A. L. Burt, [1902]. 548 pp. [MS/NUC 253:129]

It is not certain that HPL had this volume; MS lists only "Homer, Burt." *AG* 21

464. ———. *The Odyssey.* Translated by Alexander Pope, Esq. <1725–26>. To Which Is Added *The Battle of the Frogs and Mice.* London: Printed for G. B. Whittaker, 1827. 513 pp. [MS/NUC 253:176]

CF 2.54, 3.155

465. Hooker, Sir Joseph Dalton (1817–1911). *Botany.* <1876> 3d ed., rev. and corr. New York: American Book Co., [1896]. 129 pp., 68 plates. [X/NUC 253:685]

CE 2.195

466. Horace (Q. Horatius Flaccus) (65–8 B.C.E.). *Horace.* Translated by Philip Francis, with an Appendix, Containing Translations of Various Odes, &c., by Ben Jonson, Cowley, Milton, Dryden, Pope, &c. <1831> New York: Harper & Brothers, 1835. 2 vols. [MS/NUC 254:547]

The second volume also contains Phaedrus, tr. Christopher Smart (1765). Note HPL's own translation of Horace's *Odes* 3.9 (*AT* 192). *ES* 379

467. ———. *Horace.* Translated by Philip Francis.... New York: Harper & Brothers, 1838. 2 vols. [X/eBay [vol. 2 only]/MS/NUC 254:547]

A reprint of the above edition.

468. ———. *Opera: Oeuvres d'Horace.* Edition Classique avec Notice et Commentaires en français par F. Dübner. Paris: J. Lecoffre, 1887. xxii, 492 pp. [MS/BN 73:660]

469. ———. *The Works of Q. Horatius Flaccus.* The Original Text Being Reduced to the Natural Order and Construction, with Stirling's Translation Interlinearly Arranged by P. A. Nuttall. Philadelphia: D. McKay, [1884?]–[19—?]. 502 pp. [MS/NUC 254:541]

No date cited by MS; there are at least 3 printings. *CE* 1.137; 5.285n1

470. Houdini, Harry [pseud. of Ehrich Weiss (1874–1926)]. *A Magician among the Spirits.* New York: Harper & Brothers, 1924. xix, 294 pp. [X/HPL/MS/NUC 254:49]

A debunking of spiritualism. Author's inscribed copy to HPL: "To my friend Howard Lovecraft, / Best Wishes, / Houdini. / 'My brain is the key that sets me free.'" *CE* 3.11

471. Howard, John. *The Illustrated Scripture History for the Young.* <1852> Philadelphia: J. D. Carson & Co., [1859?]. 2 vols. [Grill-Binkin/OCLC]

HPL had Vol. 1 only. L. W. Currey, offering this book for sale, notes: "An early hectographed Lovecraft bookplate is affixed to the rear cover, which is also embellished with numerous penciled and inked Latin names and phrases."

472. Howe, Daniel Wait (1839–1920). *The Puritan Republic of the Massachusetts Bay in New England.* Indianapolis: Bowen-Merrill Co., 1899. xxxviii, 422 pp. [MS/NUC 257:44]

473. Howitt, William (1792–1879). *The Northern Heights of London.* London: Longmans, Green & Co., 1869. xxvi, 590 pp. [MS/NUC 257:304]

474. [Howland, Mrs Avis C. (1795–1842)]. *Rhode-Island Tales, and Tales of Old Times.* By a Friend of Youth of Newport, R.I. New York: Mahlon Day, 1839. 172 pp. [MS/NUC 257:309]

Poems. Includes "Little Ellen and Other Pleasing Poetic Stories" by A[bby] L[ee], pp. 129–72. Given to HPL by Gervaise Butler, a friend of Samuel Loveman (HPL to Lillian D. Clark, 21–22 May 1930; *LFF*).

475. Hudson, W[illiam] H[enry] (1841–1922). *Green Mansions: A Romance of the Tropical Forest.* <1904> [HPL to Duane W. Rimel, 16 April 1935 (*FLB* 266)/NUC 258:410–12]

ES 66 *FLB* 271

476. Hughes, Rupert (1872–1956). *The Golden Ladder.* New York & London: Harper & Brothers, 1924. 354 pp. [HPL to Lillian D. Clark, 29–30 September 1924; *LFF*/NUC 259:212]

An historical novel about the owner of the Morris-Jumel Mansion in New York City, by a popular American novelist of the period. Gift of J. C. Henneberger.

477. Hugo, Victor (1802–1885). *Hans of Iceland.* <1825> [HPL]

No ed. cited by HPL. Translation of *Han d'Islande* (1823). *SHL* 51

478. Huish, Robert (1777–1850). *Memoirs of George IV.* New York: Adams, Victor & Co., 1875. 499 pp. [X/MS/NUC 259:529]

479. Humboldt, Alexander, freiherr von (1769–1859). *The Travels and Researches of Alexander von Humboldt.* New York: J. & J. Harper, 1833. 367 pp. [MS/NUC 260:112]

480. Humelbergius Secundus, Dick [pseud.]. *Apician Morsels; or, Tales of the Table, Kitchen, and Larder.* New-York: J. & H. Harper, 1829. 212 pp. [MS/NUC 260:204]

481. Hussey, Christopher (1899–?), ed. *The Old Homes of Britain: The Southern Counties—Kent, Sussex, Hampshire, Surrey and Middlesex.* London: Country Life; New York: Charles Scribner's Sons, [1928]. 80 pp. [MS/NUC 261:612]

482. Hutton, Maurice (1856–1940). *The Greek Point of View.* New York: George H. Doran Co., [1925]. 207 pp. [MS/NUC 262:224]

483. Huysmans, Joris-Karl (1848–1907). *Against the Grain (A Rebours).* <1884> Translated by John Howard. Introduction by Havelock Ellis. New York: Albert & Charles Boni, 1930. 331 pp. [HPL/NUC 262:348]

For the influence of this novel upon HPL's "The Hound" (1922), see Steven J. Mariconda, "The Hound—A Dead Dog?," in *H. P. Lovecraft: Art, Artifact, and Reality* (New York: Hippocampus Press, 2013), 155–61. This copy obtained in October 1932 (*SL* 4.91), but HPL must have read some edition earlier than this one. *ES* 67, 68, 69, 72, 74, 76, 79 *OFF* 199 *RB* 149 *JVS* 104 *CLM* 299 *MWM* 265

484. ———. *Down There.* Translated by Keene Wallis. New York: Albert & Charles Boni, 1924. 317 pp. [NUC 262:353]

Translation of *La-Bàs* (1891). "I once owned this book, but it was lost amidst the calamities of a friend to whom I had lent it in 1925" (HPL to Robert Bloch, 3 December 1936 [*RB* 180]). *ES* 68, 75, 76, 79, 167 *RB* 149, 178, 356 *JVS* 121

485. Hyde, Edna. *From under a Bushel: A Book of Verse.* With an introduction by Samuel Loveman. Saugus, MA: Charles A. A. Parker, 1925. 90 pp. [HPL to Lillian D. Clark, 10 May 1928; *LFF*/NUC 262:437]

This may not be the book in question. In his letter to Clark, HPL notes that Samuel Loveman gave him a book of Hyde's poems "which had become a drug on the market." Hyde published another slim book of poems—*Turmoil* (Saugus, MA: Charles A. A. Parker, [1926?])—but this is only 20 pp., so probably *From under a Bushel* is the book HPL is referring to.

486. *Illustrated Family Christian Almanac.* New York: American Tract Society. [MS/NUC 264:603]

HPL had the issues for 1854 and 1856.

487. *Indian Notes: Published Quarterly in the Interest of the Museum of the American Indian, Heye Foundation.* New York, 1924–30. 7 vols. [MS/NUC 266:353]
HPL had only Vol. 3 (1926).

488. Ingram, John H[enry] (1842–1916). *Edgar Allan Poe: His Life, Letters, and Opinions.* London: J. Hogg, 1880. 2 vols. [MS/NUC 267:437]
Obtained in New York in September 1922 (HPL to Lillian D. Clark, 13–16 September 1922; *LFF*).

489. ———. *The Haunted Homes and Family Traditions of Great Britain.* Illustrated ed. London: Gibbings, 1901. xi, 641 pp. [HPL/MS/NUC 267:438]
MTS 54, 62, 81, 111, 113

490. *Interesting Homes of New England, from Original Photographs.* Boston: Burroughs & Co., 1915. 77 plates. [MS/NUC 268:609]

491. Irving, Washington (1783–1859). *The Alhambra.* <1832> New York: G. P. Putnam's Sons, 1889. 496 pp. [MS/NUC 272:163]

492. ———. *Bracebridge Hall.* <1822> Illustrated by [Randolph] Caldecott. New York: Hurst, n.d. 288 pp. [MS/NUC 272:177]

493. ———. *A History of New-York, from the Beginning of the World to the End of the Dutch Dynasty.* <1809> [HPL to Lillian D. Clark, 29–30 September 1924; *LFF*/NUC 272:197f.]
No ed. cited by HPL. *RB* 212n1

494. ———. *The Sketch-Book of Geoffrey Crayon, Gent.* <1819–20> Hudson Edition. New York: G. P. Putnam's Sons, 1880–88. 532 pp. [MS/NUC 272:162–65]
Contents: The Author's Account of Himself; The Voyage; Roscoe; The Wife; Rip van Winkle; English Writers on America; Rural Life in England; The Broken Heart; The Art of Book-Making; A Royal Poet; The Country Church; The Widow and Her Son; A Sunday in London; The Boar's Head Tavern, Eastcheap; The Mutability of Literature; Rural Funerals; The Inn Kitchen; The Spectre Bridegroom; Westminster Abbey; Christmas; The Stage Coach; Christmas Eve; Christmas Day; The Christmas Dinner; London Antiques; Little Britain; Stratford-on-Avon; Traits of Indian Character; Philip of Pokanoket; John Bull; The Pride of the Village; The Angler; The Legend of Sleepy Hollow; L'Envoy.
No date given by MS; there are at least 4 dates for the Hudson Edition.

495. ———. *Tales of a Traveler* [*sic*]. <1824> New York: American Book Co., 1894. 418 pp. [MS/NUC 272:282]

Contents: [Strange Stories by a Nervous Gentleman:] The Great Unknown; The Hunting Dinner; The Adventure of My Uncle; The Adventure of My Aunt; The Bold Dragoon; The Adventure of the German Student; The Adventure of the Mysterious Picture; The Adventure of the Mysterious Stranger; The Story of the Young Italian; [Buckthorne and His Friends:] Literary Life; A Literary Dinner; The Club of Queer Fellows; The Poor-Devil Author; Notoriety; A Practical Philosopher; Buckthorne; Grave Reflections of a Disappointed Man; The Booby Squire; The Strolling Manager; [The Italian Banditti:] The Inn at Terracina; The Adventure of the Little Antiquary; The Belated Travellers; The Adventure of the Popkins Family; The Painter's Adventure; The Story of the Bandit Chieftain; The Story of the Young Robber; The Adventure of the Englishman; [The Money-Diggers:] Hell-Gate; Kidd and the Pirate; The Devil and Tom Walker; Wolfert Webber; The Adventure of the Black Fisherman.

SHL 45–46, 60

496. Isham, Norman Morrison (1864–1943). *The Meeting House of the First Baptist Church in Providence: A History of the Fabric.* Providence: [Printed at the Akerman-Standard Co.,] 1925. xiii, 33 pp. [MS/NUC 272:492]

HPL frequently refers to Isham as a leading authority on Providence architecture.

497. Jackson, Charles Loring (1847–1935). *The Gold Point and Other Strange Stories.* Boston: Stratford Co., 1926. 275 pp. [HPL/NUC 274:567]

Contents: The Gold Point; The Moth; An Uncomfortable Night; Mr. Smith; The Cube; Sister Hannah; Linden; The Travelling Companion; Lot 13; An Undiscovered "Isle in the Far Sea"; The Three Nails; A Remarkable Case.

Jackson was best known as a leading American organic chemist. This is his only volume of fiction. *ES* 231

498. James, Henry (1843–1916). *The Two Magics: The Turn of the Screw; Covering End.* <1898> New York: Macmillan Co., 1911. 393 pp. [HPL/RHB/NUC 276:566]

Given to HPL by August Derleth (*ES* 280). *SHL* 27, 68 *ES* 78, 256, 280, 409 *FLB* 24, 30, 47, 76, 146, 252, 307 *CLM* 237

499. James, M[ontague] R[hodes] (1862–1936). *Ghost-Stories of an Antiquary.* London: Edward Arnold, 1904. xi, 270 pp. [HPL/OCLC]

Contents: Canon Alberic's Scrap-Book; Lost Hearts; The Mezzotint; The Ash-Tree; Number 13; Count Magnus; "Oh, Whistle, and I'll Come to You, My Lad"; The Treasure of Abbot Thomas.

No ed. cited by HPL. First read in December 1925 (HPL to Lillian D. Clark, 13 December 1925; *LFF*). *SHL* 91–95 *ES* 30, 80, 81, 101, 329 *FLB* 47

500. ———. *More Ghost Stories of an Antiquary.* London: Edward Arnold, 1911. vii, 274 pp. [HPL/OCLC]

Contents: A School Story; The Rose Garden; The Tractate Middoth; Casting the Runes; The Stalls of Barchester Cathedral; Martin's Close; Mr. Humphreys and His Inheritance.

No ed. cited by HPL. *SHL* 91–95 *ES* 30, 109, 334

501. ———. *A Thin Ghost and Others.* <1919> London: Edward Arnold, 1925. 152 pp. [X/HPL/NUC 267:618]

Contents: The Residence at Whitminster; The Diary of Mr. Poynter; An Episode of Cathedral History; The Story of a Disappearance and an Appearance; Two Doctors.

SHL 91–95 *ES* 31, 80, 81, 117, 334

502. ———. *A Warning to the Curious.* London: Edward Arnold, 1925. 199 pp. [HPL/OCLC]

Contents: The Haunted Doll's House; The Uncommon Prayer-Book; A Neighbour's Landmark; A View from a Hill: A Warning to the Curious; An Evening's Entertainment.

No ed. cited by HPL. *SHL* 91–85 *ES* 31, 101, 329

503. Jebb, R[ichard] C[laverhouse] (1841–1905). *Greek Literature.* <1877> New York: American Book Co., [188-?]–[1927?]. 176 pp. [X/NUC 278:591–92]

CE 2.191

504. Jefferies, Richard (1848–1887). *The Gamekeeper at Home.* <1878> New ed. Boston: Roberts Brothers, 1890. 221 pp. [MS/NUC 279:61]

On game preservation, hunting, and country life.

505. Jenks, William (1778–1866), ed. *The Comprehensive Commentary on the Holy Bible.* Brattleboro, VT: Fessenden & Co., 1835–38. 5 vols. [HPL to R. H. Barlow, 23 July 1936 (*OFF* 357n9)/NUC 53:228]

HPL notes that he had recently received (from "the old lady downstairs," i.e., Alice Sheppard) "a stupendous Biblical Commentary . . . in 5 huge volumes printed in Brattleboro, Vt. in 1835."

506. Jervis, William Henley (1813–1883). *The Student's France: A History of France from the Earliest Times to the Establishment of the Second Empire in 1852.* New York: Harper & Brothers, 1869. xii, 730 pp. [MS/NUC 280:49]

CE 2.192

507. Johnson, Clifton (1865–1940). *The New England Country.* Boston: Lee & Shepard, 1893. x, 121 pp. [HPL to Lillian D. Clark, 16 February 1925; *LFF*/OCLC]

No ed. cited by HPL. Obtained in February 1925.

508. ———. *What They Say in New England: A Book of Signs, Sayings and Superstitions.* Boston: Lee & Shepard, 1897. 263 pp. [MS/NUC 282:24]

Obtained in New York in January 1925 (HPL to Annie E. P. Gamwell, 10 February 1925).

509. Johnson, Fanny Kemble (1868–1950). *Silver Wings and Other Poems.* Philadelphia: Walter C. Chiles, 1891. [vi], 60 pp. [HPL to Edward H. Cole, 30 April 1935/OCLC]

Gift of Ernest A. Edkins.

510. Johnson, Gaylord. *Nature's Program.* Garden City, NY: Doubleday, Page & Co., 1926. 181 pp. [X/NUC 282:120]

511. Johnson, Samuel (1709–1784). *The Beauties of Samuel Johnson, LL.D., Consisting of Maxims and Observations, Moral, Critical, and Miscellaneous.* London: G. Kearsley, J. Walker, 1797. cxv, 294 pp. [MS/NUC 282:394]

512. ———. *A Dictionary of the English Language.* <1755> 12th ed., corr, & rev. with Considerable Additions from the 8th ed. of the Original. Montrose, Scotland: Printed by D. Buchanan, Sold by J. Fairbairn, 1802. [564] pp. [MS/NUC 282:399/OCLC]

HPL obtained his copy from Walter Raleigh Danforth, a distant relative (see *ET* 75). *CF* 1.60 *OFF* 242 *ES* 379

513. ———. *The Idler.* <1758–60> With Additional Essays. Philadelphia: Printed by Tesson & Lee for S. F. Bradford & J. Conrad, 1803. 2 vols. [MS/NUC 282:410]

HPL had only Vol. 1. *CE* 2.189 *ES* 379

514. ———. *Johnson's History of Rasselas, Prince of Abyssinia.* <1759> Edited with an Introduction on Methods of Study Fred N. Scott. Boston: Leach, Shewell, & Sanborn, [1891]. v, 214 pp. [MS/NUC 282:445]

515. ———. *A Journey to the Western Islands of Scotland.* <1775> 1st. American Ed. Baltimore: P. H. Nicklin & Co.; Boston: Farrand, Mallory & Co., 1810. 284 pp. [MS/NUC 282:415]
ET 46–47

516. ———. *Lives of the Most Eminent English Poets, with Critical Observation on Their Works.* <1779–81> With Notes Corrective and Explanatory by Peter Cunningham, and a Life of the Author by Thomas Babington Macaulay. New York: Derby & Jackson, 1857. 2 vols. [MS/NUC 282:423]
CF 2.410 *ES* 391

517. ———. *The Rambler.* <1750–52> With an Historical and Biographical Preface by Alexander Chalmers. Philadelphia: E. Earlie, 1812. 4 vols. [MS/NUC 282:436]
CE 1.51 *ES* 379

518. *Johnsoniana: A Collection of Miscellaneous Anecdotes and Sayings of Dr. Samuel Johnson, Gathered from Nearly a Hundred Different Publications.* Printed Separately from Croker's Edition of Boswell's *Life of Johnson.* London: H. G. Bohn, 1845. vi, 335, 240 pp. [MS/NUC 282:566]

519. Jonson, Ben (1572?–1637). *The Complete Plays of Ben Jonson.* London: J. M. Dent; New York: E. P. Dutton (Everyman's Library), [1910]. 2 vols. [MS/NUC 284:441]
CE 1.41 *MF* 428 *RB* 120

520. Joy, James Richard (1863-1957). *An Outline History of England.* New York: Chautauqua Press, 1890. 311 pp. [MS/NUC 285:644]

521. Jung-Stilling, Johann Heinrich (1740–1817). *Theory of Pneumatology, in Reply to the Question, What Ought to Be Believed or Disbelieved concerning Presentiments, Visions, and Apparitions, According to Nature, Reason, and Scripture.* Translated from the German, with Copious Notes, by Samuel Jackson. London: Longman, Rees, Orme, Brown, Green & Longman, 1834. xxii, 460 pp. [HPL/MS/NUC 286:569]

522. Juvenal (D[ecimus] Junius Juvenalis) (60?–140?). *The Satires of Decimus Junius Juvenalis.* With a Literal Interlinear Translation on the Hamiltonian System by Hiram Corson. With a Life of Juvenal by William Gifford, Esq. Philadelphia: David McKay, [1868]. 253 pp. [MS/NUC 287:264]
AT 389 *MTS* 33 *ET* 32

523. ——— [et al.]. *The Satires of Juvenal, Persius, Sulpicia, and Lucilius.* Literally Translated into English Prose by the Rev. Lewis Evans. To Which Is

Added the Metrical Version of Juvenal and Persius by the Late William Gifford <1802>. London: George Bell & Sons, 1910. lx, 512 pp. [MS/NUC 287:272]

524. Kames, Henry Home, Lord (1696–1782). *Elements of Criticism.* <1762> By Henry Home of Kames. Edited by Prof. James R. Boyd. New York: A. S. Barnes & Co., 1857. 486 pp. [MS/NUC 288:472]

An historically significant work of criticism by a leading member of the Scottish Enlightenment.

525. Keats, John (1795–1821). *The Poetical Works of John Keats.* New-York: Wiley & Putnam, 1846. 2 vols. in 1. [MS/NUC 291:315]

CF 1.265 *SHL* 33 *ET* 139

526. Keetels, Jean Gustave. *An Analytical and Practical French Grammar.* <1872> New York: Clark & Maynard, 1878. 523 pp. [X—JHL/NUC 291:507]

Front flyleaf inscribed "Susie Phillipps [*sic*], 194 [written over 276] Angell St, Prov" (i.e., Sarah Susan Phillips Lovecraft, HPL's mother) and "H. P. Lovecraft, 598 Angell St., Providence, R.I." HPL's manuscript notations, in Latin, are found on the free endpaper facing the inscription: "Hic liber mihi est" [this is my book] and "Lingua Latina melior quam Gallica est" [the Latin language is better than French].

527. Kellogg, Vernon Lyman (1867–1937). *Human Life as the Biologist Sees It.* New York: Henry Holt & Co., 1922. vii, 140 pp. (Brown University: The Colver Lectures, 1921.) [MS/NUC 292:445]

CE 2.195

528. Keltie, Sir John Scott (1840–1927), ed. *The Works of the British Dramatists.* Edinburgh: W. P. Nimmo, 1870. 549 pp. [MS/NUC 292:635]

Contents: Plays by John Lyly, George Peele, Robert Greene, Christopher Marlowe, Ben Jonson, Beaumont and Fletcher, John Webster, John Marston, Philip Massinger, John Ford, Thomas Heywood, and James Shirley.

529. Kendrick, Asahel C[lark] (1809–1895). *An Introduction to the Greek Language: Containing an Outline of the Grammar, with Appropriate Exercises.* <1841> 2nd ed., rev. & enl. Hamilton, NY: S. C. Griggs; New York: M. H. Newman & Co., 1847. 172 pp. [X/NUC 293:168]

The book bears HPL's signature, address ("598 Angell St."), and apparent date of acquisition ("Aug 31 1905") on the front endpaper. The bookseller listing this item writes that the book also has "Lovecraft's home-made index to vocabulary section, pages [145] to [174]—a penciled Greek alphabet running vertically down page [145] and fore edges pp. [147]–172 trimmed in varying lengths to create 14 tabs which Lovecraft has labeled accordingly, and with his penciled note on p. [174], 'This book was indexed by H P Lovecraft Sun Sep 24 1905.'" The bookseller gives the date as 1846, but no such date is listed in NUC or OCLC.

530. King, Basil (1859–1928). *The Spreading Dawn: Stories of the Great Transition.* New York: Harper & Brothers, 1927. viii, 316 pp. [HPL/MS/NUC 296:282]

Contents: The Spreading Dawn; The Ghost's Story; Heaven; Abraham's Bosom; Going West; The Last Enemy.

The title story is a sentimental romance that was made into a silent film in 1917. At least a few of the other stories are presumably weird. The author was a Canadian clergyman.

531. King, Moses (1853–1909), ed. *King's Hand-Book of Boston.* 7th ed., rev. & enl. Cambridge, MA: Moses King, 1885. 387 pp. [MS/NUC 296:452]

532. ———, ed. *King's Pocket-Book of Providence, R.I.* Providence: Tibbitts & Shaw, 1882. 124 pp. [MS/NUC 296:453]

533. [Kinglake, Alexander William (1809–1891).] *Eōthen; or, Traces of Travel Brought Home from the East.* New ed. New-York: G. P. Putnam, 1850. x, 232 pp. [MS/NUC 296:594]

A significant book about travels in the Middle East. Obtained in New York in September 1924 (HPL to Lillian D. Clark, 29–30 September 1924; *LFF*).

534. Kingsley, Charles (1819–1875). *The Heroes; or, Greek Fairy Tales for My Children.* <1856> Philadelphia: H. Altemus, 1895. 208 pp. [MS/NUC 296:667]

Contents: Perseus; The Argonauts; Theseus.
Sometimes published (and here printed on the spine) as *The Greek Heroes.*

535. ———. *Poems.* 2nd ed. Boston: Ticknor & Fields, 1856. 284 pp. [MS/NUC 296:679]

536. Kipling, Rudyard (1865–1936). *The Mark of the Beast, and The Head of the District.* Girard, KS: Haldeman-Julius Co., [19—]. 62 pp. [HPL to Lillian D. Clark, 6 August 1925; *LFF*/NUC 297:301]
SHL 72–73

537. ———. *The Phantom 'Rickshaw and Other Tales.* <1888> [HPL]

No ed. cited by HPL; contents differ widely among the several collections with this title. *SHL* 72

538. Kirk, William (1880–?), ed. *A Modern City: Providence, Rhode Island and Its Activities*. Chicago: University of Chicago Press, 1909. ix, 363 pp. [MS/NUC 297:586]

    Contents: Introduction, by William Herbert Perry Faunce; Geography, by Charles Wilson Brown; Population, by William Macdonald; Industry, by William Babcock Weeden; Labor, by William Kirk; Government, by James Quayle Dealey; Finance, by Henry Brayton Gardner; Education, by George Grafton Wilson; Art, by William Carey Poland; Philanthropy, by Mary Conyngton; Religion, by Lester Bradner.

    Obtained in New York in February 1925 (HPL to Lillian D. Clark, 16 February 1925; *LFF*).

539. Kittredge, George Lyman (1860–1941). *The Old Farmer and His Almanack*. Boston: W. Ware & Co., 1904. xiv, 403 pp. [MS/NUC 298:296]

    "I suppose ya know that Prof. Kittredge of Harvard has written a book of old New England lore based on the Farmer's Almanack—its contents & history. I have this volume—you really ought to read it! It's as much a part of a New England education as Friends' Beans!" (*JFM* 147). Kittredge was also a celebrated Shakespearean scholar. *CE* 3.263

540. Knight, Cornelia (1757–1837), and Thomas Raikes (1777–1848). *Personal Reminiscences by Cornelia Knight and Thomas Raikes*. Edited by Richard Henry Stoddard. New York: Scribner, Armstrong & Co., 1875. xvi, 339 pp. [MS/NUC 300:199]

    Knight was a author, painter, and companion to Charlotte Augusta, Princess of Wales. Raikes was a well-known merchant and dandy of the day.

541. Knowles, James D[avis] (1798–1838). *Memoir of Roger Williams, the Founder of the State of Rhode-Island*. Boston: Lincoln, Edmunds & Co, 1834. 437 pp. [X/MS/NUC 300:584]

    Signed twice, first as "H. P. Lovecraft, Gent., Providence, Rhode-Island," then as "H. P. Lovecraft" with double underlining.

542. Kosztolányi, Dezső (1885–1936). *The Bloody Poet: A Novel about Nero*. By Desider Kostolanyi. With Prefatory Letter by Thomas Mann. Translated out of the German by Clifton P. Fadiman. New York: Macy-Masius, 1927. 344 pp. [HPL to August Derleth, [1 April 1929] (*ES* 190)/NUC 304:410] *CLM* 305

543. Krause, Ernst Ludwig (1839–1903). *Erasmus Darwin*. Translated from the German by W. S. Dallas. With a Preliminary Notice by Charles Darwin. New York: D. Appleton & Co., 1880. iv, 216 pp. [MS/NUC 305:555]

Translation of *Erasmus Darwin und seine Stellung in der Geschichte der Descendenz-Theorie* (1880).

544. Kugler, Francis [i.e., Franz Theodor] (1808–1858). *The Pictorial History of Germany during the Reign of Frederick the Great: Comprehending a Complete History of the Silesian Campaigns, and the Seven Years War*. Illustrated by Adolph Menzel. London: H. G. Bohn, 1845. 616 pp. [MS/NUC 308:222]

545. Kuntz, Eugene B., D.D. (1865–1944). *Thoughts and Pictures*. Author's Edition. Haverhill, MA: Co-operatively published by H. P. Loveracft [*sic*] and C. W. Smith, January, 1932. [22] pp. [X—JHL/Josiah]

HPL edited the book and wrote the foreword. Sewn wrappers. With a foreword by H. P. Lovecraft. This copy bears an inscription in pencil in the cover signed by Samuel Loveman: "This pamphlet was actually ghostwritten by H. P. Lovecraft." Loveman means that HPL revised the poems in the process of editing the book. *CE* 1.392–93; 2.143–44, 152

546. Lamb, Charles (1775–1834). *Complete Works in Prose and Verse*. Edited and Prefaced by R. H. Shepherd. Boston: De Wolfe, Fiske, [1874]. xv, 776 pp. [MS/NUC 312:568]

CF 2.417

547. ———. *Detached Thoughts on Books and Reading: Being One of the Last Essays of Elia*. <1833> Norwood, MA: Plimpton Press, 1910. [38] pp. [MS/NUC 312:579]

548. ———, and Mary Lamb (1764–1847). *Tales from Shakespeare*. <1807> Edited, with an Introduction, the Rev. Alfred Ainger. New York: Thomas Y. Crowell Co., 1895. 395 pp. [MS/NUC 312:627]

CE 2.187

549. La Motte-Fouqué, Friedrich Heinrich Karl (1777–1843). *Undine and Sintram*. <1811; 1815> Boston: Estes & Lauriat, [18—]. 313 pp. [HPL/RHB/NUC 313:367]

Contains: Undine; The Two Captains; Auslauga's Knight; Sintram and His Companions.

Translator not identified. *CE* 2.226; 5.174 *SHL* 49–50 *RB* 381 *JVS* 365

550. Lardner, Dionysius (1793–1859). *Popular Lectures on Science and Art, Delivered in the Principal Cities and Towns of the United States.* New York: Greeley & McElrath, 1846. 2 vols. [MS/NUC 316:302]

551. Larned, J[osephus] N[elson] (1836–1913). *A History of England, for the Use of Schools and Academies.* With Topical Analyses, Research Questions and Bibliographical Notes by Homer P. Lewis. Boston: Houghton Mifflin, [1900]. xxiii, 674 pp. [MS/NUC 316:417]
CE 2.192

552. Laswell, George D. *"Corners and Characters of Rhode Island."* Providence: Oxford Press, 1924. n.p. [MS/NUC 317:411]
Reprint of columns from the [Providence] *Evening Bulletin.* HPL mentions them frequently in his letters to his aunts during his stay in New York (1924–26), as he had asked Lillian D. Clark to send him the columns as they appeared.

553. *Leavitt's Farmer's Almanack and Miscellaneous Year Book 1862.* Concord, NH: Mirror Press of Russell & Davis, [1861]. [MS/NUC 321:455]
JFM 147

554. *Leavitt's Farmer's Almanack and Miscellaneous Year Book 1927.* Boston, [1926]. [MS/NUC 321:455]
This may not be the volume in question.

555. Lecky, W[illiam] E[dward] H[artpole] (1838–1903). *History of European Morals from Augustus to Charlemagne.* <1869> 3d ed., rev. New York: D. Appleton & Co., 1881. 2 vols. [MS/NUC 322:192]

556. Lederer, Charles (1856–1925). *Drawing Made Easy: A Book That Can Teach You How to Draw.* <1913> Chicago: Hall & McCreary, 1927. 347 pp. [MS/NUC 322:380]
MS gives date as 1929, but no data available. Perhaps obtained in January 1929 in Boston ("I have just acquired ... a treatise on *drawing*": HPL to Lillian D. Clark, 6 January 1929; *LFF*). *CE* 2.201

557. Lee, Guy Carleton (1862–1936). *The True History of the Civil War.* <1903> 2nd ed. Philadelphia: J. B. Lippincott Co., 1908. 421 pp. [MS/NUC 322:685]

558. Lee, Sarah (Wallis) Bowdich. *Anecdotes of the Habits and Instincts of Animals.* <1852> By Mrs. R. Lee. With Illustrations by Harrison Weir. London:

Griffith, Farrar, Okeden & Welsch; New York: E. P. Dutton, [1891]. viii, 312 pp. [MS/NUC 742:337]

559. Le Fanu, Joseph Sheridan (1814–1873). *The House by the Churchyard.* <1863> London: Macmillan & Co., 1899. viii, 456 pp. [HPL/MS/NUC 323:365]

HPL called this novel "an insufferably dull & Victorian specimen. In reading it, it was all I could do to keep awake!" (*ES* 693). Elsewhere HPL writes: "I have never read Le Fanu's 'Green Tea', so may possibly have misjudged him" (*DS* 334). "I at last have the *Omnibus [of Crime]*, and have read 'Green Tea'. It is certainly better than anything else of Le Fanu's that I have ever seen, though I'd hardly put it in the Poe-Blackwood-Machen class" (*DS* 342). *MTS* 15 *ES* 216, 416

560. Leith, W. Compton [pseud. of Ormonde M. Dalton (1866–1945)]. *Sirenica*. With an Introduction by William Marion Reedy. Portland, ME: Printed for Thomas Bird Mosher, 1927. xvi, 142 pp. [MS/NUC 325:245]

On sirens. NUC supplies a quotation: "The Muses and the Sirens together mean all art, and the Sirens alone romance. . . . Their bondsman . . . shall give up his soul to the lure of divine impossible things" (170, 174). Given to HPL by MWM (*ES* 216). *ES* 211 *JFM* 211–12, 224 *DS SL* 495

561. Leland, Charles Godfrey (1824–1903). *Abraham Lincoln and the Abolition of Slavery in the United States.* New York: H. M. Caldwell, [1881]. 250 pp. [MS/NUC 325:345]

562. Leonard, Sterling A[ndrus] (1888–1931), Harold Y[oung] Moffett, [and Maurice W. Moe (1882–1940)], ed. *Junior Literature.* New York: Macmillan Co., 1930f. [MS/NUC 327:140]

HPL had Vols. 2 and 3. Vol. 2 contains HPL's "Sleepy Hollow To-day," pp. 545–46 (originally part of a letter to MWM, published as "Observations on Several Parts of America"). *SL* 2.249–50

563. Le Queux, William (1864–1927). *The Closed Book, concerning the Secret of the Borgias.* London: Smart Set Publishing Co, 1904. 350 pp. [MS/NUC 327:480]

564. Lester, John C. (1835–1901), and D[aniel] L[ove] Wilson (1849–1902). *Ku Klux Klan: Its Origin, Growth and Disbandment.* With Introduction and Notes by Walter L. Fleming. New York: Neale Publishing Co., 1905. 198[+10] pp. [MS/NUC 328:458]

The book is of course about the original Ku Klux Klan as it was shortly after the Civil War. A new incarnation of the Klan emerged around 1915.

565. Level, Maurice (1875–1926). *Tales of Mystery and Horror.* Translated from the French by Alys Eyre Macklin, with an Introduction by Henry B. Irving. New York: Robert M. McBride & Co., 1920. xiii, 303 pp. [HPL/MS/NUC 329:492/Tuck 1:272]

Contents: The Debt Collector; The Kennel; Who; Illusion; In the Light of the Red Lamp; A Mistake; Extenuating Circumstances; The Confession; The Test; Porissette; The Father; For Nothing; In the Wheat; The Beggar; Under Chloroform; The Man Who Lay Asleep; Fascination; The Bastard; That Scoundrel Miron; The Taint; The Kiss; The Maniac; The 10.50 Express; Blue Eyes; The Empty House; The Last Kiss.
Obtained in New York in 1922. *SHL* 53 *ES* 85

566. ———. *Those Who Return (L'Ombre).* Translated from the French by B[érengère] Drillien. New York: Robert M. McBride & Co., 1923. 243 pp. [HPL/MS/NUC 329:492]

A novel. Obtained in August 1927 (*ES* 102). *ES* 85, 104

567. Lewis, Matthew Gregory (1775–1818). *The Monk: A Romance.* <1796> London: Brentano's, [1924]. 3 vols. in 1. [HPL/RHB/NUC 330:579]

This copy acquired December 1934 (*ES* 676). *CE* 2.225; 4.40 *SHL* 38–39 *SL* 5.244 *MTS* 20, 79, 183, 194 *ES* 34, 47 *OFF* 207 *JFM* 359, 360 *RB* 20, 124 *JVS* 251 *FLB* 122, 253, 259, 266

568. Liddell, Henry George (1811–1898). *A History of Rome from the Earliest Times to the Establishment of the Empire.* New York: Harper & Brothers, 1858–99. x, 768 pp. [MS/NUC 332:103f.]

No date cited by MS; there are 26 Harper printings. *CE* 2.192

569. ———, and Robert Scott (1811–1887). *A Greek-English Lexicon.* <1843> [NUC 332:99f.]

The standard Greek-English lexicon, still in use today in a revised edition. No ed. cited by HPL at *AG* 13; see also *SL* 5.233, where HPL states that he inherited his "tattered" copy from his uncle, Franklin Chase Clark. Elsewhere HPL says his downstairs neighbour, Alice Sheppard, gave him a new copy (*OFF* 356). *OFF* 242

570. Lincoln, John Larkin. *In Memoriam: John Larkin Lincoln 1817–1891.* Boston: Houghton Mifflin, 1894. iv, 641 pp. [MS/NUC 333:641]

A collection of his essays on classical philology.

571. Lindsay, Miss B. (d. 1917). *The Story of Animal Life*. New York: McClure, Phillips & Co., 1904. 196 pp. [MS/NUC 334:376]

572. Lippitt, Charles Warren (1846–1924). *The Battle of Rhode Island*. Newport, RI: Newport Historical Society, 1915. 23 pp. [HPL to Lillian D. Clark, 6 July 1925; *LFF*/NUC 335:284]

   Lippitt was a former governor of Rhode Island (1895–97). The battle took place in 1778.

573. Livingstone, David (1813–1873). *Missionary Travels and Researches in Africa*. New York: Harper & Brothers, 1857. xxiv, 732 pp. [X—JHL/NUC 336:625]

   Signed "Howard Phillips Lovecraft, June 16, 1898."

574. Livy (T[itus] Livius) (59 B.C.E.–17 C.E.). *Selections from the First Five Books, Together with the Twenty-first and Twenty-second Books Entire*. With an Interlinear Translation . . . by I. W. Bieber. Philadelphia: David McKay, [1872]. 601 pp. [MS/NUC 336:690]

   CE 2.28

575. ———. *The History of Rome*. Translated from the Original, with Notes and Illustrations, by George Baker. London: Jones & Co., 1830. 2 vols. [MS/NUC 336:658]

   Obtained from Dauber & Pine bookshop where Samuel Loveman worked (HPL to Lillian D. Clark, 12 April 1929; *LFF*).

576. Locker-Lampson, Frederick (1821–1895). *London Lyrics*. New York: White, Stokes & Allen, 1884. x, 108 pp. [MS/NUC 337:585]

   Vers de société of the sort written by Rheinhart Kleiner (and perhaps imitated by HPL in such poems as "A Year Off" [1925]).

577. ———. *London Lyrics*. New York: Stokes, 1891. x, 108 pp. [MS/NUC 337:586]

578. Lohr, Friedrich. *A Day in Ancient Rome*. Being a Revision of Lohr's *Aus dem alten Rom*, with Numerous Illustrations by Edgar S. Shumway. New York: Chautauqua Press, 1885. 96 pp. [MS/NUC 338:667]

   Lohr's treatise appeared in German in 1883.

579. London, Jack (1876–1916). *The Star Rover*. New York: Macmillan, 1915. 329 pp. [HPL/OCLC]

   No ed. cited by HPL.

580. Long, Frank Belknap, Jr. (1901–1994). *The Goblin Tower.* Cassia, FL: Dragon-Fly Press, 1935. 25 pp. [NUC 340:69]

HPL helped the publisher, R. H. Barlow, set type on the edition. *MTS* 366, 369, 377 *AG* 218, 224 *RK* 233 *ES* 727 *OFF* 207, 216, 218, 220, 224, 234, 235–36, 251, 252, 258, 259, 261, 307 *ET* 312, 317, 319, 320 *RB* 159n3, 166, 246, 320, 321 *JVS* 276 *FLB* 130, 296, 307, 312, 316, 317, 321 *CLM* 55n9, 57, 82–83, 114

581. ———. *The Man from Genoa and Other Poems.* With a Preface by Samuel Loveman. Athol, MA: W. Paul Cook, 1926. 31 pp. [NUC 340:69]

Designed as one of a trilogy of publications, along with HPL's *The Shunned House* (#592) and Loveman's *Hermaphrodite* (#593). *MTS* 10, 133, 253 *AG* 218, 220 *ES* 40n2, 240, 468 *OFF* 54, 176, 228, 304n2 *MF* 42, 47 *JFM* 86–87 *ET* 312 *RB* 321

582. Longfellow, Henry Wadsworth (1807–1882). *Poems of Henry Wadsworth Longfellow.* Boston: Houghton Mifflin, 1887. xviii, 492 pp. [MS/NUC 340:257]

583. Lossing, Benson J[ohn] (1813–1891). *A History of the Civil War 1861–65 and the Causes That Led Up to the Great Conflict.* New York: War Memorial Association, 1912. 512 pp. [MS/NUC 342:76]

Presumably a reprint or reworking of Lossing's *Pictorial History of the Civil War* (1866–74). This edition contains many reproductions of the photographs of Matthew Brady taken during the war.

584. Lounsbury, Thomas R[aynesford] (1838–1915). *History of the English Language.* New York: Henry Holt & Co., 1879. x, 371 pp. [MS/NUC 342:651]

HPL lent the volume to C. L. Moore in 1936 (see *CLM* 134, 135). *CE* 2.192

585. Lovecraft, H[oward] P[hillips] (1890–1937). *The Cats of Ulthar.* [Cassia, FL: The Dragon-Fly Press,] Christmas 1935. 10 pp. [X—JHL/Joshi]

This celebrated volume bears the inscription by R. H. Barlow, who printed the book, on the flyleaf: "Dear HP—Here is the booklet I so long ago promised! There were forty copies on ordinary paper, and only two on Red Lion text. This is one of the latter." On the grey paper front cover Barlow has written "ULTHAR" in black pen. *OFF* 309, 313, 314, 319, 344, 350 *ET* 321 *RB* 246 *FLB* 131, 312 *CLM* 108, 313n34

586. ———. *Charleston.* [New York: H. C. Koenig, 1936.] 20 pp. [HPL to Clark Ashton Smith, 23 April 1936 (*DS* 638)/Josiah]

In his letter to Smith, HPL reports receiving copies from the publisher. It is unclear whether this is the original version or another printed a few weeks later, wherein HPL revised his original letter describing Charleston sites into a more formal essay. The publication is mimeographed, with photostatic reproductions of HPL's drawings of Charleston architectural features.

587. ———. *The Crime of Crimes*. Llandudno, Wales: A. Harris, [1915]. [4] pp. [HPL to Arthur Harris, 23 August 1915/Joshi]

In his letter to Harris, HPL notes receiving copies of this, his first separately published work (a poem about the sinking of the *Lusitania*).

588. ———. *Further Criticism of Poetry*. Louisville, KY: Press of George G. Fetter Co., 1932. 13 pp. [HPL to August Derleth, [late September 1932] (*ES* 502)/OCLC]

A criticism of amateur journals that was deemed too long to publish in the *National Amateur*, hence was published separately. HPL notes in his letter to Derleth: "I have a goodly supply of copies." *CE* 2.152 *AG* 169 *MF* 457n20, 585n9 *ET* 220, 221 *JVS* 112n1, 326n3 *CLM* 100

589. ———. *Looking Backward*. Haverhill, MA: C. W. Smith, [1920]. 38 pp. [Joshi]

An essay on the "halcyon days" of amateur journalism (1885–95). HPL had given a copy of this book to R. H. Barlow (one copy in JHL bears an inscription by HPL to Barlow [see Joshi]), so the item must have once been in his possession. The publication is a kind of offprint of the serialisation of the article (an account of amateur journalism in 1885–95) in the *Tryout* (February–June 1920).

590. ———. *The Materialist Today*. [North Montpelier, VT: Driftwind Press, 1926.] 8 pp. [X/OCLC]

Presentation copy from the publisher, Walter J. Coates, inscribed: "Howard P. Lovecraft from Walter J. Coates, Editor of 'Drift Wind' in whose columns October—1926 this article originally appears. North Montpelier, Vt. May 30, 1926." *MTS* 99

591. ———. *The Shadow over Innsmouth*. Illustrated by Frank Utpatel. Everett, PA: Visionary Publishing Co., 1936. 158 pp. [HPL to August Derleth, 16 December 1936 (*ES* 761)/OCLC]

HPL reports receiving copies in early December and sending copies out soon thereafter. In his letter to Derleth he writes: "Under separate cover I'm sending with my compliments a copy of 'Innsmouth', corrected as far as possible, and a damn poor job for all that!" Many references to this book throughout HPL's letters.

592. ———. *The Shunned House.* Athol, MA: The Recluse Press, 1928. 59 pp. [X/NUC 343:105]

See #581. Of HPL's copy of this volume Roy A. Squires (*Catalogue 8*) has remarked: "Bound in full leather, hand-tooled with raised bands, by Robert H. Barlow, who in pencil on the first flyleaf inscribed: 'For HPL—Who only wrote it—With the compliments of the binder. R.H.B. June 9, 1935. On the occasion of his second visit.'" Many references to this book throughout HPL's letters.

593. Loveman, Samuel (1887–1976). *The Hermaphrodite: A Poem.* With a Preface by Benjamin De Casseres. Athol, MA: W. Paul Cook, 1926. 33 pp. [X—JHL/OCLC]

See #581. Bears the inscription: "For Howard P. Lovecraft with the compliments of W. Paul Cook." *CE* 5.152 *MTS* 7, 8, 10, 12, 42, 48, 98, 253–54 *AG* 121 *ES* 56, 74, 193, 468, 471 *OFF* 54, 172, 228, 295 *JFM* 61, 122–23 *ET* 26 *JVS* 332

594. ———. *The Hermaphrodite and Other Poems.* Caldwell, ID: The Caxton Printers, 1936. 130 pp. [X—JHL/RHB/NUC 343:158]

Preface by Benjamin De Casseres. *MTS* 379, 380 *AG* 222n5, 224 *ES* 676n1, 707, 723 *OFF* 262, 275, 291, 292, 295 *JFM* 403 *JVS* 252n12 *FLB* 131n1 *CLM* 140

595. Lowell, James Russell (1819–1891). *The Earlier Essays of James Russell Lowell.* Edited, with an Introduction and Notes, by Ernest Godrey Hoffsten. New York: Macmillan Co., 1916. xx, 247 pp. [MS/NUC 343:372]

596. ———. *My Study Windows.* <1871> Boston: Houghton Mifflin, 1886. 433 pp. [MS/NUC 343:382]

Contents: My Garden Acquaintance; A Good Word for Winter; On a Certain Condescension in Foreigners; A Great Public Character [Josiah Quincy]; Carlyle; Abraham Lincoln; The Life and Letters of James Gates Percival; Thoreau; Swinburne's Tragedies; Chaucer; Library of Old Authors; Emerson, the Lecturer; Pope.

CE 2.192

597. ———. *The Poetical Works of James Russell Lowell.* Boston: J. R. Osgood, 1876. ix, 406 pp. [MS/NUC 343:387]

JVS 168

598. Lowrie, Sarah D[ickson] (1870–1957), and Mabel Stewart Ludlum. *The Sesqui-Centennial High Street.* Philadelphia: J. B. Lippincott Co., 1926. 96 pp. [MS/NUC 343:521]

On spine: *The Book of the Street.*

599. Lucian of Samosata (125?–180?). [*Selected Works.*] [HPL to MWM, [August 1922] (*MWM* 105)]

Not identified. HPL writes that he picked up a volume of Lucian's "Dialogues of the Dead, Trip to Moon, etc." There is no such volume of this exact title. Presumably HPL is referring to some selection of Lucian's works that includes *Dialogues of the Dead* and *True History* (although Lucian wrote other works involving a trip to the moon).

600. Lucretius (T[itus] Lucretius Carus) (98?–50 B.C.E.?). *De Rerum Natura Libri Sex.* Recognovit Iacobus Bernaysius [i.e., Jakob Bernays]. Lipsiae [i.e., Leipzig]: Sumptibus et Typis B. G. Teubneri, 1879. xii, 198 pp. [MS/NUC 344:468]

CE 2.26 *AG* 89 *MWM* 458, 460

601. [Ludlow, Fitz Hugh (1836–1870).] *The Hasheesh Eater: Being Passages from the Life of a Pythagorean.* New York: Harper & Brothers, 1857. 371 pp. [MS/NUC 344:552]

Obtained in New York in January 1925 (HPL to Lillian D. Clark, 22 January 1925; *LFF*). Gift of Samuel Loveman. "Have I *read* Fitzhugh [*sic*] Ludlow's *Hasheesh-Eater?* Why, Sir, I possess it upon mine own shelves; & wou'd not part with it for any inducement whatever! I first read a reprint in 1922, but was later honour'd by a gift of the original edition (without author's name) of 1857" *RK* 228–29 *MWM* 442–43

602. Lynch, J[oseph] Bernard. *Props: Tales of the Pawnshop and Others Stories.* Boston: Meador Publishing Co., 1932. 224 pp. [MS/NUC 347:273]

Lynch was a member of the Hub Club (an amateur journalism group in Boston associated with the National Amateur Press Association) whom HPL met frequently. This book may have been given to HPL by Lynch.

603. Lynch, John Gilbert Bohun (1884–1928), ed. *The Best Ghost Stories.* Boston: Small, Maynard & Co., [1924]. xvii, 326 pp. [HPL/RHB/NUC 347:278]

Contents: The Shadow of Midnight, by Maurice Baring; The Thing in the Hall, by E. F. Benson; The Willows, by Algernon Blackwood; The Old Nurse's Story, by Mrs [Elizabeth] Gaskell; The Tractate Middoth, by M. R. James; Thurnley Abbey, by Perceval Landon; The Fountain, by Elinor Mordaunt; Not on the Passenger-List, by Barry Pain; The Fall of the House of Usher, by Edgar Allan Poe; The Victim, by May Sinclair.

Given to HPL by August Derleth c. late January 1933 (*ES* 539n2). *JFM* 313

604. Macaulay, Thomas Babington (1800–1859). *Lays of Ancient Rome; with Ivry and The Armada.* <1842> Illustrated by J. R. Weguelin. New York: Bay View Publishing Co., n.d. 235 pp. [MC/OCLC]

Contents: Horatius; The Battle of Lake Regillus; Virginia; The Propecy of Capys.

In "Gems from *In a Minor Key*" (1915; *AT* 223), HPL parodies Macaulay's "Horatius." HPL's "The Prophecy of Capys Secundus" (1921; *AT* 364–65) uses the structure of "The Prophecy of Capys" to discuss a number of amateur writers. *SL* 1.314–15 *MF* 162 *JFM* 76 *ET* 58

605. ———. *Macaulay's Life of Samuel Johnson.* <1856> Edited by Gamaliel Bradford, Jr. Boston: Leach, Shewell & Sanborn, [1895]. iii, 73 pp. [MS/NUC 348:477]

Not a biography as such but a long article for the *Encyclopaedia Britannica*.

606. ———. *Miscellaneous Works of Lord Macaulay.* Edited by His Sister Lady Trevelyan. New York: Harper & Brothers, 1880–1915. 5 vols. [MS/NUC 348:483]

No date cited by MS; there are 4 Harper printings.

607. Macchioro, Vittorio (1880–1958). *A Lightning Spark for Pompeian Visitors.* Naples: American & British Club/Mary E. Raiola, [19—]. 44 pp. [MS/NUC 349:147]

608. ———. *The Villa of Mysteries in Pompeii.* Naples: Mary E. Raiola, [192-?] or Naples: Richter, [1931?]. 27 pp. [MS/NUC 349:147]

609. Macdonald, Alice Edith (Middleton), Lady (1861–1935). *The Fortunes of a Family (Bosville of New Hall, Gunthwaite and Thorpe) through Nine Centuries.* Edinburgh: Printed by T. & A. Constable, 1928. xi, 264 pp. [MS/NUC 350:28]

Lady Macdonald was a correspondent of Elizabeth Toldridge (*ET* 46). This volume and the next may have been sent to HPL by Lady Macdonald herself at Toldridge's suggestion (see *ET* 85). *ET* 47–48, 73, 74, 237

610. ———. *The House of the Isles.* Edinburgh: Printed by T. & A. Constable, [1925]. 168 pp. [MS/NUC 350:28]

About the Macdonald family in Scotland. *ET* 27–29, 35, 46, 73, 85, 237

611. MacDonald, George (1824–1905). *Lilith: A Romance*. New York: Dodd, Mead, 1895. vi, 351 pp. [HPL/MS/NUC 350:98]

SHL 75. HPL notes in *SHL* that he preferred "the first and simpler of the two versions" of the novel; but this earlier version has yet to be published, and HPL knew of it only in a paraphrase by Greville MacDonald in an introduction to a later edition (London: George Allen & Unwin, 1924). It is interesting that William Raeper, in *George MacDonald* (Lion Publishing, 1987) remarks of the earlier version that it "is much less threatening than the published version, as it is rational, coherent and ordered." No doubt this is why HPL preferred it. His copy is, of course, the later version. *CE* 5.234 *ES* 88, 95

612. Macdonald, William (1863–1938), ed. *Documentary Source Book of American History, 1606–1898*. New York: Macmillan Co., 1908. xii, 616 pp. [X—JHL/NUC 350:207]

613. [McDougall, Frances Harriet (Whipple) Greene (1805–1878).] *Might and Right*. By a Rhode Islander. Providence: A. H. Stillwell, 1844. 345 pp. [MS/NUC 350:277]

614. Machen, Arthur (1863–1947). *The Canning Wonder*. New York: Alfred A. Knopf, 1926. xiii, 277 pp. [MS/NUC 351:316]

A nonfiction account of a mysterious disappearance in the 18th century. Given to HPL by Vrest Orton (HPL to Lillian D. Clark, 12 February 1926; *LFF*). *MTS* 201

615. ———. *Far Off Things*. New York: Alfred A. Knopf, 1923. 230 pp. [MS/NUC 351:316]

Autobiography. *SHL* [81] *SL* 1.356

616. ———. *Hieroglyphics: A Note upon Ecstasy in Literature*. London: Grant Richards, 1902. New York: Alfred A. Knopf, 1923. [HPL]

No ed. cited by HPL (he probably had the Knopf ed.). Read in July 1925 (HPL to Lillian D. Clark, 30–31 July 1925; *LFF*). *SL* 1.356 *JFM* 33, 49 *FLB* 298

617. ———. *The Hill of Dreams*. London: E. Grant Richards, 1907. New York: Alfred A. Knopf, 1923. [HPL]

No ed. cited by HPL (he probably had the Knopf ed.). *CE* 1.343n6 *SHL* 81 *SL* 1.233–34, 356; 2.181, 308; 4.373–74 *MTS* 10, 11, 13, 25, 29, 45, 73, 78, 80–81, 85, 92, 142 *ES* 29, 30, 38, 116, 219, 251 *OFF* 49, 227 *JFM* 33, 47 *ET* 31, 57, 61 *RB* 407 *JVS* 22, 76, 82–83, 104, 209 *FLB* 26, 30, 47, 206, 213, 224, 307, 321 *CLM* 32, 159–60, 360 *DS* 247, 526

618. ———. *The House of Souls.* <1906> New York: Alfred A. Knopf, 1923. xvii, 286 pp. [HPL/RHB/NUC 351:318]

Contents: A Fragment of Life; The White People; The Great God Pan; The Inmost Light.

The 1906 (London: E. Grant Richards) also includes *The Three Impostors* and "The Red Hand." *CF* 2.436 *CE* 5.264 *SHL* 82–84 *SL* 1.356 *MTS* 336 *RK* 229 *ES* 29, 200, 215, 219, 222, 251, 265, 402, 473, 622–23 *OFF* 49 *MF* 52 *JFM* 33, 66 *ET* 57, 61 *RB* 215, 407 *JVS* 35, 49, 59, 75–76, 79, 82 *FLB* 26, 27, 30–31, 34, 47, 77, 135, 150, 208, 263 *CLM* 267, 275, 276, 302, 360 *DS* 300, 332, 336, 396

619. ———. *The London Adventure: An Essay in Wandering.* New York: Alfred A. Knopf, 1924. 170 pp. [HPL/Schiff/NUC 351:319]

Read in July 1925 (HPL to Lillian D. Clark, 27 July 1925; *LFF*). *SL* 1.356

620. ———. *The Secret Glory.* London: Martin Secker, 1922. New York: Alfred A. Knopf, 1922. [HPL]

No ed. cited by HPL (he probably had the Knopf ed.). Read in July 1925 (HPL to Lillian D. Clark, 27 July 1925; *LFF*). The copy that HPL purchased in 1924 at the Scribner bookstore (*SL* 1.356) was later destroyed by fire when he lent it to Bernard Austin Dwyer (*DS* 381), but HPL presumably acquired another copy later.

621. ———. *The Shining Pyramid.* London: Martin Secker, 1925. 188 pp. [HPL/MS/NUC 351:321]

Contents: The Shining Pyramid; Out of the Earth; The Happy Children; The Secret of the Sangraal; The Mystic Speech; In Convertendo; The Martyr; Education and the Uneducated.

Not identical to a volume of the same title edited by Vincent Starrett (1923). *SHL* 87 *SL* 2.12 *MTS* 85

622. ———. *Things Near and Far.* New York: Alfred A. Knopf, 1923. 250 pp. [HPL/MS/NUC 351:322]

Autobiography. *CE* 5.164 *SHL* [81] *SL* 1.356

623. ———. *The Three Impostors.* <1895> New York: Alfred A. Knopf, 1930. xix, 287 pp. [HPL/MS/NUC 351:322]

Contents: [*The Three Impostors:*] Prologue; Adventure of the Gold Tiberius; The Encounter of the Pavement; Novel of the Dark Valley; Adventure of the Missing Brother; Novel of the Black Seal; Incident of the Private Bar; The Decorative Imagination; The Recluse of Bayswater; Novel of the White Powder; Strange Occurrence in Clerkenwell; History of the Young Man with Spectacles; Adventure of the Deserted Residence. The Red Hand.

"The Red Hand" is not part of the episodic novel *The Three Impostors*. This copy given to HPL by Wilfred B. Talman; HPL reports having a previous one, but it perished in a fire at the home of Bernard Austin Dwyer, who had borrowed the book (HPL to Lillian D. Clark, 16 July 1931; *LFF*). *CE* 5.169, 171, 264 *SHL* 84–87 *SL* 1.281, 304 *MTS* 55 *OFF* 49, 88n1, 238 *ES* 29, 30, 35, 36, 37, 38, 334, 337, 628 *JVS* 76, 82, 321 *FLB* 26, 27, 30, 34, 50 *CLM* 248, 302, 360 *DS* 300

624. McKenna, Stephen (1888–1967). *The Oldest God.* Boston: Little, Brown, 1926. 353 pp. [HPL/MS/NUC 352:114]

A weird novel about a man at a party who may be a monster. *ES* 60, 150, 152

625. Mackenzie, Henry (1745–1831). *The Man of Feeling.* <1771> [HPL to Lillian D. Clark, 29–30 September 1924; *LFF*/NUC 352:208f.]

An important novel in the "school of sensibility." HPL states only that he obtained a "5¢ paper edition."

626. Macpherson, Hector (1888–?). *Practical Astronomy with the Unaided Eye.* London: T. C. & E. C. Jack; New York: Dodge Publishing Co., 1912. 94 pp. [MS/NUC 353:576/OCLC]

627. Macpherson, James (1736–1796). *The Poems of Ossian.* <1765> New York: C. Wells, 1841. 492 pp. [RHB/OCLC]

SHL 33

628. MacPhilpin, John, ed. *The Apparitions and Miracles at Knock: Also the Official Depositions of the Eyewitnesses.* New York: D. & J. Sadlier & Co., 1880. 142 pp. [HPL/MS/NUC 353:624; 744:411/OCLC]

629. McSpadden, J[oseph] Walker (1874–1960), ed. *Famous Psychic Stories.* New York: Thomas Y. Crowell Co., [1920]. viii, 305 pp. [HPL/MS/NUC 354:27]

Contents: The Old White Maid, by Nathenial Hawthorne; The Facts in the Case of M. Valdemar, by Edgar Allan Poe; The Dream Woman, by Wilkie Collins; The Open Door, by Margaret Oliphant; The Stalls of Barchester Cathedral, by M. R. James; The Man Who Went Too Far, by E. F. Benson [*SHL* 76]; Moxon's Master, by Ambrose Bierce; The Beast with Five Fingers, by W. F. Harvey; From the Loom of the Dead, by Elia W. Peattie; The Ghoul, by Evangeline W. Blashfield; The Shadows on the Wall, by Mary E. Wilkins Freeman; The Widow's Mite, by I. K. Funk.
Given to HPL by August Derleth (*ES* 513).

630. Macy, William Francis (1867–?). *The Story of Old Nantucket.* Nantucket: The Inquirer and Mirror, 1915. vii, 108 pp. [MS/NUC 354:114]

631. ———, ed. *The Nantucket Scrap Basket: Being a Collection of Characteristic Stories and Sayings of the People of the Town and Island of Nantucket, Massachusetts.* Nantucket: The Inquirer and Mirror, 1916. xii, 183 pp. [MS/NUC 354:113]

The source of Daniel Webster's description of Nantucket as "the unknown city in the ocean," for HPL's essay of that title (*CE* 4.259).

632. Mahabharata, The. *The Song Celestial; or, Bhagavad Gita: From the Mahabharata.* Translated from the Sanskrit Text by Sir Edwin Arnold. New York: Truslove, Hanson & Comba, 1900. 111 pp. [MS/AC 1900–04, p. 678]

633. Mahaffy, J[ohn] P[entland] (1839–1919). *Old Greek Life.* <1876> New York: D. Appleton & Co., 1879. 101 pp. [X/NUC 355:547]

CLM 306

634. ———. *A Survey of Greek Civilization.* Meadville, PA: Flood & Vincent, 1896. 337 pp. [MS/NUC 355:550]

CE 2.192 *SL* 2.186) *CLM* 306

635. Mais, S[tuart] P[etrie] B[rodie] (1885–1975). *The Cornish Riviera.* London: Great Western Railway Co., 1934. viii, 167 pp. [MS/NUC 356:439]

636. Malory, Sir Thomas (1415?–1471). *Le Morte d'Arthur.* <1485> London: J. M. Dent; New York: E. P. Dutton (Everyman's Library), [1906]–[1935]. 2 vols. [MS/NUC 357:671f.]

No date cited by MS; there are at least 11 printings. *CE* 2.86, 186 *SHL* 31 *CLM* 103

637. Mandeville, Sir John (14th c.). *The Voyages and Travels of Sir John Maundeville, Kt.* New York: Cassell, 1886. 192 pp. [HPL to MWM, [August 1922] (*MWM* 105)/OCLC]

HPL's ownership of this specific volume is conjectural; HPL has written merely: "Voyages of Mandeville."

638. Mann, Henry (1848–1915). *Our Police: A History of the Providence Force from the First Watchman to the Latest Appointee.* Providence: J. M. Beers, 1889. 519 pp. [MS/NUC 359:184]

HPL states that he had had a copy since childhood, but had "foolishly allowed [it] to slip through my fingers." This copy was purchased from Arthur Eddy's bookshop in Providence through C. M. Eddy, Jr. in February 1925 (HPL to Lillian D. Clark, 16 February 1925; *LFF*).

639. Marcet, Jane (Haldimand) (1769–1858). *Conversations on Natural Philosophy, in Which the Elements of That Science Are Familiarly Explained, and Adapted to the Comprehension of Young Pupils.* <1819> Improved by appropriate questions, for the examination of scholars; also by illustrative notes and a dictionary of philosophical terms. By J. L. Blake. Eighth American edition Boston: Lincoln & Edmands, 1826. 252 pp. [X—JHL/NUC 360:612]

640. Marryat, Capt. Frederick (1792–1848). *The Phantom Ship.* London: Henry Colburn, 1839. [HPL/OCLC]

   No ed. cited by HPL. *SHL* 46. HPL was unaware that the story "The Werewolf," which he believed to be a separate work, is simply an extract from this novel.

641. Marsh, John (1788–1868). *An Epitome of General Ecclesiastical History, from the Earliest Period to the Present Time.* New York: Printed by Vanderpool & Cole, 1827. 420[+32] pp. [MS/NUC 363:423]

642. Marsh, Richard (1857–1915). *The Beetle: A Mystery.* <1897> London: Eveleigh Nash & Grayson, [19—]. 338 pp. [HPL/MS/OCLC]

   Given to HPL by August Derleth (*ES* 260, 280). *SHL* 74 *OFF* 207 *JFM* 49

643. Martial (M[arcus] Valerius Martialis) (40?–104?). *Epigrams of Martial, &c., with Mottos from Horace, &c.* Translated . . . with Notes . . . by the Rev. Mr. [William] Scott. London: Printed for J. Willkie, J. Walter, & H. Parker, 1773. xxiv, 262 pp. [MS/NUC 364:262]

   With Latin text.

644. *Marvel Tales.* Edited by William L. Crawford. [HPL]

   HPL had a complete set, beginning with the May 1934 issue. Many references to this periodical in HPL's letters.

645. Mather, Cotton (1663–1728). *Magnalia Christi Americana; or, The Ecclesiastical History of New-England, from Its First Planting in the Year 1620, unto the Year of Our Lord, 1698.* London: Printed for T. Parkhurst, 1702. 7 parts in 1. [HPL/NUC 369:75]

   HPL owned the first edition, a family inheritance. HPL's epigraphs from Lactantius in "The Festival" (1923) and Borellus (actually a paraphrase of Borellus by Mather) in *The Case of Charles Dexter Ward* (1927) were taken from this volume (see *CB* 87 and Schultz's note ad loc.).

   CF 1.211, 400; 2.60, 252 *CE* 4.132, 133; 5.236n22, 237, 256 *SL* 3.306 *AG* 123, 142 *RK* 225 *OFF* 231, 238, 415n15 *ES* 379 *JFM* 16, 239 *RB* 129 *DS* 455

646. Maturin, Charles Robert (1782?–1824). *Melmoth the Wanderer*. <1820> London: Richard Bentley & Son, 1892. 3 vols. [HPL/NUC 370:151]

Given to HPL by W. Paul Cook (*FLB* 253). HPL did not read the entire novel previous to writing his account of it in *SHL*, but read "two anthology excerpts" (*JFM* 90)—i.e., #428 and #824. *CE* 2.225; 5.175 *SHL* 39–42 *SL* 2.36; 3.239; 4.98, 130, 144 *MTS* 7, 8, 11, 20, 22, 129, 176, 183, 207 *AG* 176 *ES* 32, 33, 34, 35, 46, 47, 96, 537, 567, 582 *OFF* 50 *MF* 202, 526 *JFM* 209 *ET* 231 *RB* 20, 347 *JVS* 78, 121, 125, 333

647. Maunder, Edward Walter (1851–1928). *The Science of the Stars*. London & Edinburgh: T. C. & E. C. Jack; New York: Dodge Publishing Co., [1912]. vii, 95 pp. [MS/OCLC]

648. Maupassant, Guy de (1850–1893). *A Selection from the Writings of Guy de Maupassant*. With a Critical Preface by Paul Bourget . . . and an Introduction by Robert Arnot. New York: D. A. McKinlay & Co., 1803. 6 vols. [HPL to MWM, [August 1922] (*MWM* 105)/NUC 370:441]

No ed. cited by HPL, but this is the only edition of Maupassant published up to 1922 that is in 6 volumes. *SHL* 52–53, 65

649. Maurice, Michael [pseud. of Conrad Arthur Skinner (1889–?)]. *Not in Our Stars*. Philadelphia: J. B. Lippincott Co., [1923]. 288 pp. [MS/NUC 549:56]

A partly weird novel of precognition and time travel, but not appearing on HPL's lists of his weird library. With inscription: "To H. P. Lovecraft,—Another swaying of the Curtain.—With compliments of E. A. Edkins, Feb 10—1933." *JVS* 125

650. Maurois, André (1885–1967). "The Weigher of Souls." Translated by Hamish Miles. *Scribner's Magazine* 89, No. 3 (March 1931): 235–50, 334–49. [MS]

The complete text of the short novel. Later published as a book (London: Cassell; New York: D. Appleton & Co., 1931).

651. Melville, Herman (1819–1891). *Moby-Dick; or, The White Whale*. <1851> Boston: Dana Estes & Co., 1892. 545 pp. [X/NUC 375:24]

Gift of George Kirk. *CE* 2.188; 5.156, 159 *ES* 67, 208, 300 *JFM* 364 *JVS* 165

652. Mencken, H[enry] L[ouis] (1880–1956). *The American Language*. New York: Alfred A. Knopf, 1919. [MS]

No ed. cited by MS; there are 10 printings and 4 eds. through 1937. MS also mentions: "H. L. MENCKEN (Paper bound edition)." *CE* 2.192

653. Meredith, Owen [pseud. of Edward Robert Bulwer Lytton, earl of Lytton (1831–1891)]. *Lucile.* <1860> New York: Thomas Y. Crowell Co., [1883]–[189-?]. 369 pp. [MS/NUC 348:7–8]

No date cited by MS; there are at least 3 Crowell printings.

654. Merritt, A[braham] (1882–1943). *The Face in the Abyss.* New York: Horace Liveright, 1931. 343 pp. [HPL/Tuck 2:309]

OFF 144, 162 *ES* 543–44, 545, 547 *FLB* 87–88, 97, 219, 281 *CLM* 96

655. ———. *Thru the Dragon Glass.* Jamaica, NY: ARRA Press (Conrad Ruppert), [1932]. 24 pp. [HPL/HPL to Richard Ely Morse, 21 May 1934/ISFDB]

Given to HPL by R. H. Barlow.

656. Milton, John (1608–1674). *Paradise Lost.* <1667> Illustrated by Gustave Doré <1866>. [NUC 385:309f.]

See HPL to Clark Ashton Smith, 17 November 1930: "my own [edition] being the less uncommon Doré one" (*DS* 276). *CF* 1.55, 61 *RK* 68 *JFM* 141

657. ———. *Prose Works.* New York: Hurst, [1865]. viii, 486 pp. [MS/NUC 385:284]

658. *Miniature Almanack for the Year of Our Lord, 1837.* Concord, NH: John F. Brown, [1836]. [MS/*American Imprints for 1836*, p. 274]

659. Miniter, Edith (1869–1934). *Our Natupski Neighbors.* New York: Henry Holt & Co., 1916. 346 pp. [X/NUC 386:104]

A realistic novel about Polish immigrants in Massachusetts, written by an amateur journalism associate of HPL. This copy inscribed: "For Howard P. Lovecraft, with regards from the author, Edith Miniter, April 1921." *CE* 1.181, 380–81, 383, 384; 4.31n16

660. Minto, William (1845–1893). *The Literature of the Georgian Era.* Edited with a Biographical Introduction by William Knight. New York: Harper & Brothers, 1895. lvi, 362 pp. [MS/NUC 386:485]

CE 2.191

661. Mitchell, David Andrew (1883–1926?). *Mitchell's Guide to the Game of Chess.* Philadelphia: David McKay, 1915. 83 pp. *or* 1920 or 1924. 117 pp. [MS/NUC 387:654]

In a letter to Lillian D. Clark (4–6 November 1924; *LFF*), HPL notes that, when his wife Sonia was in the hospital, he "went downtown to negotiate some purchases—book on chess at Brentano's." This was probably the volume in question, and therefore HPL probably secured the 1924 printing.

662. Mitchell, Edwin Valentine (1890–1960). *The Art of Authorship*. New York: Loring & Mussey, 1935. 128 pp. [HPL to August Derleth, 10 November 1935 (*ES* 718)/NUC 387:676]

Given to HPL by the publisher.

663. Mitchell, John Ames (1845–1918). *The Last American: A Fragment from the Journal of Khan-Li, Prince of Dimph-Yoo-Chur and Admiral in the Persian Navy*. <1889> 7th ed. New York: Frederick A. Stokes & Brothers, [1891?]. 78 pp. [MS/NUC 388:33]

HPL notes having a 7th ed. (HPL to R. H. Barlow, 28 January 1933 [*OFF* 49]).

664. Mitchell, Samuel Augustus (1790–1868). *Mitchell's Ancient Atlas, Classical and Sacred*. Philadelphia: Butler, 1844. [HPL to Fritz Leiber, 19 December 1936 (*CLM* 304)/OCLC]

HPL does not specify which edition he owned. There were 7 editions down to 1874.

665. ———. *Mitchell's Ancient Geography*. Philadelphia: Cowperthwait, DeSilver & Butler, 1855. 216 pp. [MS/NUC 388:88]

CLM 304

666. Mitford, Mary Russell (1797–1855). *Our Village*. <1824–32> Brontë, Emily (1818–1848). *Wuthering Heights*. <1847> New York: Century Co., 1906. ix, 92, v, 279 pp. [HPL/MS/OCLC]

CE 2.188, 226; 5.158, 175 *SHL* 48–49 *MTS* 19 *ES* 200 *JFM* 90 *JVS* 289

667. Mitton, Geraldine Edith (1868–1955). *Hampstead and Marylebone*. Edited by Sir Walter Besant. London: A. & C. Black, 1902. ix, 111 pp. [MS/NUC 388:317]

668. *The Modern Encyclopedia: A New Library of World Knowledge*. Edited by A. H. McDannald. New York: Grosset & Dunlap, 1935. 1334 pp. [HPL to Richard F. Searight, 16 April 1935/NUC 388:565–66/CBI 1933–1937, p. 1624]

CE 2.202 *ES* 683–84 *OFF* 224 *JFM* 362 *ET* 301 *JVS* 264

669. Moe, Maurice W[inter] (1882–1940). *Imagery Aids*. Wauwatosa, WI: Kenyon Press, 1931. [ii, 32 pp.] [MS]

Moe, of course, was a correspondent of HPL. This book, which MS listed with #814 and #951, may have been revised by HPL.

670. Monnier, Marc (1827–1885). *The Wonders of Pompeii.* Translated from the Original French <1870>. New York: Scribner, Armstrong & Co., 1872. 250 pp. [MS/NUC 391:131]

Translation of *Pompeii et les Pompéiens* (1864).

671. Montgomery, David Henry (1837–1928). *The Leading Facts of American History.* Boston: Ginn & Co., 1890. xli, 359, lxvii pp. [NUC 392:277]

See *RK* 72, where he notes that he composed the verses "C. S. A. 1861–1865: To the Starry Cross of the SOUTH" "on the back of a half-tone illustration in Montgomery's 'American History'—a book still on my shelves." *CE* 5.33

672. *The Monthly Visitor and Entertaining Pocket Companion.* London, 1797–1802. 15 vols. [MS/NUC 392:414]

HPL had only Vol. 1 (1797).

673. Moore, C[atherine] L[ucille] (1911–1987). *Werewoman.* 1934. Privately prepared, typewritten ribbon copy on the rectos of [iii] 29 [ii] pages, 8½ × 11". [C. L. Moore to HPL and R. H. Barlow, 20 August 1935 (*CLM* 56)]

Inscribed by Moore and bound in half morocco and heavy paper-covered boards, with an additional inscription on an adhesive label affixed to front fly. A notation appears on the final leaf, indicating that this is one of three copies. This uncollected Northwest Smith story was first published in *Leaves* No. 2 (Winter 1938–39).

674. Moore, Thomas (1779–1852). *The Epicurean: A Tale.* London: Printed for Longman, Rees, Orme, Brown, & Green, 1827. [HPL]

No ed. cited by HPL. Based upon Moore's poem *Alciphron. CE* 2.226 *SHL* 46 *MTS* 37, 69, 73

675. ———. *The Poetical Works of Thomas Moore.* Philadelphia: Carey & Hart, 1844.. 518 pp. [MS/OCLC]

CF 1.238, 430 *SHL* 33, 46 *MTS* 73, 81

676. ———, and William Jerdan (1782–1869). *Personal Reminiscences of Moore and Jerdan.* Edited by Richard Henry Stoddard. New York: Scribner, Armstrong & Co., 1875. 293 pp. [MS/NUC 393:459]

677. Morand, Paul (1888–1976). *Black Magic.* Translated from the French by Hamish Miles. Illustrated by Aaron Douglas. New York: Viking Press, 1929. vi, 218 pp. [MS/NUC 394:35]

On African Americans. Given to HPL by Henry S. Whitehead (HPL to Lillian D. Clark, 10 May 1931; *LFF*). *ES* 341

678. Morey, William C[arey] (1843–1925). *Outlines of Greek History, with a Survey of Ancient Oriental Nations.* New York: American Book Co., 1903. 378 pp. [MS/NUC 394:603]

SL 2.186

679. Morison, James Cotter (1832–1888). *Macaulay.* London: Macmillan & Co., 1882. 186 pp. (English Men of Letters.) [MS/NUC 395:325]

680. Morley, Henry (1822–1894), ed. *A Miscellany Containing: Richard of Bury's Philobiblion; The Basilikon Doron of King James I.; Monks and Giants, by John Hokham [sic] Frere; The Cypress Crown, by de la Motte-Fouqué . . . and The Library: A Poem, by George Crabbe.* London: George Routledge & Sons, 1888. 272 pp. [L. W. Currey, *Catalogue 74* (Fall 1983)/NUC 395:444]

681. Morell, Sir Charles [pseud. of James Ridley (1736–1765)]. *Tales of the Genii.* <1764> Translated from the Persian [i.e., written] by Sir Charles Morell. London: T. Davidson, 1824. [MS/NUC 494:350]

Stories based on the *Arabian Nights.*

682. Morris, William (1834–1896). *The Defence of Guenevere and Other Poems.* <1858> London: Ellis & White, 1875. vii, 248 pp. [X/NUC 396:136]

683. Morse, Edward S[ylvester] (1838–1925). *Mars and Its Mystery.* Boston: Little, Brown, 1906. viii, 192 pp. [MS/NUC 396:321]

684. Morse, Jedidiah (1761–1826). *Geography Made Easy: Being an Abridgment of the American Universal Geography.* <1784> 8th ed. Boston: I. Thomas & E. T. Andrews, 1802. 432 pp. [MS/NUC 396:346]

HPL quotes a paragraph from this book (about the newly constructed city of Washington, D.C.) in his letter to Lillian D. Clark (21 April 1925; *LFF*). *CE* 4.79

685. ———. *Geography Made Easy.* <1784> 19th ed. Boston: Thomas & Andrews, 1818. 432 pp. [MS/NUC 396:346]

MS gives date of 1812, but this is the date of the 15th, not 19th, ed.

686. ———, and Elijah Parish. *A Compendious History of New-England: To Which Is Added a Short Abstract of the History of New-York and New-Jersey.* Charlestown, MA: Printed by S. Etheridge, 1820. 324 pp. [MS/NUC 396:345]

687. Morse, Richard Ely (1909–1986). *Winter Garden.* Amherst, MA: Poetry Society of Amherst College, 1931. 59 pp. [X/MS/NUC 396:370]

Morse was a correspondent of HPL. This copy bears the inscription: "For Howard Lovecraft, Magnus Magister, in return for all his gracious kindness and friendship and for all the shuddering pleasure of his tales and verse with admiration and gratitude from Richard Ely Morse." *FLB* 322, 329

688. Mowry, William Augustus (1829–1917). *Elements of Civil Government, Local, State, and National.* New York: Silver, Burdett & Co., 1890. 211 pp. [MS]

No ed. cited by MS.

689. Mulock, Mrs. [Dinah Maria (Mulock) Craik, 1826–1887]. *A Brave Lady.* By Mrs. Mulock. New York: Harper & Brothers, 1870–1903. 456 pp. [MS/NUC 126:221]

No date cited by MS; there are 6 Harper eds.

690. ———. *A Hero and Other Tales.* By Mrs. Mulock. New York: Harper & Brothers, 1853. 269 pp. [MS/NUC 126:224]

691. ———. *John Halifax, Gentleman.* By Mrs. Mulock. New York: Harper & Brothers, 1856–79. 485 pp. [MS/NUC 126:226f.]

No date cited by MS; there are at least 15 Harper eds.

692. ———. *My Mother and I: A Girl's Love-Story.* By Mrs. Mulock. New York: Harper & Brothers, 1874–1904. 287 pp. [MS/NUC 126:231]

No date cited by MS; there are at least 5 Harper eds.

693. ———. *A Noble Life.* By Mrs. Mulock. New York: Harper & Brothers, 1866–1916. 302 pp. [MS/NUC 126:231f]

No date cited by MS; there are at least 8 Harper eds.

694. Munro, Wilfred Harold (1849–1934). *Picturesque Rhode Island.* Providence: J. A. & R. A. Reid, 1881. 304 pp. [MS/NUC 401:590]

695. Murillo, Bartolome Estaban (1617–1682). *The Masterpieces of Murillo (1618 [sic]–1682).* Sixty Reproductions of Photographs from the Original Paintings by F. Hanfstaengl. New York: Frederick A. Stokes Co., 1907. 64 pp. [MS/NUC 402:170]

696. Murray, Lindley (1745–1826), ed. *Introduction to the English Reader; or, A Selection of Pieces, in Prose and Poetry.* <1827> [MS/NUC 402:526]

MS gives only the date; there are 4 different 1827 eds.

697. ———, ed. *Sequel to The English Reader: Elegant Selections in Prose and Poetry*. New-York: Collins & Co., 1831. 299 pp. [MS/NUC 402:536]

698. Myers, P[hilip] V[an] N[ess] (1846–1937). *Ancient History*. Boston: Ginn & Co., 1904. xvi, 639 pp. (+ 47 leaves of plates). [HPL to Fritz Leiber, 19 December 1936 (*CLM* 303–4)/NUC 403:613]
No ed. cited by HPL.

699. Nasmyth, James (1808–1890), and James Carpenter (1840–1899). *The Moon: Considered as a Planet, a World, and a Satellite*. <1874> 4th ed. New York: James Pott & Co.; London: John Murray, 1903. xviii, 315 pp. [MS/OCLC]

700. Neale, Arthur, ed. *The Great Weird Stories*. New York: Duffield & Co., 1929. 409 pp. [HPL/MS/NUC 409:6/Ashley 852]
Contents: The Great Keinplatz Experiment, by Sir Arthur Conan Doyle; In Letters of Fire, by Gaston Leroux; The Red Room, by H. G. Wells; The Two Sisters of Cologne, by Anonymous; The Woman's Ghost Story, by Algernon Blackwood; Almodoro's Cupid, by William Waldorf Astor; The Ghost's Double, by L. F. Austin; In the Valley of the Sorceress, by Sax Rohmer; The Mark of the Beast, by Rudyard Kipling; The Man Who Lived Backwards, by Allen Upward; The Ghost of a Head, by Anonymous; The Black Cat, by Edgar Allan Poe; The Tapestried Chamber, by Sir Walter Scott; The Legend of Dunblane, by Anonymous; The Shining Pyramid, by Arthur Machen; A Night in an Old Castle, by G. P. R. James; The Trial for Murder, by Charles Dickens; The Power of Darkness, by E. Nesbit; The Warder of the Door, by L. T. Meade and Robert Eustace; The Doppelgänger, by Anonymous.
ES 207

701. Nepos, Cornelius (99?–24 B.C.E.?). [*Lives of Eminent Commanders.*] Literally Translated with Notes by John Selby Watson. Philadelphia: David McKay, [1899]. 171 pp. [MS/NUC 410:340]

702. Nevin, John Williamson (1803–1886). *A Summary of Biblical Antiquities*. Philadelphia: American Sunday-School Union, [1849]. 447 pp. [MS/NUC 412:135]

703. *The New and Complete Universal Self-Pronouncing Encyclopedia, for Home, School and Office; A Compendium of Information and Instruction on All Subjects*. Edited by Charles Annandale . . . A. R. Spofford, Isaac T. Johnson, Walter Hart

Blumenthal, and a corps of eminent specialists. Philadelphia: "International" Press, 1905. 8 vols. [MS/NUC 412:186]

704. *New Biographical Dictionary.* By the Editors of the Cassell's Standard Reference Books, Dictionaries, &c. Rev. ed. Philadelphia: David McKay, [1899]. 741 pp. [MS/NUC 412:212]

705. *The New England Almanac and Farmer's Friend.* New London: E. C. Daboll. [MS/NUC 412:296]

HPL had the issues for 1856, 1860, 1871, 1872, 1873, and 1878. The first two are by Nathan Daboll, the others by David A. Daboll.

706. *The New-England Primer: Improved, for the More Easy Attaining the True Reading of English: To Which Is Added The Assembly of Divines, and Mr. Cotton's Catechism.* <1760?> Albany, NY: Joel Munsell, 1777. [80] pp. [X—JHL/Josiah]

HPL had 3 different eds., but does not identify them; see *ES* 380. The above copy is inscribed: "His Liber Emptus erat / A.b. XII. KAL. Dec. MDCCCCIV / ab / H. P. Lovecraft, / 598 Angell St., / Providence, R.I." ("this book was purchased on 18 November 1904 by H. P. Lovecraft . . ."). *CE* 2.34; 4.64 *RK* 17 *ES* 380

707. New York (City) Metropolitan Museum of Art. *Guide to the Collections.* New York: [Gilliss Press,] 1919–37. [MS/NUC 414:242–43]

No date cited by MS; there are 10 printings and 3 eds.

708. ———. *Handbook of the Classical Collection.* <1917> By Gisela M. A. Richter. [4th ed.] New York: [Gilliss Press,] 1922. xxxiv, 278 pp. [MS/NUC 414:244]

709. ———. *The Tomb of Perneb.* New York: [Gilliss Press,] 1916. 79 pp. [MS/NUC 414:259]

This volume probably helped to provide background information for HPL's ghostwritten tale "Under the Pyramids" (1924).

710. *New York Street Cries, in Rhyme.* New-York: Mahlon Day, 1825. xxvi, 31 pp. [HPL to Elizabeth Toldridge, 24 August 1932 (*ET* 218)/OCLC]

In his letter to Toldridge, HPL writes that "I have a little illustrated book of street cries—owned by a great-grandfather—published in N.Y. about 1830."

711. Newcomb, Simon (1835–1909). *Astronomy for Everybody.* <1902> New York: McClure, Phillips & Co., 1904. xv, 333 pp. [MS/NUC 417:36] *ET* 109

712. ———. *Popular Astronomy.* <1878> New York: Harper & Brothers, 1880. xviii, 571 pp. [MS/NUC 417:43]

713. *The North American Tourist.* New York: A. T. Goodrich, [1839]. ix, 506 pp. [MS/NUC 422:77]

714. O'Brien, Edward J[oseph Harrington] (1890–1941). *The Dance of the Machines: The American Short Story and the Industrial Age.* New York: Macaulay Co., 1929. 274 pp. [MS/NUC 425:632]

"Read Edward J. O'Brien's exposé of commercial fiction—*The Dance of the Machines.* I've just picked up a copy for a quarter—as a remainder" (*SL* 4.73). *CE* 1.405 *SL* 4.91 *JFM* 180, 181, 205 *JVS* 104, 359

715. ———, ed. *The Best Short Stories of 1928 and the Yearbook of the American Short Story.* New York: Dodd, Mead, 1928. xiv, 429 pp. [MS/NUC 51:223]

Contains a "Biographical Notice" by HPL, p. 324. Other mentions of him on pp. 312, 404. *CE* 5.206, 286, 291 *SL* 2.202, 212, 236 *MTS* 195, 197, 231 *ES* 121, 781 *ET* 22, 118, 151n1 *RB* 26n2, 43n6 *FLB* 15, 17 *DS* 153

716. Olcott, William Tyler (1873–1936). *A Field Book of the Stars.* New York: G. P. Putnam's Sons, 1907. xiii, 163 pp. [MS/NUC 429:139]

717. Oliver, John A. Westwood, ed. *Astronomy for Amateurs.* London: Longmans, Green, 1888. vii, 316 pp. [MS/NUC 429:586]

718. Onions, Oliver (1873–1961). *Ghosts in Daylight.* London: Chapman & Hall, 1924. 236 pp. [HPL/MS/NUC 430:653]

Contents: The Ascending Dream; The Honey in the Wall; The Dear Dryad; The Real People; The Woman in the Way.

"I have Onions's 'Ghosts in Daylight' . . . I didn't care much for the various tales" (HPL to J. Vernon Shea, 14 February 1936 [*JVS* 282]).

719. Orton, Vrest (1897–1986). *Dreiserana: A Book about His Books.* New York: [Printed at the Stratford Press,] 1929. ix, 84 pp. [MS/NUC 433:551]

The first bibliography of Dreiser. Orton was an associate and correspondent of HPL. *JFM* 184

720. Osborn, Edward Bolland (1867–1967). *The Heritage of Greece and the Legacy of Rome.* New York: George H. Doran, [1924] or [1925]. 192 pp. [MS/NUC 433:652]

Originally published as *Our Debt to Greece and Rome* (1924). *CE* 2.192

Ovid 123

721. ———. *The Middle Ages*. Garden City, NY: Doubleday, Doran, 1928. viii, 246 pp. [MS/NUC 433:652]
 CE 2.192

722. Overman, Frederick (1803–1852). *Practical Mineralogy, Assaying and Mining*. <1851> 11th ed. Philadelphia: P. Blakiston, Son & Co., 1882. x, 230 pp. [MS/NUC 435:493]

723. Ovid (P[ublius] Ovidius Naso) (43 B.C.E.–17 C.E.). *Art of Love*. Translated. [MS]
 No ed. cited by MS save place of publication: "London." *MWM* 278; *SL* 4.285

724. ———. *Excerpta ex Scriptis Publii Ovidii Nasonis*. <1827> Accedunt Notulae Anglicae et Quaestiones. In Usum Scholae Bostoniensis. Cura B. A. Gould. Bostoniae: B. B. Mussey, 1843. vii, 287 pp. [X/MS/NUC 435:677]
 Contents: *Metamorphoses; Heroides; Fasti; Nux, Elegia; Tristia;* Notulæ; Quæstiones.
 The bookseller listing this item reports that it contains "Lovecraft's extensive translation (?) notes to the first four sections of the book (pages 15 to 58)" (by which he presumably means extracts from Books I–IV of the *Metamorphoses*). The bookseller gives the date as 1848, but no such date is listed in NUC or OCLC. MS gives the date as 1843.

725. ———. *The Heroycall Epistles of the Learned Poet Publius Ouidius Naso, in English Verse*. Set Out and Translated by George Tuberuile. London: Henry Denham, 1567. [14], [322] pp. [OCLC]
 The oldest book in HPL's library, bought in New York in September 1922 for $2.00. See HPL to Lillian D. Clark, 29 September 1922 (*LFF*).

726. ———. *The Metamorphoses of Ovid*. Literally Translated, with Notes and Explanations, by Henry T. Riley. New York: Hinds, Noble & Eldridge, [190-?]. 2 vols. [MS/NUC 435:650]
 Cf. "Ovid's Metamorphoses" (1900?; *AT* 25–28), a translation of the first 88 lines of the *Metamorphoses*. *CE* 2.28; 3.11, 184, 196; 5.272n1 *SL* 4.285

727. ———. [*Opera Omnia.*] Ex Recognitione Rudolphi Merkelii [i.e., Rudolf Merkel]. Lipsiae [i.e., Leipzig]: B. G. Teubneri, 1881–84. 3 vols. [X/NUC 435:554]
 CE 2.28 *JFM* 133–34

728. ———. *Ovid.* Translated by Dryden, Pope, Congreve, Addison, and Others. New-York: Harper & Brothers, 1837. 2 vols. [MS/NUC 435:575]

> HPL had only Vol. 2. Contains the *Metamorphoses* ("Garth" translation) and the *Epistles*. MWM 45 ES 379

729. ———. *Selections from the Metamorphoses and Heroides of Publius Ovidiius Naso.* With a Literal and Interlinear Translation on the Hamiltonian System as Improved by Thomas Clark . . . by George William Heilig. Philadelphia: David McKay, [1889]. 464 pp. [MS/NUC 435:682]

730. Oxenford, John (1812–1877), and C. A. Feiling, ed. & tr. *Tales from the German: Comprising Specimens from the Most Celebrated Authors.* London: Chapman & Hall, 1844. xiv, 446 pp. [HPL/MS/BLC 244: 263/NUC 436:211]

> *Contents:* Libussa, by J. H. Musaeus; The Criminal from Lost Honour, by Friedrich Schiller; The Cold Heart, by Wilhelm Hauff; The Wonders in the Spessart, by Karl Immermann; Nose the Dwarf, by Wilhelm Hauff; Axel: A Tale of the Thirty Years' War, by C. F. Van der Velde; The Sandman, by E. T. W. [*sic*] Hoffmann; Michael Kohlhaas, by Heinrich von Kleist; The Klausenburg, by Ludwig Tieck; The Moon, by Jean Paul Friedrich Richter; The Elementary Spirit, by E. T. W. Hoffmann; St. Cecilia; or, The Power of Music, by Heinrich von Kleist; The New Paris, by J. W. Goethe [*sic*]; Ali and Gulhyndi, by Adam Oehlenschlaeger; Alamontade, by Heinrich Zschokke; The Jesuits' Church in G———, by E. T. W. Hoffmann; The Severed Hand, by Wilhelm Hauff.

731. Owen, Frank [pseud. of Roswell Williams (1893–1968)]. *The Wind That Tramps the World: Splashes of Chinese Color.* New York: Lantern Press, 1929. 118 pp. [X/MS/NUC 436:49/Tuck 2:461]

> *Contents:* The Wind That Tramps the World; Pale Pink Porcelain; The Month the Almonds Bloom; The Inverted House; The Blue City; The Frog; The Snapped Willow.
>
> Collection of short stories first published in *Weird Tales*. Inscribed: "From W. Paul Cook, Esq. H. P. Lovecraft, Providence, R.I. September 1932."

732. [Packard, Frederick Adolphus (1794–1867).] *The Union Bible Dictionary.* Philadelphia: American Sunday-School Union, 1837. 648 pp. [MS/NUC 437:75]

733. [———.] *The Union Bible Dictionary.* Rev. ed. Philadelphia: American Sunday-School Union, [1855]. 690 pp. [MS/NUC 437:75]

734. Page, Thomas Nelson (1853–1922). *Robert E. Lee, the Southerner.* New York: Charles Scribner's Sons, 1909. xiii, 312 pp. [MS/NUC 437:407]

Biography by an important Southern novelist.

735. Pain, Barry (1865–1928). *An Exchange of Souls.* London: Eveleigh Nash, 1911. 256 pp. [HPL/MS/NUC 437:582]

A novel about personality exchange (perhaps an influence on "The Thing on the Doorstep" [1933] or "The Shadow out of Time" [1934–35]). HPL listed Pain's "The Undying Thing" (from *Stories in the Dark*) among items to mention in the revised *SHL*, but never in fact cited it.

736. Palgrave, Francis T[urner] (1814–1897), ed. *The Golden Treasury: Selected from the Best Songs and Lyrical Poems in the English Language.* London: Macmillan, 1861. 332 pp. [MS/OCLC]

No other information provided by MS save: "(Paper bound edition)." Perhaps the most celebrated poetry anthology in English literature. *CE* 1.405; 2.191 *ES* 753 *JFM* 323 *RB* 213 *FLB* 153

737. Palmer, Edward Henry (1840–1882). *The Caliph Haroun Alraschid and Saracen Civilization.* New York: G. P. Putnam's Sons, 1881. 228 pp. [MS/NUC 438:698]

738. Parker, Richard Green (1798–1869). *Aids to English Composition, Prepared for Students of All Grades.* <1844> 5th ed. New York: Harper & Brothers, 1850. 429 pp. [X/NUC 442:445/OCLC]

HPL referred to this work as "redolent of the scholarship of the Poe period . . . [it] is really what I grew up on" (*JVS* 110). *ES* 380 *JVS* 58

739. Parkman, Francis (1823–1893). *The Conspiracy of Pontiac and the Indian War after the Conquest of Canada.* <1851> 10th ed., rev., with additions. Boston: Little, Brown, 1886. 2 vols. [MS/NUC 442:593]

740. Parsons, Theophilus (1797–1882). *Laws of Business for All the States and Territories of the Union and the Dominion of Canada.* <1876> New rev. ed. Hartford, CT: S. S. Scranton, 1889. 864 pp. [MS/NUC 443:348]

Perhaps originally purchased by HPL's grandfather Whipple Phillips.

741. Parsons, Thomas William (1819–1892). *Poems.* Boston: Ticknor & Fields, 1854. 189 pp. [MS/NUC 443:360]

Obtained in New York in September 1924 (HPL to Lillian D. Clark, 29–30 1924; *LFF*). Parsons was an American poet most noted for his partial translation of Dante's *Divine Comedy*.

742. Pater, Walter (1839–1894). *Marius the Epicurean: His Sensations and Ideas.* <1885> New York: Boni & Liveright (Modern Library), [1921]. vi, 384 pp. [RHB/NUC 444:435]

CE 2.189 *SL* 1.341 *ES* 146 *ET* 38. Cf. the citation of Pater's *Renaissance* at *CB* 85.

743. [Paterson, William (1745–1806).] *Glimpses of Colonial Society and Life at Princeton College 1766–1773.* By One of the Class of 1763. Edited by W. Jay Mills. Philadelphia: J. B. Lippincott Co., 1903. 182 pp. [MS/NUC 444:489]

Given to HPL by George Kirk (HPL to Lillian D. Clark, 27–28 May 1930; *LFF*).

744. Pattee, Fred Lewis (1863–1950). *The House of the Black Ring.* Harrisburg, PA: Mount Pleasant Press, 1916. v, 324 pp. [HPL/MS/NUC 445:38]

Given to HPL by Anne Tillery Renshaw, who was acquainted with the author (*JVS* 258; see also 300). Pattee reviewed HPL's *Supernatural Horror in Literature* (Abramson ed.) in *American Literature* 18, No. 2 (May 1946): 175–77.

745. Pearson, James Larkin (1879–1981). *Pearson's Poems.* Boomer, NC: Published by the author, 1924. 374 pp. [X—JHL/NUC 446:595]

Pearson was a colleague of HPL's in the amateur journalism movement. *CE* 1.356

746. Peck, Harry Thurston (1856–1914), ed. *Harper's Dictionary of Classical Literature and Antiquities.* New York: American Book Co., 1896. 1701 pp. [MS/NUC 447:68]

CE 2.186, 191 *CLM* 304

747. Pellisson, Maurice (1850–1915). *Roman Life in Pliny's Time.* [As by Maurice Pellison.] Translated from the French by Maud Wilkinson. With an Introduction by Frank Justus Miller. Meadville, PA: Flood & Vincent, 1897. xviii, 315 pp. [MS/NUC 448:75]

CE 2.192 *SL* 2.186 *CLM* 304

748. Pelton, W[illiam] F[rederick] (1858–1944). *The Master-Key to the Apocalypse: A Reply to the Higher Critics and the Millennarians.* London: Simpkin, Marshall, Hamilton, Kent, 1926. 250 pp. [MS/NUC 448:128]

A book of biblical criticism.

749. Pennell, H[enry] Cholmondeley (1837–1915), ed. *The Muses of Mayfair: Selections from the Vers de Société of the Nineteenth Century.* London: Chatto & Windus, 1874. xv, 382 pp. [MS/NUC 448:473]

750. *People's Cyclopedia: A Complete Library of Reference Containing the Exact Knowledge of the World.* Under the Chief Editorship of Charles Leonard-Stuart and George J. Hagar. New York: Syndicate Publishing Co., [1914]. 5 vols. [MS/NUC 449:453]

751. Pepys, Samuel (1633–1703). *The Diary of Samuel Pepys, from 1659 to 1669, with Memoir.* Edited by Lord Braybrooke. London: Frederick Warne, 1825. xii, 639 pp. [MS/NUC 449:560]

    First publication of Pepys' diary. *CE* 2.187

752. Percy, Thomas (1729–1811), ed. *Reliques of Ancient English Poetry.* <1765> London: J. M. Dent; New York: E. P. Dutton (Everyman's Library), [1906]–[1932]. 2 vols. [Schiff/NUC 450:1]

    No date cited; there are at least 4 Everyman eds. Celebrated anthology that helped to revive interest in older English literature. *CF* 1.62 *RK* 86, 184

753. Perutz, Leo (1884–1957). *The Master of the Day of Judgment.* Translated from the German by Hedwig Singer. New York: Charles Boni, 1930. 195 pp. [HPL/MS/NUC 452:255]

    Obtained in October 1932 (*SL* 4.91). Translation of *Der Meister des jüngsten Tages* (1923). A non-supernatural mystery/horror novel. *ES* 260n1 *JVS* 104, 321n3

754. Petronius (T[itus] Petronius Arbiter) (fl. 1st c. C.E.). *The Satyricon of T. Petronius Arbiter.* Burnaby's Translation, 1694. With an Introduction by Martin Travers. London: Simpkin, Marshall, Hamilton, Kent, [1923]. xvi, 226 pp. [Schiff/NUC 453:491]

    Sold to HPL by Samuel Loveman (HPL to Lillian D. Clark, 10 May 1928; *LFF*). Copy dated "May 1928." *SHL* 31; cf. "The Rats in the Walls" (*CF* 1.391), where Trimalchio (the central figure in the segment of the *Satyricon* entitled "Trimalchio's Dinner") is cited.

755. *The Phantagraph.* Edited by Donald A. Wollheim. 1935–37. [HPL]

    HPL had a complete set of the journal. He appeared frequently in its pages. There were 14 issues from July/August 1935 to March/April 1937. Many references to the periodical in HPL's letters.

756. [Phillips, Sir Richard (1767–1840).] *A Geographical View of the World, Embracing the Manners, Customs, and Pursuits of Every Nation.* By the Rev. J.

Goldsmith [pseud.]. 1st American ed., rev., corr., & improved by James G. Percival. New-York: E. Hopkins & W. Reed, 1826. 406, 46 pp. [MS/NUC 456:190]

757. *Picturesque Homes of Ireland.* [MS]
Not located.

758. Pindar (518–438 B.C.E.). *The Extant Odes of Pindar.* Translated into English with an Introduction and Short Notes by Ernest Myers. London: Macmillan & Co., 1912. 176 pp. [MS/NUC 458:641]
A prose translation.

759. Pittenger, William (1840–1904). *Capturing a Locomotive: A History of the Secret Service in the Late War.* Washington, DC: National Tribune, 1885. 354 pp. [MS/NUC 460:145]

760. ———. *The Debater's Treasury: Comprising a List of 200 Questions with Notes and Arguments.* Philadelphia: Penn Publishing Co., 1891. 141 pp. [MS/NUC 460:145]
No ed. cited by MS.

761. Plarr, Victor (1863–1929). *In the Dorian Mood.* London: John Lane; New York: George H. Richmond, 1896. 111 pp. [MS/NUC 461:14]
Poems.

762. Plato (429?–347 B.C.E.). *The Republic of Plato in Ten Books.* Translated from the Greek by H. Spens. Introduction by Richard Garnett. London: J. M. Dent; New York: E. P. Dutton (Everyman's Library), [1906f.]. xv, 348 pp. [MS/NUC 461:197f.]
No date cited by MS. *JFM* 375

763. Plutarch (50?–120?). *Lives.* Translated from the Original Greek: With Notes, Critical and Historical: And a Life of Plutarch. By John Langhorne and William Langhorne. Baltimore: W. & J. Neal, 1836. xx, 738 pp. [MS/NUC 462:262]

764. ———. *Plutarch's Lives.* The Translation Called Dryden's. Corrected from the Greek and Revised by A[rthur] H[ugh] Clough. New York: A. L. Burt, [188-?]. 5 vols. [MS/NUC 462:267]
HPL had only 2 vols. Dryden only supervised the original translation (1683). *CF* 1.42

765. Poe, Edgar Allan (1809–1849). *The Gold Bug.* Forward by Hervey Allen. Notes on the Text by Thomas Ollive Mabbott. Garden City, NY: Doubleday, Doran, 1929. xxxiii, 91 pp. [RHB/NUC 462:513]

Given to HPL by "The Man from Genoa" (i.e., Frank Belknap Long). Mabbott (1897–1968) not only wrote an important early critical notice of HPL, "H. P. Lovecraft: An Appreciation" (in HPL's *Marginalia* [1944]), but spent years working on a landmark critical edition of Poe, dying just as the first volume (1969) was in the press.

766. ———. *Marginalia.* Edited, and with an Introduction by Isaac Goldberg. Girard, KS: Haldeman-Julius, [1924]. 64 pp. [NUC 462:523]

Obtained in August 1925 (cf. HPL to Lillian D. Clark, 13 August 1925; *LFF*).

767. ———. *The Poems of Edgar Allan Poe.* Edited by Andrew Lang. London: Kegan Paul, Trench, 1881. xxvi, 172 pp. [HPL to Edward H. Cole, 30 January 1935/NUC 462:535]

Gift of Ernest A. Edkins.

768. ———. *Tales of Mystery and Imagination.* Illustrated by Harry Clarke. New York: Tudor Publishing Co., 1933. 412 pp. [X/NUC 462:563]

HPL was given this copy by R. H. Barlow in January 1934; after HPL's death it was given to Clark Ashton Smith. This copy bears Smith's signature, dated 25 May 1937. *ET* 293

769. ———. *The Works of Edgar Allan Poe.* The Raven Edition. New York: P. F. Collier & Son, 1903. 5 vols. [HPL/MS/NUC 462:487]

CF 1.100n, 3.19, 145 *AT* 19 *SHL* 54–60. Many references to individual works by Poe in HPL's letters.

770. ———. *The Works of Edgar Allan Poe.* The Cameo Edition. With an Introduction by Edwin Markham. New York: Funk & Wagnall's, 1904. 10 vols. [MS/NUC 462:488]

HPL had only Vol. 9: *Essays and Philosophy*, which contains, among other things, *Eureka*. Obtained in New York in 1922 (HPL to Lillian D. Clark, 13–16 September 1922; *LFF*). *AG* 43

771. *The Poetical Works of Milton, Young, Gray, Beattie, and Collins.* Philadelphia: Grigg & Elliot, 1841. 543 pp. [MS/NUC 463:35]

772. Pope, Alexander (1688–1744). *The Poetical Works of Alexander Pope.* Edited, with a Critical Memoir, by William [Michael] Rossetti. Illustrated by Thomas Seccombe. London: E. Moxon, Son & Co., 1873; *or* London:

William Collins, Sons & Co., n.d.; *or* London: Ward, Lock & Co., n.d. xxxix, 600 pp. [MS/NUC 465:355, 361]

CE 1.32

773. Powys, John Cowper (1872–1963). *One Hundred Best Books.* <1916> Girard, KS: Haldeman-Julius, 1923. 62 pp. [HPL to Frank Belknap Long, 4 September 1923/NUC 468:540]

774. Prescott, William H[ickling] (1796–1859). *History of the Conquest of Mexico, with a Preliminary View of the Ancient Mexican Civilization, and the Life of the Conqueror Hernando Cortes.* <1849> New York: A. L. Burt, [19—?]. 2 vols. in 1. [X/NUC 470:254]

The book dealer selling this volume reports: "H. P. Lovecraft's copy with his ownership signature and address on the front fly: H.P. Lovecraft, 598 Angell St., Providence, R.I., U.S.A. and with a few numbers in his hand on the front pastedown." Cited in a footnote to "The Transition of Juan Romero" (*CF* 1.102n).

775. Prime, William Cowper (1825–1905). *Pottery and Porcelain of All Times and Nations.* New York: Harper & Brothers, 1878. 531 pp. [MS/NUC 471:369]

776. Prior, Matthew (1664–1721). *Poetical Works.* With Memoir and Critical Dissertation by George Gilfillan. Edinburgh: James Nichol, 1858. xx, 475 pp. [MS/NUC 471:698]

CF 1.49

777. Proctor, Richard Anthony (1837–1888). *Half-Hours with the Telescope.* <1868> 13th Impression. London: Longmans, Green, 1902. viii, 109 pp. [MS/NUC 472:336]

CE 3.130, 261, 294

778. Pronti, Domenico (1750?–?). *Nuova raccolta di 100 vedutine antiche della città di Roma e sue vicinanze.* Roma: Presso il Suddetto Incisore, 1795. 2 vols. in 1. [MS/NUC 472:613]

MS lists date as 1819, but no data available.

779. Providence Franklin Society. *Report on the Geology of Rhode Island.* Providence: The Society, 1887. 130 pp. [MS/NUC 473:509]

780. Providence Sunday Journal. *Half a Century with the* Providence Journal. [Providence:] The Journal Co., 1904. xiii, 235 pp. [MS/NUC 473:513]

781. Pyle, Katharine (1863–1938). *Once upon a Time in Rhode Island.* [Garden City, NY: Doubleday, Page & Co., 1914.] 204 pp. [MS/NUC 476:205]

782. Quackenbos, John D[uncan] (1848–1926). *Illustrated History of Ancient Literature, Oriental and Classical.* New York: Harper & Brothers, 1882. 432 pp. [MS/NUC 476:301]

   CE 2.191

783. Quatrefages de Breau, Armand de (1810–1892). *The Human Species.* [Translated from the French.] New York: D. Appleton & Co., 1881. x, 498 pp. [MS/NUC 751:146]

   Translation of *L'Espèce humain* (1877). Quatrefages is one of the anthropological authorities cited by Akeley in "The Whisperer in Darkness" (*CF* 2.476).

784. Quiller-Couch, Sir Arthur (1863–1944). *Noughts and Crosses: Stories, Studies, and Sketches.* <1891> By "Q." London: Cassell, 1893. viii, 263 pp. [HPL/MS/NUC 477:388]

   Contents: The Omnibus; Fortunio; The Outlandish Ladies; Statement of Gabriel Foot, Highwayman; The Return of Joanna; Psyche; The Countess of Bellarmine; A Cottage in Troy; Old Aeson; Stories of Bleakirk; A Dark Mirror; The Small People; The Mayor of Gantick; The Doctor's Foundling; The Gifts of Feodor Himkoff; Yorkshire Dick; The Carol; The Paradise of Choice; Beside the Bee-hives; The Magic Shadow.

785. ———. *Old Fires and Profitable Ghosts: A Book of Stories.* New York: Charles Scribner's Sons, 1900. vi, 384 pp. [HPL/MS/NUC 477:388]

   Contents: Oceanus; The Seventh Man; A Room of Mirrors; A Pair of Hands; The Lady of the Ship; Frozen Margit; Singular Adventure of a Small Free-Trader; The Mystery of Joseph Laquadem; Prisoners of War; A Town's Memory; The Lady of the Red Admirals; The Penance of John Emmet; Elisha; "Once Aboard the Lugger"; Which?

786. ———. *Wandering Heath: Stories, Studies, and Sketches.* By "Q." New York: Charles Scribner's Sons, 1896. 276 pp. [HPL/MS/NUC 477:397]

   Contents: Prologue; The Roll-Call on the Reef; The Looe Die-hards; My Grandfather, Hendry Watty; Jetsam; Wrestlers; The Bishop of Eucalyptus; Widdershins; Visitors at the Gunnel Rock; Letters from Troy; Legends; Experiments.

787. Radcliffe, Ann (1764–1823). *The Mysteries of Udolpho: A Romance.* <1794> London: George Routledge & Sons, [1882]–[192-]. [HPL/RHB/OCLC]

No date cited by HPL or RHB; there are at least 6 Routledge eds. Three of the eds. have an introduction by D. Murray Rose. *CE* 2.225; 5.158, 173 *SHL* 37, 42 *SL* 5.244 *MTS* 174, 176, 183, 188, 193 *OFF* 187, 237 *ES* 34, 47 *RB* 20 *FLB* 253

788. [Rand, William Wilberforce (1816–1904), ed.] *A Dictionary of the Holy Bible.* New York: American Tract Society, [1859]. 534 pp. [MS/NUC 480:577]

789. Rand, McNally & Co. *Rand-McNally 15¢ Pocket Atlas of the World.* Chicago: Rand, McNally & Co., 1902. 286 pp., 119 pp. maps. [MS/NUC 480:593]

790. Raymond, George Lansing (1839–1929). *Poetry as a Representative Art: An Essay in Comparative Aesthetics.* <1886> 7th ed., rev. New York: G. P. Putnam's Sons, 1921. 356 pp. [MS/NUC 483:40]

MS lists date as 1927, but no data available (perhaps a stenographer's error). "... no one could peruse Brander Matthews' 'Study of Versification', Gummere's 'Handbook of Poetics', or Prof. Raymond's 'Poetry as a Representative Art' without enlightenment & profit" (*ET* 21).

791. Read, Francis (1811?–1896). *Westminster Street, Providence, as It Was about 1824. From Drawings Made by Francis Read and Lately Presented by His Daughter, Mrs. Marinus Willett Gardner, to the Rhode Island Historical Society.* Providence: Printed for the Society, 1917. 1 p., 7 plates. [HPL to Lillian D. Clark, 25 November 1925; *LFF*/NUC 483:261]

Given to HPL by Lillian D. Clark. The author's daughter's name was surely a partial influence for that of Marinus Bicknell Willett in *The Case of Charles Dexter Ward* (1927).

792. *The Recluse.* Edited by W. Paul Cook. 1927. [HPL]

Contains HPL's "Supernatural Horror in Literature" (original version), pp. 23–59. Many references to the periodical in HPL's letters.

793. Reeve, Clara (1729–1807). *The Old English Baron.* <1777/1778> [HPL]

No ed. cited by HPL. First published (1777) as *The Champion of Virtue*; retitled *The Old English Baron* in 1778. *CE* 2.225 *SHL* 35–36 *MTS* 20 *JFM* 35, 90

794. Rennell, James Rennell Rodd, baron (1858–1941). *Rose Leaf and Apple Leaf.* As by "Rennell Rodd." With an Introduction by Oscar Wilde. Philadelphia: J. M. Stoddart & Co., 1882. 102 pp. *or* Portland, ME: Thomas Bird Mosher, 1906. viii, 100 pp. [HPL to Donald Wandrei, 10 December 1927 (*MTS* 190)/NUC 501:326]

A poetry collection.

795. Renshaw, Anne Tillery (1890?–1953?). *Salvaging Self Esteem: A Program for Self-Improvement*. Washington, DC: Renshaw School of Speech, [1937]. 107 pp. [MS/NUC 488:611]

796. ———. *Well Bred Speech: A Brief, Intensive Aid for English Students*. [Washington, DC: Standard Press, 1936.] 98 pp. [MS/NUC 488:611]

HPL worked on the revision of this book, but few of his revisions were incorporated in the published version. The essay "Suggestions for a Reading Guide" (title not HPL's) was to have been the last chapter of the book. Extensive notes and some whole chapters by HPL, as well as galleys of the book corrected by HPL, survive at JHL; the chapters were published in *ET*. Renshaw was an amateur associate of HPL's from the 1910s. CE 2.8–9, 202–3 *ES* 750n2 *OFF* 341, 358, 361, 363 *JFM* 392 *ET* 339, 344, 375–80, 381–85, 388–92 *RB* 179n1, 289n1, 398n1 *JVS* 377n4, 379n6 *FLB* 332 *CLM* 123n3, 205n20, 345n1

797. *The Republic of Letters: A Republication of Standard Literature*. New York: G. Dearborn, 1834f. [MS/NUC 489:199]

HPL apparently had only Vols. 1 and 2 (1834).

798. Reynolds, Beatrix, and James Gabelle, comps. *George Washington in the Hearts of His Countrymen: An Anthology 1732–1932*. [Ridgewood, NJ: Garen Publishing Co., 1932.] 105 pp. [X—JHL/NUC 491:158]

Given to HPL by Elizabeth Toldridge in late October 1932 (*ET* 217–18, 221–22).

799. Reynolds, Sir Joshua (1723–1792). *The Masterpieces of Reynolds*. Sixty Reproductions from the Original Paintings by F. Hanfstaengl. New York: Frederick A. Stokes Co., 1906. 67 pp. [MS/NUC 491:262]

800. *The Rhode Island Almanac for the Year* . . . Newport: Printed and Sold by Oliver Farnsworth; Providence: Printed and Sold by Hugh H. Brown; [etc.]. [MS/NUC 491:630]

HPL had the issues for 1789, 1803, 1825, 1828, 1832 (by Isaac Bickerstaff [pseud.]), 1833 (by R. T. Paine), 1834, 1835, 1840, 1843, 1849, 1852, 1866, 1867, 1870 (all by Isaac Bickerstaff [pseud.]), and 1883 (by George A. Stockwell).

801. Rhode Island Historical Society. *Collections*. Providence, 1827–1941. 34 vols. [MS/NUC 491:638; 91:90; 564:692]

HPL owned:
Vol. 4 (1838): John Callendar, *An Historical Discourse on the Civil and Religious Affairs of the Colony of Rhode-Island*. 270 pp.

Vol. 5 (1843): William Reed Staples, *Annals of the Town of Providence, from Its First Settlement to the Organization of the City Government, in June, 1832.* 670 pp.

802. *Rhode Island Imprints: A List of Books, Pamphlets, Newspapers, and Broadsides Printed at Newport, Providence, Warren, Rhode Island between 1727 and 1800.* Providence: The [Rhode Island Historical] Society, 1915. 88 pp. [MS/NUC 491:644]

Prepared by the John Carter Brown Library.

803. Richardson, Charles Francis (1851–1913). *The Choice of Books.* <1881> New York: John B. Alden, 1885. 208 pp. [X/MS/NUC 493:137]

804. Richman, Irving Berdine (1861–1938). *Rhode Island: A Study in Separatism.* Boston: Houghton Mifflin, 1905. x, 395 pp. [MS/NUC 493:434]

805. Rickword, Edgell (1898–1982). *Rimbaud, the Boy and the Poet.* New York: Alfred A. Knopf, 1924. xiii, 234 pp. [MS/NUC 494:161]

806. Riley, James Whitcomb (1849–1916). *Old-Fashioned Roses.* <1888> 17th ed. London: Longmans, Green, 1897. ix, 145 pp. [MS/NUC 495:293]

Poems.

807. Roberts, Peter (1859–1932). *Immigrant Races in North America.* New York: Young Men's Christian Association, 1910. 109 pp. [X/MS/NUC 497:664]

Inscribed: "H. P. Lovecraft / 598 Angell St., / Providence, / R.I., / U.S.A."

808. Rogers, Samuel (1763–1855). *The Poetical Works of Samuel Rogers.* New York: Worthington, 1885. 451 pp. [MS/NUC 501:277]

Poet who is often called "the last Augustan."

809. ———. *Recollections.* Edited by William Sharpe. Boston: Bartlett & Miles, 1859. xxii, 253 pp. [MS/NUC 501:277]

810. Roget, Peter Mark (1779–1869). *Thesaurus of English Words and Phrases.* New ed., enlarged & improved, partly from the author's notes, & with a full index, by John Lewis Roget. New York & Chicago: John R. Anderson & Co., 1882. xlv, 429, 271 pp. [X/MS/NUC 501:326]

This copy obtained in September 1933 (*JVS* 167); HPL probably had an earlier copy. L. W. Currey notes: "[HPL] has added between 100 and 200 words and phrases of his own to various entries, spread through the volume." *CE* 2.191, 202 *AT* 19 *SL* 2.226 *RK* 35 *OFF* 298, 306, 315 *ES* 259 *JVS* 38, 61

811. Rohmer, Sax [pseud. of Arthur Sarsfield Ward, 1883–1959]. *Brood of the Witch-Queen*. <1918> New York: A. L. Burt, 1926. 278 pp. [HPL/MS/NUC 648:117/Tuck 2:369]

SHL 74 *MTS* 113 *OFF* 9 *ES* 29, 30, 31n1, 250 *RB* 35

812. Rollin, Charles (1661–1741). *The Ancient History of the Egyptians, Carthaginians, Assyrians, Babylonians, Medes and Persians, Macedonians, and Grecians*. <1734–39> Translated from the French. New-York: G. Long, 1828. 4 vols. [MS/NUC 502:155]

Translation of *Histoire ancienne des Égyptiens, des Carthaginois, des Assyriens, des Babyloniens, des Mèdes et des Perses, des Macédoniens, des Grecs* (1730–38).

813. Roscoe, Sir Henry Enfield (1833–1915). *Chemistry*. New York: American Book Co., [189-]. 132 pp. [X/NUC 504:35]

814. Rountree, Richard Jerome. *An Introduction to the Appreciation of Music*. Wauwatosa, WI: Kenyon Press, 1930. 63 pp. [MS/NUC 506:554]
Revised by HPL? Cf. #669.

815. Rowson, Mrs Susanna (Haswell) (1762–1824). *Charlotte Temple: A Tale of Truth*. <1791> New York: Hurst, 1889. 135 pp. [MS/NUC 507:494]

816. Rudwin, Maximilian J[osef] (1885–1946), ed. *Devil Stories: An Anthology*. New York: Alfred A. Knopf, 1921. xix, 332 pp. [X/HPL/MS/NUC 509:55]

Contents: The Devil in a Nunnery, by Francis Oscar Mann; Belphagor; or, The Marriage of the Devil, by Niccolò Macchiavelli; The Devil and Tom Walker, by Washington Irving; From the Memoirs of Satan, by Wilhelm Hauff; St John's Eve, by Nicolai Gogol (tr. Isabel F. Hapgood); The Devil's Wager, by William Makepeace Thackeray; The Painter's Bargain, by William Makepeace Thackeray; Bon-Bon, by Edgar Allan Poe; The Printer's Devil, by Anonymous; The Devil's Mother-in-Law, by Fernán Caballero (tr. John H. Ingram); The Generous Gambler, by Charles Baudelaire (tr. Arthur Symons); The Three Low Masses, by Alphonse Daudet (tr. Robert Routeledge); Devil-Puzzlers, by Frederic Beecher Perkins; The Devil's Round, by Charles Deulin (tr. Isabel Bruce); The Legend of Mont St Michel, by Guy de Maupassant; The Demon Pope, by Richard Garnett; Lucifer, by Anatole France (tr. Alfred Allinson); The Devil, by Maxim Gorky (tr. Leo Wiener); The Devil and the Old Man, by John Masefield.

Given to HPL by Samuel Loveman, who has written on the flyleaf: "For Howard / As a token of his friend's esteem." Loveman had dedicated his poem "To Satan" (*Conservative*, July 1923) to HPL.

817. Ruoff, Henry W[oldmar] (1865–1935), comp. *Universal Manual of Ready Reference*. Springfield, MA: King-Richardson Co., 1904. 741 pp. [MS/NUC 510:47]

818. Ruskin, John (1819–1900). *Modern Painters*. <1843–60> New York: John Wiley & Sons, 1888. 5 vols. in 4. [MS/NUC 510:315]

   HPL had only 2 vols. *CE* 2.200

819. ———. [*Selected Works.*] Chicago: Bedford, Clarke, [188-]. 6 vols. in 1. [MS/NUC 510:347]

820. Russell, W[illiam] Clark (1844–1911). *The Flying Dutchman; or, The Death Ship.* <1888> New York: Hurst, 1893. 256 pp. [HPL/RHB/MS/OCLC]

   First published as *The Death Ship*.

821. ———. *The Frozen Pirate*. London: Sampson, Low & Co., 1887. 2 vols. [HPL/MS]

   No ed. cited by HPL or MS. Read by HPL at the age of eight or nine (HPL to Richard F. Searight, 13 October 1934). A tale of Antarctic adventure that may have minimally influenced *At the Mountains of Madness*.

822. Russell, William (1798–1873). *Orthophony; or, The Cultivation of the Voice in Elocution*. <1846> 34th ed. Boston: Ticknor & Fields, 1869. 300 pp. [Grill-Binkin/NUC 510:674]

823. Saint-Pierre, Jacques Henri Bernadin de (1737–1814). *The Shipwreck; or, The Adventures, Love, and Constancy of Paul and Virginia*. <1788> New York: S. King, 1821. 34 pp. [MS/OCLC]

   MS gives date as 1823, but no data available. *Paul et Virginie* is a sentimental adventure novel that enjoyed tremendous popularity in the late 18th and early 19th centuries.

824. Saintsbury, George (1843–1933), ed. *Tales of Mystery*. New York: Macmillan Co., 1891. xxix, 319 pp. [HPL/RHB/NUC 515:467]

   Given to HPL by Frank Belknap Long. Contains selections from the work of Ann Radcliffe, M. G. Lewis, and Charles Robert Maturin. Saintsbury was one of the premier critics of English literature in the 19th century. *SHL* 42 *SL* 1.199

825. Sallust (C[aius] Sallustius Crispus) (86–35 B.C.E.). *Opera*. Adapted to the Hamiltonian System by a Literal and Analytical Translation by James

Hamilton. Philadelphia: David McKay, [1885]–[190-]. 309 pp. [MS/NUC 516:381]

No date cited by MS; there are at least 2 printings.

826. Saltus, Edgar (1855–1921). *The Lords of the Ghostland: A History of the Ideal.* <1907> New York: Brentano's, 1922. 215 pp. [MS/NUC 516:682]

On religion. Read in February 1925 (HPL to Annie E. P. Gamwell, 10 February 1925).

827. Sargent, Epes (1813–1880). *The Standard Fourth Reader: Part Two: With Spelling and Defining Lessons, Exercises in Declamation, etc.* Boston: J. L. Shorey, 1867. xvi, 336 pp. [MS/NUC 520:684]

828. Savile, Frank Mackenzie. *Beyond the Great South Wall: The Secret of the Antarctic.* <1899> New York: Grosset & Dunlap, 1901. 322 pp. [HPL/MS/NUC 522:354/OCLC]

A novel of Antarctic exploration that may have influenced *At the Mountains of Madness*.

829. Saxe, John Godfrey (1816–1887). *Poems.* <1850> 8th ed. Boston: Ticknor, 1855. 192 pp. [MS/NUC 522:550]

830. Sayers, Dorothy L[eigh] (1893–1957), ed. *The Omnibus of Crime.* <1928> Garden City, NY: Garden City Publishing Co., 1931. 1177 pp. [HPL/MS/NUC 522:694]

Contents [Mystery and Horror section only]: The Open Door, by Mrs [Margaret] Oliphant; The Story of the Bagman's Uncle, by Charles Dickens; The Trial for Murder, by Charles Collins and Charles Dickens; Martin's Close, by M. R. James; How Love Came to Professor Guildea, by Robert Hichens; The Open Window, by Saki [pseud. of H. H. Munro]; [The Novel of] The Black Seal, by Arthur Machen; Tcheriapin, by Sax Rohmer; The Monkey's Paw, by W. W. Jacobs; The Hair, by A. J. Alan; Mrs Amworth, by E. F. Benson; Moxon's Master, by Ambrose Bierce; The Dancing Partner, by Jerome K. Jerome; Thrawn Janet, by Robert Louis Stevenson; The Avenging of Ann Leete, by Marjorie Bowen; August Heat, by W. F. Harvey; The Anticipator, by Morley Roberts; The Brute, by Joseph Conrad; Where Their Fire Is Not Quenched, by May Sinclair; Green Tea, by J. Sheridan Le Fanu; The Misanthrope, by J. D. Beresford; The Bad Lands, by John Metcalfe; Nobody's House, by A. M. Burrage; The Seventh Man, by A. T. Quiller-Couch; Proof, by N. Royde-Smith; Seaton's Aunt, by Walter de la Mare; Lukundoo, by Edward Lucas White; The Gentleman from America, by Michael Arlen; The Narrow Way, by R. Ellis Roberts; Sawney Bean (Traditional Tale of the Lowlands); The Squaw, by Bram Stoker; The Corsican Sisters,

by Violet Hunt; The End of a Show, by Barry Pain; The Cone, by H. G. Wells; The Separate Room, by Ethel Colburn Mayne.
Obtained early in 1932 (*DS* 335). See also #557. First published (1928) as *Great Short Stories of Detection, Mystery, and Horror [First Series]*. OFF 13 *ES* 208, 404, 435 *CLM* 107

831. Schmitz, Leonhard (1807–1890). *A Manual of Ancient History, from the Remotest Times to the Overthrow of the Western Empire, A.D. 476.* <1855> New York: Sheldon & Co., 1868. 466. [MS/NUC 528:100]

832. Schoonmaker, Frank (1905–1976). *Through Europe on Two Dollars a Day.* <1927> New & rev. ed. New York: Robert M. McBride, 1933. xii, 225 pp. [MS/NUC 529:468]

833. Schopenhauer, Arthur (1788–1860). *The Art of Controversy.* Translated by T. Bailey Saunders. <1896> Girard, KS: Haldeman-Julius, [1923]. 64 pp. [HPL to Frank Belknap Long, 4 September 1923/NUC 529:483; OCLC]

834. Schrevel, Cornelius (1608–1664). *Lexicon Manuale Graeco-Latinum et Latino-Graecum.* <1654> 2nd American ed. New York: Eastburn, Kirk & Co., 1814. vi, 578 pp. [MS/NUC 530:203]

835. Scott, Frederick George (1861–1944). *Elton Hazelwood: A Memoir by His Friend Harry Vane.* New York: Whittaker, 1892. 146 pp. [MS/NUC 534:66]

836. Scott, Sir Walter (1771–1832). *The Antiquary.* <1816> Philadelphia: J. B. Lippincott Co., 1887. [MS/OCLC]

837. ———. *Guy Mannering; or, The Astrologer.* <1815> Boston: DeWolfe, Fiske, [1880?]. 422 pp. [MS/NUC 534:356]
Bound with *Anne of Geierstein* (1829).

838. ———. *The Heart of Mid-Lothian.* <1818> Philadelphia: Porter & Coates, n.d. 2 vols. in 1. [MS/NUC 534:360]

839. ———. *Ivanhoe: A Romance.* <1819> Philadelphia: J. B. Lippincott Co., 1877. [MS/NUC 534:299]
CE 2.186

840. ———. *Letters on Demonology and Witchcraft.* <1830> With an Introduction by Henry Morley. London: George Routledge & Sons, 1884. 320 pp. [HPL/RHB/NUC 534:413]

Obtained in August 1927 (*ES* 102). *CE* 2.193 *SHL* 45 *JFM* 143 *RB* 190 *FLB* 208

841. ———. *The Monastery.* <1820> Boston: DeWolfe, Fiske, [1880?]. xli, 37–430 pp. [MS/NUC 534:432]

    Bound with *The Abbott* (1820).

842. ———. *The Poetical Works of Walter Scott.* With a Sketch of His Life by J. W. Lake. Complete in One Volume. Philadelphia: J. Crissy, 1837. xxviii, 443 pp. [MS/NUC 534:282]

843. ———. *The Talisman: A Tale of the Crusaders; and The Chronicles of the Canongate.* <1825; 1827> Boston: DeWolfe, Fiske, [188-?]. [MS/NUC 534:493]

    CE 2.186 *JVS* 165

844. ———. *Woodstock; or, The Cavalier.* <1826> Boston: DeWolfe, Fiske, [1880?]. 471 pp. [MS/NUC 534:512]

    Bound with *Waverley* (1814).

845. Scudder, Horace E[lisha] (1838–1902). *Boston Town.* Boston: Houghton Mifflin, 1883. 243 pp. [MS/NUC 535:215]

    Obtained in New York in February 1925 (HPL to Annie E. P. Gamwell, 10 February 1925).

846. ———, ed. *Men and Manners in America One Hundred Years Ago.* New York: Scribner, Armstrong & Co., 1876. 320 pp. [MS/NUC 535:219]

    CE 2.193

847. Seeley, Harry Govier (1839–1909). *The Story of the Earth in Past Ages.* New York: D. Appleton & Co., 1895. 186 pp. [MS/NUC 536:326]

848. Selden, John (1584–1654). *John Selden and His Table-Talk.* [Edited] by Robert Walters. New York: Eaton & Mains; Cincinnati: Curts & Jennings, 1899. 251 pp. [MS/NUC 537:344]

    Discussions of religious and political affairs by a Jacobean man of letters.

849. Serviss, Garrett P[utnam] (1851–1929). *Astronomy with an Opera-Glass.* <1888> 8th ed. New York: D. Appleton & Co., 1906. vi, 158 pp. [MS/NUC 539:366]

    CE 2.194; 3.89, 99 *ES* 732

850. ———. *Astronomy with the Naked Eye*. New York: Harper & Brothers, 1908. xiii, 246 pp. [MS/NUC 539:367]

It was from this book (p. 152) that HPL derived the quotation from Serviss at the conclusion of "Beyond the Wall of Sleep" (1919; *CF* 1.85). *CE* 2.194 *ET* 190

851. ———. *Pleasures of the Telescope*. New York: D. Appleton & Co., 1901. viii, 200 pp. [MS/NUC 539:368]

CE 2.194

852. Seton, William. *A Glimpse of Organic Life*. New York: P. O. Shea, 1897. 135 pp. [MS/NUC 539:473]

853. Sewell, Elizabeth M[issing] (1815–1906). *The Child's First History of Rome*. <1849> New York: D. Appleton & Co., 1883. 255 pp. [MS/NUC 540:102f.]

854. ———. *A First History of Greece*. <1852> New York: D. Appleton & Co., 1883. 358 pp. [MS/NUC 540:104]

855. Seymour, G[eorge] S[teele] (1878–1945), ed. *A Bookfellow Anthology*. Chicago: The Bookfellows, 1925–36. 12 vols. [X—JHL/MS/NUC 540:258]

HPL had only Vol. 1 (1925). It includes a poem by Frank Belknap Long ("A Sonnet for Seamen," p. 93); this copy is Long's autographed presentation copy to HPL. *JFM* 82

856. Shackleton, Robert (1860–1923). *The Book of Boston*. Philadelphia: Penn Publishing Co., 1917. 332 pp. [MS/NUC 540:366]

857. Shakespeare, William (1564–1616). *The Complete Works of William Shakespeare*. With Historical and Analytical Editions to Each Play . . . by J. O. Halliwell . . . and Other Eminent Commentators. London: J. Tallis & Co., 1860. 3 vols. [MS/NUC 540:514]

858. *Mr. William Shakespeare's Comedies, Histories, Tragedies, and Poems*. The Text Newly Edited with Glossarial, Historical, and Explanatory Notes by Richard Grant White. Boston: Houghton Mifflin, 1883–84. 6 vols. [MS/NUC 540:529]

CF 1.71 *SHL* 31–32. Many references to Shakespeare's individual works in HPL's letters.

859. ———. *Shakespeare's Complete Works.* Edited with Notes by William J. Rolfe. New York: Harper & Brothers, 1898; *or* New York: American Book Company, 1898f. [MS]

There is no indication how many volumes are in the former edition; the latter contains 37 volumes. It is unclear how many volumes HPL owned; MS writes only "Shakespeare set—Rolfe."

860. Sharpless, Isaac (1848–1920), and George Morris Philips (1851–1920). *Astronomy for Schools and General Readers.* <1882> Philadelphia: J. B. Lippincott Co., 1906. 315 pp. [MS/NUC 542:75]

861. Shaw, George Bernard (1856–1950). *Back to Methuselah: A Metabiological Pentateuch.* New York: Brentano's, 1921. ciii, 300 pp. [NUC 542:175]

Given to HPL by Sonia H. Greene (*RK* 213). *AG* 104, 116

862. Shaw, Thomas B[udd] (1813–1862). *Outlines of English Literature.* <1849> With a sketch of American literature by Henry T. Tuckerman. New York: Sheldon & Co., 1852. 489 pp. [HPL to Edward H. Cole, 14 December 1914/NUC 542:325]

863. [Shaw, William.] *The Life of Hannah More: With a Critical Review of Her Writings.* By the Rev. Sir Archibald McSarcasm [pseud.]. London: T. Hurst, [etc.], 1802. viii, 208 pp. [MS/NUC 542:335]

A satirical work.

864. Shelley, Mary (1797–1851). *Frankenstein; or, The Modern Prometheus.* <1818> New-York: H. G. Daggers, 1845. 114 pp. [HPL/MS]

In a letter to R. H. Barlow (*OFF* 231) HPL remarks that he owned "a pretty old edition—New York, evidently around 1830." It is unclear what edition HPL is referring to. *CE* 2.225 *SHL* 44–45 *MTS* 18, 20, 22, 40, 207 *AG* 73 *OFF* 28, 238 *ES* 37, 513 *ET* 257

865. Shelley, Percy Bysshe (1792–1822). *The Poetical Works of Percy Bysshe Shelley.* Edited by Edward Dowden. New York: Thomas Y. Crowell Co., [188-]. viii, 705 pp. [MS/NUC 542:683]

866. Shenstone, William (1714–1763). *The Poetical Works of William Shenstone.* With Life, Critical Dissertation, and Explanatory Notes by the Rev. George Gilfillan. New York: D. Appleton & Co., 1854. xxviii, 284 pp. [MS/NUC 543:57]

867. Sheridan, Richard Brinsley (1751–1816). *The Works of Richard Brinsley Sheridan: Dramas, Poems, Translations, Speeches, and Unfinished Sketches.* Edited by F. Stainforth. London: Chatto & Windus, 1874. viii, 656 pp. [MS/NUC 543:265]
CE 2.188 *AG* 156 *RK* 118 *JFM* 29, 34

868. Sherwin, Oscar (1902–1976). *Mr. Gay: Being a Picture of the Life and Times of the Author of* The Beggar's Opera. New York: John Day Co., 1929. 184 pp. [MS/NUC 543:439]

869. Shiel, M[atthew] P[hipps] (1865–1947). *The Lord of the Sea.* <1901> Introduction by Carl Van Vechten. New York: Alfred A. Knopf, 1924. xvii, 299 pp. [HPL/MS/NUC 543:571]
Given to HPL by Richard Ely Morse (HPL to Richard Ely Morse, 30 November 1935). *ES* 573, 575

870. ———. *Prince Zaleski.* Boston: Roberts Brothers, 1895. 207 pp. [HPL/RHB/MS/NUC 543:571]
Contents: The Race of Orven; The Stone of the Edmundsbury Monks; The S.S.
Given to HPL by Samuel Loveman. *MTS* 26, 37, 41 *ES* 49, 50, 52, 573, 575, 580, 729, 733

871. ———. *The Purple Cloud.* <1901> New York: Vanguard Press, [1930]. ix, 294 pp. [HPL/RHB/NUC 543:572]
Given to HPL by Richard Ely Morse (HPL to Richard Ely Morse, 30 August 1932). HPL had, however, read the book in 1927, from a copy lent to him by Frank Belknap Long (see *ES* 90, 91), which means he read a copy of the 1901 edition; Shiel radically revised the text for a 1929 edition, of which the above is a reprint. The earlier chapters, recounting an expedition to the Arctic, could have influenced the analogous portion of *At the Mountains of Madness* (1931). *SHL* 74 *MTS* 110, 111, 114, 131, 134, 135 *ES* 179, 190, 191n2, 209, 573, 575, 667 *RB* 242 *FLB* 340 *CLM* 267, 307

872. Shirley, William (1694–1771). *Correspondence of William Shirley, Governor of Massachusetts and Military Commander in America, 1731–1760.* Edited by Charles Henry Lincoln. New York: Macmillan Co., 1912. 2 vols. [MS/NUC 544:190]

873. *Shudders: A Collection of Uneasy Tales.* [Edited by Charles Birkin.] London: Philip Allan, 1932. 254 pp. [HPL/MS/Ashley 717]
Contents: Of Persons Unknown, by H. Russell Wakefield; Toys, by Tod Robbins; Accusing Shadows, by Elliott O'Donnell; Professor Pownall's

Oversight, by H. Russell Wakefield; The Harlem Horror, by Charles Lloyd [pseud. of Charles Birkin]; The Trunk, by Philip Murray; The Third Coach, by H. Russell Wakefield; The Crimson Blind, by Mrs [H. D.] Everett; The Haunted Spinney, by Elliott O'Donnell; The Patch, by Philip Murray; That Dieth Not, by H. Russell Wakefield.
ES 624

874. Sinclair, May (1863–1946). *The Intercessor and Other Stories*. New York: Macmillan Co., 1932. 222 pp. [HPL/RHB/NUC 547:523]

Contents: The Mahatma's Story; Jones's Karma; Heaven; The Intercessor; The Villa Désirée.
   Given to HPL by August Derleth (*ES* 598). HPL also read Sinclair's *Uncanny Stories* (1923; cf. *SHL* 77) from a volume lent to him by Arthur Leeds (HPL to Lillian D. Clark, 15 April 1926; *LFF*). *ES* 594, 595, 596, 599, 603 *JVS* 181

875. Singleton, Esther (1865–1930). *The Furniture of Our Forefathers*. With Critical Descriptions of Plates by Russell Sturgis. Garden City, NY: Doubleday, Page, 1922. 8 parts in 1. [MS/NUC 548:48]
CE 2.193 *SL* 1.356

876. Sitwell, Sir Osbert (1892–1969). *The Man Who Lost Himself*. London: Duckworth, 1929. viii, 288 pp. *or* New York: Coward-McCann, 1930. viii, 309 pp. [HPL/MS/NUC 548:386]
No ed. cited by HPL or MS.

877. Skinner, Charles M[ontgomery] (1852–1907). *Myths and Legends of Our New Possessions and Protectorate*. Philadelphia: J. B. Lippincott Co., 1900. 354 pp. [MS/NUC 549:52]
On myths in Cuba, Puerto Rico, and the Philippines.

878. ———. *Myths and Legends of Our Own Land*. Philadelphia: J. B. Lippincott Co., 1896. 2 vols. [MS/NUC 549:52]
HPL derived certain folklore elements in "The Shunned House" and "The Dunwich Horror" from this volume. *CE* 2.191

879. Smellie, William (1740–1795). *The Philosophy of Natural History*. <1790> With an Introduction and Various Additions and Alterations . . . by John Ware. Boston: Hilliard, Gray & Co., 1835. viii, 327 pp. [MS/NUC 550:181]

880. Smith, Clark Ashton (1893–1961). *The Double Shadow and Other Fantasies*. [Auburn, CA:] The Auburn Journal, 1933. 30 pp. [MS/NUC 550:531]

Contents: The Voyage of King Euvoran; The Maze of the Enchanter; The Double Shadow; A Night in Malnéant; The Devotee of Evil; The Willow Landscape.

SHL 72 *SL* 4.214 *MTS* 322, 326 *ES* 559n5 *OFF* 70n1, 320 *MF* 631n4, 634, 655 *JFM* 333n1 *ET* 246, 251 *RB* 26n4, 47, 56, 188n1 *JVS* 145n3, 174 *FLB* 17n3, 31, 143 *CLM* 31, 33, 35, 41–42, 48, 240, 243 *DS* 422

881. ———. *Ebony and Crystal: Poems in Verse and Prose.* [Auburn, CA: The Auburn Journal, 1922.] 152 pp. [X/HPL/RHB/NUC 550:531]

Contents: Arabesque; Beyond the Great Wall; To Omar Khayyam; Strangeness; The Infinite Quest; Rosa Mystica; The Nereid; In Saturn; Impression; Triple Aspect; Desolation; The Orchid; A Fragment; Crepuscle; Inferno; Mirrors; Belated Love; The Absence of the Muse; Dissonance; To Nora May French; In Lemuria; Recompense; Exotique; Transcendence; Satiety; The Ministers of Law; Coldness; The Desert Garden; The Crucifixion of Eros; The Exile; Ave atque Vale; Solution; The Tears of Lilith; A Precept; Remembered Light; Song; Haunting; The Hidden Paradise; Cleopatra; Ecstasy; Union; Psalm; In November; Symbols; *The Hashish Eater; or, The Apocalypse of Evil;* The Sorrow of the Winds; Artemis; Love Is Not Yours, Love Is Not Mine; The City in the Desert; The Melancholy Pool; The Mirrors of Beauty; Winter Moonlight; To the Beloved; Requiescat; Mirage; Inheritance; Autumnal; Chant of Autumn; Echo of Memnon; Twilight on the Snow; Image; The Refuge of Beauty; Nightmare; The Mummy; Forgetfulness; Flamingoes; The Chimaera; Satan Unrepentant; The Abyss Triumphant; The Motes; The Medusa of Despair; Laus Mortis; The Ghoul and the Seraph; At Sunrise; The Land of Evil Stars; The Harlot of the World; The Hope of the Infinite; Love Malevolent; Palms; Memnon at Midnight; Eidolon; The Kingdom of Shadows; Requiescat in Pace; Alexandrines; Ashes of Sunset; November Twilight; Sepulture; Quest; Beauty Implacable; A Vision of Lucifer; Desire of Vastness; Anticipation; A Psalm to the Best Beloved; The Witch in the Graveyard; *Poems in Prose:* The Traveller; The Flower-Devil; Images (Tears, The Secret Rose, The Wind and the Garden, Offerings, A Coronal); The Black Lake; Vignettes (Beyond the Mountains, The Broken Lute, Nostalgia of the Unknown, Grey Sorrow, The Hair of Circe, The Eyes of Circe); A Dream of Lethe; The Caravan; The Princess Almeena; Ennui; The Statue of Silence; Remoteness; The Memnons of the Night; The Garden and the Tomb; In Cocaigne; The Litany of the Seven Kisses; From a Letter; From the Crypts of Memory; A Phantasy; The Demon, the Angel, and Beauty; The Shadows.

Author's presentation copy to HPL. Copy #219 of 500. HPL reviewed the volume in *L'Alouette* 1, No. 1 (January 1924): 20–21 (*CE* 2.73–74). *CE* 1.353 *MTS* 8, 81, 215 *OFF* 67 *ES* 51, 281 *MF* 652n3, 655 *ET* 251 *RB* 187, 206 *JVS* 38 *FLB* 50 *CLM* 33, 35, 42, 48 *DS* 48–49, 194, 422

882. ———. *Odes and Sonnets.* Preface by George Sterling. San Francisco: Book Club of California, 1918. 28 pp. [HPL/NUC 550:531]

Contents: Preface, by George Sterling; Nero; Ode to the Abyss; To the Darkness; The Retribution; Satan Unrepentant; Alexandrines; Exotique; Ave atque Vale; The Ministers of Law; The Refuge of Beauty; The Crucifixion of Eros; The Harlot of the World; Belated Love; The Medusa of Despair; Memnon at Midnight.

George Kirk's presentation copy to HPL, dated 15 August 1922. *SL* 1.195

883. ———. *Sandalwood.* [Auburn, CA: The Auburn Journal, 1925.] 43 pp. [HPL/RHB/NUC 550:531]

Contents: Semblance; The Song of Aviol; We Shall Meet; Forgotten Sorrow; Departure; You Are Not Beautiful; Query; Enigma; Incognita; The Secret; The End of Autumn; The Love-Potion; The Song of Cartha; Afterwards; Contradiction; The Last Oblivion; Autumn Orchards; Remembrance; The Wingless Archangels; Moon-Dawn; Lunar Mystery; Enchanted Mirrors; Duality; A Valediction; Selenique; Alienage; Adventure; Plum-Flowers; Song; Minatory; Maya; Interrogation; Consolation; A Meeting; The Barrier; Apologia; Estrangement; Loss; A Catch; Don Juan Sings; On Reading Baudelaire; To the Chimera; *Nineteen Poems from the French of Charles Pierre Baudelaire:* Rêve Parisien; Semper Eadem; L'Idéal; La Géante; La Muse Vénale; L'Examen de Minuit; La Musique; Hymne à la Beauté; Parfum Exotique; Mœsta et Errabunda; Ciel Brouillé; La Fontaine de Sang; Harmonie du Soir; L'Aube Spirituelle; Le Vin des Amants; Obsession; Alchimie de la Douleur; Horreur Sympathétique [*sic*]; L'Irrémédiable.

Author's presentation copy to HPL. Copy #12 of 250. *MTS* 215 *ES* 281 *DS* 111

884. ———. *The Star-Treader and Other Poems.* San Francisco: A. M. Robertson, 1912. 99 pp. [HPL/RHB/NUC 550:531]

Contents: Nero; Chant to Sirius; The Star-Treader; The Morning Pool; The Night Forest; The Mad Wind; Song to Oblivion; Medusa; Ode to the Abyss; The Soul of the Sea; The Butterfly; The Price; The Mystic Meaning; Ode to Music; The Last Night; Ode on Imagination; The Wind and the Moon; Lament of the Stars; The Maze of Sleep; The Winds; The Masque of Forsaken Gods; A Sunset; The Cloud-Islands; The Snow-Blossoms; The Summer Moon; The Return of Hyperion; Lethe; Atlantis; The Unrevealed; The Eldritch Dark; The Cherry-Snows; Fairy Lanterns; Nirvana; The Nemesis of Suns; White Death; Retrospect and Forecast; Shadow of Nightmare; The Song of a Comet; The Retribution; To the Darkness; A Dream of Beauty; The Dream-Bridge; Pine Needles; To the Sun; The Fugitives; Averted Malefice; The Medusa of the Skies; A Dead City; The Song of the Stars; Copan; A Song of Dreams; The Balance; Saturn; Finis.

Given to HPL by Alfred Galpin (HPL to Lillian D. Clark, 13–16 September 1922; *LFF*). *SL* 1.194–95 *MTS* 369 *AG* 273–75 *ES* 281 *OFF* 67, 176 *ET* 26 *RB* 206 *FLB* 52, 88, 93 *CLM* 42, 48 *DS* 111

885. Smith, Clark Ashton, and David H[enry] Keller (1880–1966). *The White Sybil* [by Smith] *and Men of Avalon* [by Keller]. Everett, PA: Fantasy Publications, 1934. [HPL to Richard Ely Morse, 22 December 1934/Tuck 1:251]

    FLB 113, 203, 248

886. Smith, G[rafton] Elliot (1871–1937) [et al.]. *Culture: The Diffusion Controversy*. New York: W. W. Norton, [1927]. 106 pp. [MS/NUC 551:173]

    Contents: The Diffusion of Culture, by G. Elliot Smith; The Life of Culture, by Bronislaw Malinowski; The Prosaic vs. the Romantic School in Anthropology, by Herbert J. Spinden; The Diffusion Controversy, by Alex. Goldenweiser.

    Smith is one of the anthropological authorities cited in "The Whisperer in Darkness" (*CF* 2.476).

887. Smith, T[homas] R[oger] (1830–1903). *Architecture, Gothic and Renaissance*. New & rev. ed. London: Sampson Low, Marston & Co., [1880]. xxxix, 236 pp. [MS/NUC 552:234]

    CE 2.200

888. ———, and John Slater (1847–1924). *Architecture, Classic and Early Christian*. London: Sampson Low, Marston, Searle, & Rivington, 1890. xxix, 272 pp. [MS/NUC 552:233]

    CE 2.200 *CLM* 305

889. Smith, Sir William (1813–1893). *A History of Greece, from the Earliest Times to the Roman Conquest*. <1853> Revised with an Appendix by George W. Greene. New York: Harper & Brothers, 1864. xxxiv, 704 pp. [MS/NUC 552:330]

    CE 2.192

890. ———. *A School Dictionary of Greek and Roman Antiquities*. Abridged from the Larger Dictionary. With Corrections and Improvements by Charles Anthon. New-York: Harper & Brothers, 1846. iv, 373 pp. [MS/NUC 552:338]

    CLM 304

891. ———. *A Smaller Classical Dictionary of Biography, Mythology, and Geography.* Abridged from the Larger Dictionary by William Smith. New York: American Book Co., [1852?]. 438 pp. [X—JHL/MS/NUC 552:340]
CLM 304

892. ———. *A Smaller History of Rome, from the Earliest Times to the Establishment of Empire.* <1860> With a Continuation to A.D. 476 by Eugene Lawrence. New York: Harper & Brothers, 1889. xxx, 365 pp. [MS/NUC 552:344]

893. ———. *A Smaller Latin-English Dictionary.* London: John Murray, 1867. ix, 662 pp. [MS/NUC 552:344]

894. ———, ed. *A Dictionary of Greek and Roman Antiquities.* New York: Harper & Brothers, 1846. 1124 pp. [MS/NUC 552:323]

895. ———, ed. *A Dictionary of the Bible: Comprising Its Antiquities, Biography, Geography, and Natural History.* <1860–62> Hartford: J. B. Burr, 1868. vi, 776 pp. [MS/NUC 552:326/OCLC]

896. Snider, Denton Jacques (1841–1925). *Architecture as a Branch of Aesthetic, Psychologically Treated.* St Louis: Sigma Publishing Co., 1905. 561 pp. [MS/NUC 553:56]

897. Snow, Royall H[enderson] (1898–1976). *Thomas Lovell Beddoes, Eccentric & Poet.* New York: Covici, Friede, 1928. ix, 227 pp. [HPL to Clark Ashton Smith, 11 January 1934 (*DS* 512)/NUC 353:139]

898. Spence, Lewis (1874–1955). *An Encyclopaedia of Occultism: A Compendium of Information on the Occult Sciences, Occult Personalities, Psychic Science, Magic, Demonology, Spiritism and Mysticism.* New York: Dodd, Mead, 1920. xii, 451 pp. [HPL/MS/NUC 561:266]
RB 377

899. Spencer, Truman J[oseph] (1864–1944), ed. *A Cyclopedia of the Literature of Amateur Journalism.* Hartford, CT: Truman J. Spencer, 1891. x, 512 pp. [MS/NUC 561:412]

    HPL worked with Spencer during their involvement with the NAPA in the 1930s. *CE* 1.252, 289

900. Spenser, Edmund (1552?–1599). *The Shepherd's Calendar.* <1579> [HPL to MWM, [August 1922] (*MWM* 105)]

    No ed. cited by HPL.

901. Spinden, Herbert J[oseph] (1879–1967) *Ancient Civilizations of Mexico and Central America*. New York: American Museum of Natural History, 1917, 1922, or 1928. 238, 242, or 271 pp. [MS/NUC 562:89]

No date cited by MS.

902. Spofford, Ainsworth Rand (1825–1908), and Charles Gibbon (1843–1890), ed. *The Library of Choice Literature*. Philadelphia: Gebbie & Co., 1882. 8 vols. [MS/NUC 562:319]

903. Spofford, Harriet Elizabeth (Prescott) (1835–1921); Guiney, Louise Imogen (1861–1920); and Brown, Alice (1857–1948). *Three Heroines of New England Romance: Their True Stories*. With many little picturings, authentic and fanciful, by Edmund H. Garrett. Boston: Little, Brown, 1895. 175 pp. [MS/NUC 562:327]

Contents: Priscilla, by Harriet Prescott Spofford; Agnes Surriage, by Alice Brown; Martha Hilton, by Louise Imogen Guiney; Notes, by Edmund H. Garrett.
  Biographical essays (the first is on Priscilla Alden). HPL was acquainted with Guiney, a minor poet.

904. *Spofford's Political Register and U.S. Farmer's Almanac*. Boston, T. Groom. [MS/NUC 562:330]

HPL had the issues for 1841 and 1843.

905. [Spyri, Johanna (1827–1901).] *Willis the Pilot: A Sequel to The Swiss Family Robinson; or, Adventures of an Emigrant Family Wrecked on an Unknown Coast of the Pacific Ocean*. <1858> Boston: Lee & Shepard, 1864. 350 pp. [HPL to Marian F. Bonner, 4 May 1936/NUC 666:64]

The Swiss Family Robinson (*Der Schweizerische Robinson*, 1812) was written by Johann David Wyss (1743–1818).

906. Stark, James Henry. *Stark's Illustrated Bermuda Guide*. Boston: Photo-electrotype Co., 1884. 192 pp. [MS]

No ed. cited by MS.

907. [State Street Trust Company, Boston.] *Towns of New England and Old England, Ireland and Scotland*. Printed to commemorate the landing of the Pilgrims. [Written by Allan Forbes (1874–1955).] Boston, 1920–21. [HPL to Edward H. Cole, 30 September [1923]/NUC 565:343]

Gift of Victor E. Bacon.

908. Stedman, Edmund Clarence (1833–1908). *Poets of America*. Boston: Houghton Mifflin, 1885. xviii, 516 pp. [MS/NUC 566:47]

Contents: Early and Recent Conditions; Growth of the American School; William Cullen Bryant; John Greenleaf Whittier; Ralph Waldo Emerson; Henry Wadsworth Longfellow; Edgar Allan Poe; Oliver Wendell Holmes; James Russell Lowell; Walt Whitman; Bayard Taylor; The Outlook. Landmark critical study of American poetry. *CE* 2.191

909. Steele, George McKendree (1823–1902). *Outline Study of Political Economy*. New York: Chautauqua Press, 1886. xvi, 195 pp. [MS/NUC 566:118]

910. Steele, Joel Dorman (1836–1886). *A Fourteen Weeks Course in Descriptive Astronomy*. New York: A. S. Barnes & Co.; Boston: Woolworth, Ainsworth & Co., 1873. 336 pp. [MS/NUC 566:131]

911. ———. *Fourteen Weeks in Chemistry*. <1873> [HPL to Duane W. Rimel, 19 November 1934 (*FLB* 239)/NUC 566:131–32]
CE 2.194

912. ———. *Fourteen Weeks in Human Physiology*. New York: A. S. Barnes & Co., 1873. 238 pp. [MS/NUC 566:132]

913. ———. *Fourteen Weeks in Physics*. <1878> [HPL to Duane W. Rimel, 19 November 1934 (*FLB* 239)/NUC 566:133]
CE 2.194

914. ———. *Fourteen Weeks in Zoology*. New York: A. S. Barnes & Co., 1877. 308 [i.e., 314] pp. [MS/NUC 566:133]
CE 2.195

915. ———. *The Story of the Rocks: Fourteen Weeks in Popular Geology*. Rev. ed. New York: A. S. Barnes & Co., 1877. 280 pp. [MS/NUC 566:135]

916. ———, and Esther Baker Steele (1835–1911). *A Brief History of France*. New York: American Book Co., [1875] or [1903]. 299, xxx pp. [MS/NUC 566:129]

917. ———. *Brief History of Rome: With Select Readings from Standard Authors*. New York: American Book Co., 1885. 302 pp. [MS/NUC 566:129]

918. *Stepping Stones of American History*. [By Divers Hands.] With 14 Full-Page Pictures in Color by Frank O. Small. Boston: W. A. Wilde Co., 1904. ix, 381 pp. [MS/NUC 568:2]

919. Sterne, Laurence (1713–1768). *The Beauties of Sterne: Consisting of Selections from His Works.* Boston: N. W. Whitaker, 1828. 160 pp. [MS/NUC 568:185]

920. Stevens, Frank. *Stonehenge Today and Yesterday.* <1916> Rev. ed. London: H. M. Stationery Office, 1929. 90 pp. [MS/NUC 568:405]

921. Stevenson, Robert Louis (1850–1894). *Black Canyon, Not I, and Other Stevensoniana.* New York: M. F. Mansfield & A. Wessells, 1899. [20] pp. [RHB/NUC 568:659]

922. ———. *Dr. Jekyll and Mr. Hyde and The Merry Men and Other Tales.* <1886; 1887> London: J. M. Dent; New York: E. P. Dutton (Everyman's Library), [1914]–[1932]. xii, 244 pp. [HPL/NUC 598:48–50]

Contents: The Strange Case of Dr. Jekyll and Mr. Hyde; The Merry Men; Will o' the Mill; Markheim; Thrawn Janet; Olalia; The Treasure of Franchard.

It is not certain that HPL had this volume; there are 4 Everyman eds. *SHL* 48 *OFF* 166

923. ———. *Treasure Island.* <1883>

See HPL to Lillian D. Clark, [20 July 1925; *LFF*]: "During the course of the evening McNeil gave me a defective copy of 'Treasure Island' which he had on hand—a copy with the last page missing. This I remedied by copying the missing fragment on the rear fly leaf from a complete version which McN. had." *CE* 5.163

924. Stewart, Balfour (1828–1887). *Physics.* (Science Primers.) <1872> New York: American Book Co., [1890]–[19–]. 168 pp. [X/NUC 569:160]

925. Stirling, Anna Maria Diana Wilhelmina (1865–1965). *A Painter of Dreams and Other Biographical Studies.* London: John Lane; New York: John Lane Co., 1916. xvi, 366 pp. [MS/NUC 570:58]

On English social life.

926. Stoker, Bram (1847–1912). *Dracula.* London: Constable, 1897. [HPL/MS]

No ed. cited by HPL or MS. *CE* 1.381 *SHL* 74 *SL* 1.255; 3.213–14 *MTS* 11, 20, 22, 29 *ES* 669 *OFF* 44, 81, 166, 173, 307 *JFM* 149 *RB* 188 *FLB* 298

927. Stone, Admiral Paschal (1820–1902). *A History of England.* Boston: Thompson, Brown & Co., 1879–1910. [MS/NUC 571:113–14]

No date cited by MS.

928. Stormonth, James (1824–1882). *A Dictionary of the English Language.* <1871> The Pronunciation Carefully Revised by the Rev. P. H. Help. New York: Harper & Brothers, 1885. xiv, 1233 pp. [MS/NUC 571:520]

A British dictionary that HPL preferred over Webster's. *SL* 1.324 *ET* 44, 279 *JFM* 157 *JVS* 235

929. Storr, Francis (1839–1919), and Hawes Turner. *Canterbury Chimes; or, Chaucer Tales Retold for Children.* New York: Roberts Brothers, 1879. 256 pp. [MS/NUC 571:535]

930. *Strange Tales of Mystery and Terror.* Edited by Harry Bates. [HPL]

HPL had a complete set of all 7 issues (September 1931–January 1933). He submitted several stories to it, but they were all rejected. The March 1932 issue (2, No. 1) included HPL's revision of Henry S. Whitehead's "The Trap" (73–88). Many references to this periodical in HPL's letters.

931. Stuart, Dorothy Margaret (1889–1963). *Horace Walpole.* New York: Macmillan Co., 1927. x, 229 pp. (English Men of Letters) [MS/NUC 574:236]

932. *Studies in the Poetry of Italy.* Cleveland: Chautauqua Assembly, [1901]. 2 vols. in 1. [MS/NUC 574:517]

Part 1: *Roman,* by Frank Justus Miller (1858–1939); Part 2: *Italian,* by O. Kuhns.

933. Sudbury, Charles [pseud. of Charles Gibson (1874–1954)]. *Two Gentlemen in Touraine.* New York: Duffield & Co., 1909. iv, 341 pp. [MS/NUC 198:627]

Given to HPL by Frank Earle Schermerhorn (Frank Earle Schermerhorn to HPL, 30 September 1936).

934. Suetonius (C. Suetonius Tranquillus) (69–130?). *The Lives of the Twelve Caesars.* An unexpurgated English version edited with notes and an introduction by Joseph Gavorse. New York: Modern Library, 1931. xvi, 361 pp. [X/NUC 575:573]

CLM 305

935. Sullivan, Francis Stoughton (1719–1776). *Lectures on the Constitution and Laws of England.* London: Printed for E. & C. Dilly, 1772. [MS/NUC 576:135]

MS gives title as: *A Discourse concerning the Laws and Government of England.*

936. Surrey, Henry Howard, earl of (1517?–1547). *The Poetical Works of Henry*

Howard, Earl of Surrey. Boston: Little, Brown; New York: Evans & Dickerson, 1854. lxxii, 190 pp. [MS/NUC 577:159]

937. Swift, Jonathan (1667–1745). *Gulliver's Travels*. <1726> London: J. M. Dent; New York: E. P. Dutton (Everyman's Library), [1906]. xiv, 279 pp. [MS/NUC 579:187]
CE 2.187

938. ———, and Abraham Cowley (1618–1667). *Essays*. [HPL to MWM, [August 1922] (*MWM* 105)]
Not identified. HPL writes: "Swift's and Cowley's Essays." It is unclear from this whether HPL is referring to one volume or two. There does not seem to be a single volume in which essays by Swift and Cowley were printed together, so perhaps HPL is referring to two separate volumes.

939. Swinburne, Algernon Charles (1837–1909). *Poems*. Introduction by Ernest Rhys. New York: Boni & Liveright (Modern Library), [1919] or [1925]. xvii, 231 pp. [Schiff/NUC 579:302]
No date cited. Given to HPL by George Kirk.

940. Symmes, Mrs. William B. (Cassie Mansfield Doty Symmes, 1872–1935). *Old World Footprints*. With a Preface by Frank Belknap Long, Jr. Athol, MA: Published by W. Paul Cook/The Recluse Press, 1928. 32 pp. [X/NUC 580:91]
HPL ghostwrote the preface for Long (*CE* 5.287). Symmes was Long's aunt. *MTS* 366 *OFF* 54n6, 304n2, 362 *RB* 321

941. Syntax, Doctor [pseud. of William Combe (1742–1823)]. *The Tour of Doctor Syntax in Search of the Picturesque*. <1812> New ed. New York: D. Appleton & Co, 1903. 266 pp. [MS/NUC 117:172]
Poem.

942. Tacitus, P. Cornelius (56?–115?). *The Works of Cornelius Tacitus*. With an Essay on His History and Genius, Notes, Supplements, &c., by Arthur Murphy. New ed. New York: Bangs, Brother & Co., 1855. xviii, 742 pp. [MS/NUC 581:169]
CE 2.30 *SL* 2.336

943. Talman, Wilifred Blanch (1904–1986). *Cloisonné and Other Verses*. Providence: Bear Press, Brown University, 1925. [16] pp. [HPL to Lillian D. Clark, 20 July 1925; *LFF*/OCLC]
RB 51

944. Tannahill, Robert (1774–1810). *The Poetical Works of Robert Tannahill.* With Several Additional Poems and Explanatory Notes. To Which Is Prefixed the Life of the Author. Glasgow: Fullarton & Co., 1836. 68 pp. [MS/NUC 582:560]

945. Tarbell, Frank Bigelow (1853–1920). *A History of Greek Art, with an Introductory Chapter on Art in Egypt and Mesopotamia.* Meadville, PA: Flood & Vincent, 1896. 295 pp. [MS/NUC 583:121]

CE 2.201 *CLM* 305

946. Tarbell, Ida Minerva (1857–1944). *A Short Life of Napoleon Bonaparte.* New York: S. S. McClure, 1895. viii, 248 pp. [MS/NUC 583:131]

947. Tasso Torquato (1544–1595). *Godfrey of Bulloigne; or, The Recovery of Jerusalem.* <1580> Done into English Heroical Verse, from the Italian of Tasso, by Edward Fairfax <1624>. 1st American ed. from the 7th London ed. To Which Are Prefixed, an Introductory Essay, by Leigh Hunt, and the Lives of Tasso and Fairfax, by Charles Knight. New-York: Wiley & Putnam, 1845–46. 2 vols. in 1. [MS/NUC 583:526]

948. Taylor, John (1757–1832). *Records of My Life.* New-York: J. & J. Harper, 1833. xi, 462 pp. [MS/NUC 584:614]

Taylor was a British drama critic and newspaper editor.

949. Tennyson, Alfred, Lord (1809–1892). *The Works of Alfred Lord Tennyson, Poet Laureate.* New York: Grosset & Dunlap, [1892]–[1911]. viii, 882 pp. [MS/NUC 586:588f.]

No date cited by MS; there are at least 4 Grosset & Dunlap eds. *CLM* 83, 103

950. *Terrible Tales: Italian.* Paris: Brentano's, [1891?]. 181 pp. [HPL/MS/NUC 587:316]

Contents: The Bridal Wreath; Domenico Matteo; The Betrothed; The Story of the Lady Ermenia; The Brigands; The Village Priest; Eurispe; Lanucci; The Lovers; The Unlucky Fortune.

Title from spine (on title page the title reads *The Best Terrible Tales from the Italian*). One of a set of four volumes, the other featuring tales from the French, German, and Spanish. HPL apparently did not have these other volumes.

951. Teter, George E. *An Introduction to Some Elements of Poetry.* Wauwatosa, WI: Kenyon Press, [1927]. 46 pp. [MS/NUC 587:571]

See "An Epistle to the Rt. Honble. Maurice Winter Moe, Esq. of Zythopolis" (1929): "Thanks for the gift, nor blame me if I Teter / And slip into mine antient vice of metre" (*AT* 439). Revised by HPL? Cf. #669. *CE* 1.375 *RB* 213, 359, 404 *FLB* 134

952. Thackeray, William Makepeace (1811–1863). *The Christmas Books of Mr. M. A. Titmarsh; Mrs. Perkins's Ball; Our Street; Dr. Birch; The Knickleburys on the Rhine.* New York: J. W. Lovell, [1883]. 162 pp. [MS/NUC 588:439]

953. ———. *The English Humourists of the Eighteenth Century.* <1853> Edited with an Introduction and Explanatory and Critical Notes by William Lyon Phelps. New York: Henry Holt & Co., 1900. xli, 360 pp. [MS/NUC 588:447]

Obtained in New York in September 1924 (HPL to Lillian D. Clark, 29–30 September 1924; *LFF*).

954. ———. *The History of Henry Esmond, Esq.; The Memoirs of Barry Lyndon, Esq.; Denis Duval.* <1852; 1844; 1863> Boston: Estes & Lauriat, 1883. 415, 409 pp. [MS/NUC 588:457]

AT 163

955. ———. *The History of Pendennis: His Fortunes and Misfortunes, His Friends and His Greatest Enemy.* <1850> [HPL to August Derleth, 16 May 1927 (*ES* 88)/NUC 588:462f.]

956. ———. *The Newcomes: Memoirs of a Most Respectable Family.* <1853–55> Philadelphia: J. B. Lippincott Co., 1886. 2 vols. [MS/NUC 588:419]

CE 2.188

957. ———. *The Virginians: A Tale of the Last Century.* <1857–59> New York: J. W. Lovell Co., 1880. [MS/NUC 588:525]

958. Thaxter, Celia (Laughton) (1835–1894). *Among the Isles of Shoals.* Boston: J. R. Osgood, 1873. 184 pp. [MS/NUC 589:12]

959. Thimm, Franz (1820–1899). *German Self-Taught with Complete English Pronunciation of Every Word.* Chicago: Geo. W. Ogilvie & Co., [1902]. 83 pp. [MS/NUC 590:155]

960. Thomson, Christine Campbell (1897–1985), ed. *By Daylight Only.* London: Selwyn & Blount, 1929. 286 pp. [HPL/MS/Ashley 898]

Contents: The Chain, by H. Warner Munn; The Fates, by John Dwight; Pickman's Model, by H. P. Lovecraft; The Last Laugh, by C. Franklin Miller; At Number Eleven, by Flavia Richardson [pseud. of Christine Campbell Thomson]; The Devils of Po Sung, by Bassett Morgan; The Rose Window, by C. L. Edholm; Panthers of Shevogan, by Morgan Johnson; Medusa, by Royal W. Jimerson; Piecemeal, by Oscar Cook; Bells of Oceana, by Arthur J. Burks; The Devil's Martyr, by Signe Toksvig; The Cave of Spiders, by William R. Hickey; The Witch-Baiter, by R. Anthony; The Trimmer, by Douglas Newton; Blood, by Rupert Grayson; The Tenant, by August Derleth; White Lotus Flower, by Harold Markham; In Kashla's Garden, by Oscar Schisgall; The Copper Bowl, by George Fielding Eliot.

ES 236, 238, 239, 243 *RB* 19

961. ———, ed. *Grim Death*. London: Selwyn & Blount, 1932. 254 pp. [HPL/MS/Ashley 898]

Contents: If You Sleep in the Moonlight, by J. Leslie Mitchell; Island of Doom, by Bassett Morgan; Flies, by Anthony Vercoe; Lord of the Talking Heads, by Arthur Woodward; Hellvellyn: Elvilion or Hill of Baal, by Rosalie Muspratt; House of the Living Dead, by Harold Ward; The Wings, by J. Dyott Matthews; The Great White Fear, by Oscar Cook; The Black Stone, by Robert E. Howard; The Ghost That Never Died, by Elizabeth Sheldon; Behind the Blinds, by Flavia Richardson [pseud. of Christine Campbell Thomson]; The Thing in the Cellar, by David H. Keller; Dormer Cordaianthus, by H. H. Gorst; Night and Silence, by Maurice Level; The Inn, by Guy Preston.

ES 459n1, 514n4

962. ———, ed. *Gruesome Cargoes*. London: Selwyn & Blount, 1928. 245 pp. [HPL/MS/Ashley 898]

Contents: Dead Man's Luck, by Lockhart North; When Hell Laughed, by Flavia Richardson [pseud. of Christine Campbell Thomson]; The Black Spider, by Edmund Snell; The Haunting of the Doonagh Bog, by Anthony Wharton; Drums of Fear, by Dora Christie-Murray; The Hand from the Ruins, by Harold Markham; A Celestial Hell, by Harry De Windt; The Children of Bondage, by Dagney Major; The Man Who Ordered a Double, by Rupert Grayson; When Glister Walked, by Oscar Cook; Offspring by Hell, by H. Thomson; The Tomb, by Francis Beeding; The Creeping Horror, by A. A. Rawlinson; The Green Eyes of Mbuiri, by Benge Atlee; The Padlocked House, by L. Oulton.

ES 160, 165

963. ———, ed. *Not at Night*. London: Selwyn & Blount, 1925. 240 pp. [HPL/MS/Ashley 899]

Contents: Monsters of the Pit, by Paul S. Powers; Four Wooden Stakes, by Victor Rowan; The Third Thumb-Print, by Mortimer Levitan; Lips of the Dead, by W. J. Stamper; The Devil Bed, by Gerald Dean; Death-Waters, by

Frank Belknap Long; Black Curtains, by G. Frederick Montefiore; The Plant Thing, by C. Franklin Miller; A Hand from the Deep, by Romeo Poole; The Tortoise-Shell Cat, by Greye La Spina; The Case of the Russian Stevedore, by Henry W. Whitehill; Leopard's Trail, by W. Chiswell Collins; The Last Trip, by Archie Binns; The Purple Cincture, by H. Thompson Rich.
ES 74, 75, 100, 104 *JVS* 21, 300

964. ———, ed. *The "Not at Night" Omnibus*. London: Selwyn & Blount, [1936]. 511 pp. [MS/Ashley 899]

Contents: The Curse of Yig, by Zealia Bishop [revised by HPL]; Lips of the Dead, by W. J. Stamper; The Wonderful Tune, by Jessie D. Kerruish; The Death Plant, by Michael Gwynn; The Witch-Baiter, by R. Anthony; The Library, by Hester Holland; The Inn, by Guy Preston; The Phantom Drug, by A. W. Kapfer; Pickman's Model, by H. P. Lovecraft; His Beautiful Hands, by Oscar Cook; Pigmy Island, by Edmond Hamilton; Behind the Yellow Door, by Flavia Richardson [*pseud*. of Christine Campbell Thomson]; The Crack, by Oswell Blakeston; Suzanne, by Jean Joseph Renaud; The Accursed Isle, by Mary Elizabeth Counselman; Legion of Evil, by Warden Ledge; The House of Horror, by Seabury Quinn; The Way He Died, by Guy Preston; The Horror in the Museum, by Hazel Heald [revised by HPL]; The Copper Bowl, by George Fielding Eliot; The Watcher in the Green Room, by Hugh B. Cave; Black Curtains, by G. Frederick Montefiore; The Author's Tale, by L. A. Lewis; The Chain, by H. Warner Munn; Piecemeal, by Oscar Cook; The Scream, by Hester Holland; Swamp Horror, by Will Smith and R. J. Robbins; The Seven-Locked Room, by Jessie D. Kerruish; The Chadbourne Episode, by Henry S. Whitehead; The Thing in the Cellar, by David H. Keller; The Black Hare, by Flavia Richardson [*pseud*. of Christine Campbell Thomson]; Flies, by Anthony Vercoe; The Tenant, by August Derleth; Little Red Shoes, by Gordon Chesson; The Closed Door, by Harold Ward.
JFM 400 *RB* 366, 406

965. ———, ed. *Switch On the Light*. London: Selwyn & Blount, 1931. 256 pp. [HPL/MS/Ashley 899]

Contents: The Curse of Yig, by Zealia Bishop [revised by HPL]; Murder by Proxy, by Richard Stone; Haunted Hands, by Jack Bradley; The Flame-Fiend, by N. J. O'Neail; Boomerang, by Oscar Cook; The Tapping, by J. Dyott Matthews; The Red Fetish, by Frank Belknap Long; The Pacer, by August Derleth and Mark Schorer; Flower Valley, by J. S. Whittaker; The Rats in the Walls, by H. P. Lovecraft; Suzanne, by Jean Joseph Renaud; The Thought Monster, by Amelia Reynolds Long; The Red Turret, by Flavia Richardson [pseud. of Christine Campbell Thomson]; Pigmy Island, by Edmond Hamilton; Bhuillaneadh, by R. F. Broad.
ES 448

966. ———, ed. *You'll Need a Night Light*. London: Selwyn & Blount, 1927. 254 pp. [HPL/MS/Ashley 899]

Contents: The Last Horror, by Eli Colter; The Life Serum, by Paul S. Powers; The Girdle, by Joseph McCord; Si Urag of the Tail, by Oscar Cook; The Beast, by Paul Benton; His Wife, by Zita I. Ponder; Laocoon, by Bassett Morgan; Out of the Earth, by Flavia Richardson [pseud. of Christine Campbell Thomson]; Ti Michel, by W. J. Stamper; The House of Horror, by Seabury Quinn; The Coffin of Lissa, by August Derleth; The Parasitic Hand, by R. Anthony; The Death Crescents of Koti, by Romeo Poole; Ghost of the Air, by J. M. Hiatt and Moye W. Stephens; The Horror at Red Hook, by H. P. Lovecraft.

SL 2.155, 212, 260–61 *MTS* 196, 199, 202 *MTS* 195–96 *ES* 101, 121 *RB* 19. Cf. #53.

967. Thomson, James (1700–1748). *The Seasons; with The Castle of Indolence*. <1726–30; 1748> New-York: Published by W. B. Gilley, . . . Clayton & Kingsland, Printers, 1819. 287 pp. [MS/NUC 592:218]

CE 2.188; 5.169 *SL* 3.317–18 *RK* 15, 170, 182 *ES* 386, 389, 391, 392, 393, 395 *ET* 24, 298 *JVS* 191

968. Thwing, Annie Haven (1851–1940). *The Crooked and Narrow Streets of the Town of Boston 1630–1822*. Boston: Marshall Jones Co., 1920. xi, 282 pp. [MS/NUC 593:509]

SL 1.356

969. Tibullus, Albius (50?–19 B.C.E.). *A Poetical Translation of the Elegies of Tibullus; and of the Poems of Sulpicia*. With Original Text, and Notes Critical and Explanatory, . . . by James Grainger. London: Printed for A. Millar, 1759. 2 vols. [MS/NUC 593:587]

970. Ticknor, Caroline (1866–1937). *Poe's Helen*. New York: Charles Scribner's Sons, 1916. ix, 292 pp. [MS/NUC 593:638]

On Poe and Sarah Helen Whitman.

971. Titcomb, Timothy, Esquire [pseud. of Josiah Gilbert Holland (1819–1881)]. *Titcomb's Letters to Young People, Single and Married*. <1858> 50th ed. New York: Charles Scribner's Sons, 1883. ix, 223 pp. [MS/NUC 251:373]

972. Todd, David Peck (1855–1939). *Astronomy: The Science of the Heavenly Bodies*. New York: Harper & Brothers, 1922. 384 pp. [HPL to Duane W. Rimel, 30 October 1934 (*FLB* 231)/NUC 595:682]

973. Toksvig, Signe (1891–1983). *The Last Devil.* New York: John Day Co., 1927. 306 pp. [HPL/MS/NUC 596:240]

Given to HPL by August Derleth (*ES* 256, 280). *ES* 168, 170

974. Tolstoi, Leo (1828–1910). *War and Peace.* Translated into French by a Russian Lady, and from the French by Clara Bell. New York: W. S. Gottsberger, 1887. 2 vols. [NUC 596:615]

HPL writes (*AG* 164): "'War & Peace', in two ample volumes, is among the paternally inherited section of my library." The above is probably the edition owned by HPL's father. *CE* 2.189 *JVS* 260 *FLB* 113

975. Tomes, Robert (1817–1882). *The Champagne Country.* New York: George Routledge & Sons, 1867. xv, 231 pp. [MS/NUC 597:38]

On the French province of Reims.

976. Tomlinson, Everett (1859–1931). *A Short History of the American Revolution.* New York: Doubleday, Page & Co., 1901. x, 419 pp. [MS/NUC 597:100]

977. Traill, H[enry] D[uff] (1842–1900). *The New Fiction and Other Essays on Literary Subjects.* New York: New Amsterdam Book Co., 1898. 323 pp. [MS/NUC 599:515]

Contents: The New Fiction; The Political Novel; The Politics of Literature; Matthew Arnold; Samuel Richardson; The Novel of Manners; Newspapers and English; Lucian; The Revolution of Grub Street; The Provincial Letters; The Future of Humour.

978. Treadwell, John H. *Martin Luther.* New York: G. P. Putnam's Sons, 1881. 243 pp. [MS/NUC 600:325]

979. Trench, Richard Chenevix (1807–1886). *On the Study of Words: Five Lectures.* London: John W. Parker & Son, 1851. [MS/BLC 329:132]

CE 2.192; 3.321 *CLM* 163

980. Trent, William P[eterfield] (1862–1939). *Daniel Defoe: How to Know Him.* Indianapolis: Bobbs-Merrill, [1916]. 329 pp. [MS/NUC 600:651]

981. ———, and Benjamin W. Wells (1856–1923), ed. *Colonial Prose and Poetry.* New York: Thomas Y. Crowell Co., [1903]. 3 vols. [MS/NUC 600:651]

982. *The Tribune and Political Register.* New York: G. Dearborn & Co. [MS/NUC 601:282]

HPL had the issues for 1845 and 1852, at which time the almanac was called *The Whig Almanac and United States Register.*

983. Tuckey, Janet. *Joan of Arc, "the Maid."* New York: G. P. Putnam's Sons, 1880. 224 pp. [MS/NUC 603:678]

984. Turner, Edward (1798–1837). *Elements of Chemistry, Including the Recent Discoveries and Doctrines of the Science.* <1827> Sixth American edition. With notes and emendations by Franklin Bache. Philadelphia: Thomas, Cowperthwait & Co., 1840. xvi, 666 pp. [X/NUC 605:148]

985. Twain, Mark [pseud. of Samuel Langhorne Clemens (1835–1910)]. *The Celebrated Jumping Frog of Calaveras County and Other Sketches.* Edited by John Paul [i.e., Mark Twain]. New York: C. H. Webb, 1868. 198 pp. [MS/NUC 112:160]

986. ―――. *The Innocents Abroad; or, The New Pilgrim's Progress.* <1869> [MS] No further data given by MS save that it is a "very old" ed.

987. ―――. *The Prince and the Pauper: A Tale for Young People of All Ages.* Boston: J. R. Osgood, 1882. 411 pp. [MS/NUC 112:149]

988. *Uncle Richard's Conversations about the Ancient History of London.* By a Minister Who Loves Children. Lowell, MA: Rice & Wise; Boston: D. S. King, 1842. 127 pp. [MS/NUC 607:505]

989. U.S. War Department. Inspector General's Office. *Regulations for the Order and Discipline of the Troops of the United States.* [Compiled by Baron de Steuben.] Part I. Philadelphia: Printed by Styner & Cist, in Second-Street, 1779. 154[+8] pp. [MS/NUC 624:240]

990. Upton, Winslow (1853–1914). *Star Atlas.* Boston: Ginn & Co., 1896. iv, 34 pp. [MS/NUC 625:646]

Upton was a professor at Brown University and wrote astronomy columns for the *Providence Journal.* See *FLB* 157, where HPL refers to this book and also states that it was through the influence of Upton (who was "a friend of the family") that HPL was allowed access to Brown's Ladd Observatory as a teenager.

991. Van Dusen, Washington (1857–1938). *Sonnets on Great Men and Women and Other Poems.* Philadelphia, 1929. 80 pp. [HPL to MWM, 3 August 1929 (*MWM* 230)/NUC 629:269]

Van Dusen was an amateur writer acquainted with HPL. He gave this copy to HPL.

992. Vaughan, L. Brent (1873–1950), comp. *Hill's Spanish-English and English-Spanish Dictionary.* Chicago: G. M. Hill Co., [1898]. 317 pp. [MS/NUC 631:30]

993. Velázquez de la Cavena, Mariano (1778–1860), and T. Simmone. *Ollendorff's New Method of Learning to Read, Write, and Speak the Spanish Language.* New York: D. Appleton & Co., 1850. 558 pp. [X—JHL/NUC 631:693]

994. Verne, Jules (1828–1905). *De la terre à la lune, trajet direct en 97 heures 20 minutes.* Dessins par [Henri] de Montaut. Paris: J. Hetzel, 1865–1906. [MS/NUC 634:461/BN 206:606–7]

No date cited by MS. Given to HPL by Richard Ely Morse (HPL to Richard Ely Morse, 16 September 1935).

995. ———. *From the Earth to the Moon.* <1865> [HPL/MS]

No ed. cited by MS or HPL; this is surely an English translation.

996. ———. *20,000 Leagues under the Sea.* <1869> [HPL/MS]

No ed. cited by MS or HPL; this is surely an English translation. HPL mentions "others [i.e., works by Verne] in magazines."

997. Vinal, Harold (1891–1965). *Island Born.* New York: Harold Vinal, October 1925. [vi], 28 pp. [X—JHL/NUC 638:220]

Poems. HPL met Vinal in New York in 1926 (HPL to Lillian D. Clark, 6 April 1926; *LFF*).

998. Vince, Charles (1887–?). *Barrie Marvell: His Dreams and Adventures.* Boston: Little, Brown, 1923. 146 pp. [MS/NUC 638:242]

A sentimental novel about a solitary boy. *ES* 495, 497, 499

999. Virgil (P. Vergilius Maro) (70–19 B.C.E.). *The Works of Virgil.* Translated by Joseph Davidson <1743>. New edition, revised, with additional notes by Theodore Alois Buckley. New York: Harper & Brothers, 1872f. ix, 404 pp. [X/NUC 633:635]

Flyleaf has HPL's address (598 Angell St.) in his hand. *SL* 3.317

1000. ———. *Publii Vergilii Maronis Opera; or, The Works of Virgil.* With Copious Notes . . . by the Rev. J. G. Cooper. <1827> 9th stereotype ed. New York: Pratt, Woodford & Co, 1852. xvi, 615 pp. [MS/NUC 633:603]

CF 1.38; 3.494 *CE* 1.107; 2.12, 27, 28, 29, 185; 5.67n31, 126, 272n1 *SL* 3.[313] *ES* 112 *JFM* 160 *JVS* 8, 47, 252n1

1001. ———. *The Works of P. Vergilius Maro.* With . . . an Interlinear Translation . . . Combining the Methods of Ascham, Milton, and Locke, by Levi Hart and V. R. Osborn. Philadelphia: David McKay, 1882. 131, 384 pp. [MS/NUC 633:621]

1002. ———. *The Works of Virgil.* Translated by John Dryden <1697>. London: Henry Frowde/Oxford University Press (World's Classics), 1903–25. 486 pp. [MS/NUC 633:639–40]

No date cited by MS. Cf. HPL to R. H. Barlow, 21 October 1935 (*OFF* 300).

1003. Wakefield, H[erbert] Russell (1890–1964). *Others Who Returned: Fifteen Disturbing Tales.* New York: D. Appleton & Co., 1929. 274 pp. [HPL/NUC 645:185]

Contents: Old Man's Beard; The Last to Leave; The Cairn; Present at the End; "Look Up There!"; "Written in Our Flesh"; Blind Man's Buff; A Coincidence at Hunton; Nurse's Tale; The Dune; Unrehearsed; A Jolly Surprise for Henri; The Red Hand; Surprise Item; A Case of Mistaken Identity.

Given to HPL by Henry S. Whitehead (HPL to Lillian D. Clark, 10 May 1931; *LFF*). *CE* 5.234 *SHL* 76 *ES* 234, 345 *CLM* 279

1004. ———. *They Return at Evening.* New York: D. Appleton & Co., 1928. 265 pp. [HPL/NUC 645:185]

Contents: That Dieth Not; Or Persons Unknown: "He Cometh and He Passeth By"; Professor Pownall's Oversight; The Third Coach; The Red Lodge; "And He Shall Sing . . ."; The Seventeenth Hole at Duncaster; A Peg on Which to Hang; An Echo.

Given to HPL by August Derleth (*ES* 280), although HPL notes that he owned another copy. *CE* 5.234 *SHL* 76 *MTS* 229 *ES* 150, 152, 153, 156, 159, 216 *RB* 24

1005. Walker, John (1732–1807). *A Critical Pronouncing Dictionary and Expositor of the English Language.* <1804> 3rd American ed. New-York: S. Stansbury, 1807. cxxxi, 962 pp. [MS/NUC 646:16]

"When I was ten I set to work to delete every modern word from my vocabulary, and to this end adopted an old Walker's Dictionary (1804) which was for some time my sole authority" (*MWM* 45).

1006. ———. *A Rhetorical Grammar; or, Course of Lessons in Elocution.* <1785> 1st American ed. Boston: J. T. Buckingham, 1814. 356 pp. [MS/NUC 646:26]

"I also [in verse-writing] gave the pronoun *my* its old-fashioned value 'me' or 'mih' when it did not call especial attention to the quality of possession—as recommended in Walker's (eighteenth-century) *Rhetorical Grammar*" (*SL* 5.238).

1007. [Walpole, Horace (1717–1797).] *Jeffery's Edition of the Castle of Otranto, a Gothic Story.* <1764> London: Printed by W. Backader . . . for the Publisher [Edward Jeffery], 1800. xvi, 152 pp. [HPL/OCLC]

No ed. cited by HPL. Elsewhere HPL mentions obtaining "an 1800 copy of Walpole's 'Castle of Otranto' on large paper, with long ſ's, & with a fine set of engraved illustrations coloured by hand" (HPL to Lillian D. Clark, 22 January 1925; *LFF*). *CE* 2.225; 5.150 *SHL* 33–35 *MTS* 20 *RK* 174 *ES* 34, 43, 77, 199 *JFM* 31, 90 *MWM* 469 *DS* 394

1008. Walton, George A[ugustus] (1822–1908). *A Written Arithmetic, for Common and High Schools; to Which Is Adapted a Complete System of Reviews, in the Form of Dictation Exercises.* Boston: Brewer & Tileston, 1864. 348 pp. [X—JHL/NUC 647:401]

1009. Wandrei, Donald (1908–1987). *Dark Odyssey.* With Five Illustrations by Howard Wandrei. St. Paul, MN: Webb Publishing Co., [1931]. 47 pp. [X—JHL/NUC 647:557]

Author's presentation copy to HPL, dated Easter 1931. *MTS* 199, 252, 267, 272, 275, 276, 277, 278, 279, 285 *ES* 331 *OFF* 37 *MF* 245 *JFM* 287 *RB* 34 *FLB* 50, 71

1010. ———. *Ecstasy and Other Poems.* Athol, MA: Recluse Press, 1928. 40 pp. [X—JHL/NUC 647:557]

Author's presentation copy to HPL, dated 10 April 1928. This copy also has two photographs of Wandrei pasted to the inside back cover (one of which appears in *SL* 3, facing p. 406). *MTS* 167, 169, 176, 183, 192, 198, 200, 207, 211, 212, 218, 219, 221, 231, 254, 277 *ES* 331 *OFF* 228 *MF* 245 *RB* 34 *FLB* 50

1011. Wanostrocht, Nicholas (1745–1812). *Recueil choisi de traits historiques, et de contes moraux.* <1785> Baltimore: S. Jefferis, 1810. 280 pp. [MS/NUC 647:689/OCLC]

An elementary French reader. Cf. HPL to Richard F. Searight, 22 December 1934.

1012. [Warford, Aaron.] *How to Become a Scientist.* New York: Frank Tousey, Publisher, [1891]. 61 pp. [X—JHL/NUC 648:544]

HPL's copy reads: "Bound by H. P. Lovecraft."

1013. [———.] *How to Become an Inventor.* New York: Frank Tousey, Publisher, [1891]. 61 pp. [X—JHL/NUC 648:545]

1014. Warner, Charles Dudley (1829–1900). *Baddeck, and That Sort of Thing.* <1874> Boston: Houghton Mifflin, [1902]. 191 pp. [X/MS/NUC 648:672]

   On Nova Scotia.

1015. Warren, David M. *A Primary Geography.* <1863> Philadelphia: H. Cowperthwait, 1865. 88 pp. [MS/NUC 649:137]

1016. Watson, Elkanah (1758–1842). *Men and Times of the Revolution; or, Memoirs of Elkanah Watson.* <1856> Edited by His Son, Winslow C. Watson. 2nd ed. New York: Dana & Co., 1857. 557 pp. [MS/NUC 650:681]

   CE 2.193

1017. Watts, William Lord (1850–1921). *Snoiland; or, Iceland, Its Jokulls and Fjalls.* London: Longmans, 1875. 183 pp. [MS/NUC 651:355]

1018. Webb, Thomas William (1807–1885). *Celestial Objects for Common Telescopes.* <1859> Revised and Greatly Enlarged ... by Rev. T. E. Spin. London: Longmans, Green, 1904–07. 2 vols. [MS/NUC 652:44]

   HPL had only Vol. 1 (1904). *CE* 2.167

1019. Webster, J. Provand. *The Oracle of Baal: A Narrative of Some Curious Events in the Life of Professor Horatio Charmichael, M.A.* Philadelphia: J. B. Lippincott Co., 1896. 374 pp. [HPL/MS/NUC 652:510]

   MTS 37, 69, 73

1020. Webster, John (1578?–1632?). *The White Devil and the Duchess of Malfy* [sic]. Edited by Martin W. Sampson. Boston: D. C. Heath, 1904. xliv, 422 pp. [MS/NUC 652:522]

   Obtained in New York in September 1924 (HPL to Lillian D. Clark, 29–30 September 1924; *LFF*). *SHL* 32 *ES* 120

1021. Webster, Noah (1758–1834). *An American Dictionary of the English Language.* Revised and enlarged by Chauncey Goodrich. Springfield, MA: G. & C. Merriam, 1848. lxxxiv, 1367 pp. [HPL to Annie E. P. Gamwell, 5 August 1928/NUC 652:547]

1022. ———. *An American Dictionary of the English Language.* Rev. & enl. by Chauncey A. Goodrich and Noah Porter. Springfield, MA: G. & C. Merriam, 1864. lxxii, 1768 pp. [NUC 652:549]

SL 1.300, 324; 2.226 *AG* 38 *ET* 379 *MWM* 431

In a letter to Clark Ashton Smith (24 November 1925) HPL states: "I have the same old Webster you have—1864 edition with the supplement of 1873" (*DS* 88). It is not clear what HPL means by "the supplement of 1873." There is an 1873 printing of the above title (which was revised from earlier editions), but it seems identical to the 1864 edition. There is a "Supplement of Additional Words and Definitions" published in the 1879 edition and subsequent editions.

1023. ———. *A Dictionary for Primary Schools.* New-York: F. J. Huntington, 1838. 341 pp. [MS/NUC 652:570]

1024. ———. *Webster's International Dictionary of the English Language.* Now Thoroughly Revised and Enlarged under the Supervision of Noah Porter. Springfield, MA: G. & C. Merriam, 1891. xcviii, 2011 pp. [MS/NUC 652:652]

SL 5.233 *JVS* 243

1025. Weigall, Arthur (1880–1934). *Wanderings in Roman Britain.* London: Thornton Butterworth, [1926]. 341 pp. [MS/NUC 653:531]

Purchased in New York, Christmas 1933 (HPL to R. H. Barlow, [13 January 1934]; *OFF* 100). *SL* 4.374 *MTS* 336 *OFF* 119 *ES* 133 *MF* 757 *JFM* 347 *RB* 126 *JVS* 215 *CLM* 274 *MWM* 477–79, 483–83 *DS* 526–30

1026. *Weird Tales.* Edited by Edwin Baird (1923–24) and Farnsworth Wright (1924–40). [HPL]

HPL had a complete set, beginning with the first issue (March 1923). The copies that survive are deposited in JHL. The magazine contains many stories and poems by HPL. Many references to this periodical in HPL's letters.

1027. Wells, H[erbert] G[eorge] (1866–1946). *The First Men in the Moon.* Indianapolis: Bowen-Merrill Co., [1901]. 312 pp. [HPL/MS/NUC 655:329]

HPL also notes: "(others in magazines)," by which he refers to reprints of Wells's work in *Amazing Stories* (see #32).

1028. ———. *The Outline of History.* <1920> Written with the Advice and Editorial Help of Mr. Ernest Barker, Sir H. H. Johnston, Sir E. Ray Lankester, and Professor Gilbert Murray. Garden City, NY: Garden City Publishing Co., [1920?]–[1931]. xxi, 1174 pp. [MS/NUC 655:354–57]

No date cited by MS; there are 6 Garden City Pub. Co. eds. *CE* 1.269; 2.192, 197 *ES* 190n1 *OFF* 379 *RB* 212 *JVS* 274

1029. ———. *A Short History of the World.* New York: Macmillan Co., 1922. xvi, 455 pp. [MS/NUC 655:366]
Designed as a preface to the above, not an abridgement of it.

1030. [Wessely, Ignaz Emanuel (1841–1900).] *Handy Dictionary of the Latin and English Languages.* Philadelphia: David McKay, [18—]. 198, 212 pp. [MS/NUC 229:516]

1031. ———, and C. M. Stevans. *Hill's Italian-English Dictionary.* Philadelphia: David McKay, [1904]. 216, 119 pp. [MS/NUC 657:34]

1032. West, Willis Mason (1857–1931). *Ancient History to the Death of Charlemagne.* Boston: Allyn & Bacon, 1902. xlii, 564 pp. [HPL to Fritz Leiber, 19 December 1936 (*CLM* 306)/OCLC]

1033. Westlake, Herbert Francis (1879–1925). *The New Guide to Westminster Abbey.* London: A. R. Mowbray, 1916–28. xv, 52 pp. [MS/NUC 658:164]
No date given by MS.

1034. Whipple, Edwin P[ercy] (1819–1886). *The Literature of the Age of Elizabeth.* <1869> Boston: Houghton Mifflin, 1886. 364 pp. [MS/NUC 659:378] *CE* 2.191

1035. White, Edward Lucas (1866–1934). *Andivius Hedulio: Adventures of a Roman Nobleman in the Days of the Empire.* New York: E. P. Dutton, [1923]. viii, 592 pp. [RHB/NUC 659:657]
"'Andivius' is, so far as I know, the only novel of Roman life ever published which makes any attempt to deal accurately with the setting, or to reproduce the Roman point of view" (HPL to Richard Ely Morse, 29 April 1934). *CE* 2.186 *ES* 97–98, 99, 631 *MF* 656 *ET* 41, 63, 73, 74, 234, 269 *CLM* 305

1036. ———. *Lukundoo and Other Stories.* New York: George H. Doran, 1927. 328 pp. [HPL/NUC 659:657]
Contents: Lukundoo; Floki's Blade; The Picture Puzzle; The Snout; Alfandega; The Message on the Slate; Amina; The Pigskin Belt; The House of the Nightmare; Sorcery Island.
    Given to HPL in 1933 by William Lumley (*SL* 4.271 [CAS]), although of course HPL had read it earlier than 1933. *SHL* 71 *ES* 97, 148, 631 *RB* 52, 72 *CLM* 56

1037. ———. *The Song of the Sirens and Other Stories*. New York: E. P. Dutton, 1919. xi, 348 pp. [HPL/NUC 659:657]

Contents: The Song of the Sirens; Irabas; The Right Man; Dodona; The Elephant's Ear; The Fasces; The Swimmers; The Skewbald Panther; Disvola; The Flambeau Bracket.

Given to HPL by Richard Ely Morse (HPL to Richard Ely Morse, 27 October 1932), but HPL had read it earlier. *CE* 5.63 *SHL* 71 *AG* 103 *ES* 98

1038. White, Gilbert (1720–1793). *The Natural History of Selborne*. <1789> New York: Harper & Brothers, 1842. 335 pp. [NUC 660:34]

A notable work of natural history and ecology. This copy purchased in New York for 10¢; previously he had a two-volume ed. from Cassell's (1887) (HPL to Lillian D. Clark, 8 July 1931; *LFF*). *ES* 411

1039. White, Gleeson (1851–1898). *The Cathedral Church at Salisbury: A Description of Its Fabric and a Brief History of the See of Sarum*. <1896> 3rd ed. London: George Bell & Sons, 1908. 122 pp. [MS/NUC 660:42]

1040. White, Michael, ed. *In Memoriam: Jennie E. T. Dowe*. Dorchester, MA: [W Paul Cook,] 1921. 64 pp. [HPL to Edward H. Cole, 29 September 1934/OCLC]

A tribute volume to a deceased amateur journalist. Contains HPL's poem "In Memoriam: J. E. T. D." and a prose article, "A Singer of Ethereal Moods and Fancies" (both on p. 56). *CE* 1.301

1041. White, Richard Grant (1821–1885). *Words and Their Uses, Past and Present*. New York: Sheldon & Co., 1870. 437 pp. [MS/NUC 660:246]

1042. White, W. B. *Seeing Stars*. Cleveland: Harter Publishing Co., 1935. 61 pp. [MS/NUC 660:310]

1043. White, Walter R., publisher. *Souvenir Book of Providence, Rhode Island*. Providence, [1910?]. n.p. [MS/JDR]

Photographs.

1044. Whiting, Lilian (1847–1942). *Paris the Beautiful*. Boston: Little, Brown, 1908. 399 pp. [MS/NUC 660:651]

1045. Whitman, Sarah Helen (Power) (1803–1878). *Edgar Poe and His Critics*. New York: Rudd & Carleton, 1860. 81 pp. [HPL to Frank Belknap Long, 4 June 1921/NUC 661:15]

Whitman's celebrated defence of Poe's character and achievements.

1046. ———. *Poems*. <1879> 2nd ed. Providence: Preston & Rounds, 1894. xii, 261 pp. [MS/NUC 661:16]

1047. Whitman, Walt (1819–1892). *Selections from Whitman*. Edited by Zada Thornsburgh. New York: Macmillan Co., 1927. xxxvii, 282 pp. [MS/NUC 661:49]

For HPL's satirical "Fragment on Whitman" see "In a Major Key," *The Conservative* 1, No. 2 (July 1915): 9–11 (*CE* 56–57). *RK* 47

1048. Whittier, John Greenleaf (1807–1892). *The Poetical Works of John Greenleaf Whittier*. Boston: Houghton Mifflin, 1887. 344 pp. [MS/NUC 661:292] *SL* 1.224

1049. Wilde, Oscar (1854–1900). *Fairy Tales and Poems in Prose*. New York: Boni & Liveright (Modern Library), [1918]. 214 pp. [HPL/RHB/NUC 663:280]

Contents: The Young King; The Birthday of the Infanta; The Fisherman and His Soul; The Star-Child; The Happy Prince; The Nightingale and the Rose; The Selfish Giant; The Devoted Friend; The Remarkable Rocket; Poems in Prose.

Obtained in 1920. Cf. HPL's "With a Copy of Wilde's Fairy Tales" (1920; *AT* 71–72), a poem accompanying a gift of such a volume to Alice Hamlet. Colin Wilson (*The Strength to Dream*, 1961) believes that "The Birthday of the Infanta" could have influenced "The Outsider" (1921). *SHL* 73 *ES* 64 *ET* 38, 51

1050. ———. *An Ideal Husband; A Woman of No Importance*. <1899; 1894> New York: Boni & Liveright (Modern Library), 1919. 220 pp. [MS/NUC 663:292]

1051. ———. *The Picture of Dorian Gray*. <1890> New York: Boni & Liveright (Modern Library), 1918. 255 pp. [HPL/MS/NUC 663:312]

CE 5.62 *SHL* 73 *SL* 2.98, 315 *MTS* 267 *ES* 64, 65, 66 *ET* 38 *JVS* 348

1052. ———. *Poems*. New York: Modern Library, [1917?]. ix, 275 pp. [MS/NUC 663:317]

"Wilde's poems are exquisite, but somewhat impaired by imitativeness" (*ET* 38). Obtained in New York in September 1922 (HPL to Lillian D. Clark, 29 September 1922; *LFF*). *CE* 2.189 *ES* 66, 67, 167

1053. Wilder, Thornton (1897–1975). *Childe Roland to the Dark Tower Came*. Yale Literary Magazine 84, No. 6 (June 1919): 238–40. [C. L. Moore to HPL, 27 May 1935 (*CLM* 34)/OCLC]

A short play. Gift of C. L. Moore.

1054. Wilkins, Augustus S[amuel] (1843–1905). *Roman Antiquities*. (Classical Antiquities II.) London: Macmillan, 1877. 126 pp. [HPL to Fritz Leiber, 19 December 1936 (*CLM* 304)/NUC 664:5f.]

No ed. cited by HPL. *CE* 2.192

1055. Wilkinson, William Cleaver (1833–1920). *Classic Greek Course in English*. New York: Chautauqua Press, 1892. 314 pp. [MS/NUC 664:135]

CE 2.185

1056. ———. *Preparatory Latin Course in English*. New York: Phillips & Hunt; Cincinnati: Walden & Stowe, 1883. 331 pp. [MS/NUC 664:138]

CE 2.186

1057. Williams, Blanche Colton (1879–1944). *Studying the Short Story*. Garden City, NY: Doubleday, Page, 1926. vi, 42 pp. [MS/NUC 664:536]

Williams was editor of the *O. Henry Memorial Prize Stories* from 1919 to 1932, which cited HPL's stories in several volumes.

1058. Wilson, Rufus Rockwell (1865–1949). *New York: Old and New; Its Story, Streets, and Landmarks*. Philadelphia: J. B. Lippincott Co., 1902, 1903, or 1909. 2 vols. [HPL to Lillian D. Clark, 29–30 September 1924; *LFF*/NUC 667:212]

1059. Winchell, Alexander (1824–1891). *Walks and Talks in the Geological Field*. New York: Chautauqua Press, 1886. 329 pp. [MS/NUC 667:473]

CE 2.194; 5.221 *CB* 31

1060. Winter, William (1836–1917). *Shakespeare's England*. Boston: Houghton Mifflin, 1890. 270 pp. [MS/NUC 668:469]

1061. Wister, Owen (1860–1938). *A Straight Deal; or, The Ancient Grudge*. London: Macmillan & Co., 1920. ix, 275 pp. *or* New York: Macmillan Co., 1920. vii, 287 pp. [MS/NUC 669:604]

On Anglo-American relations.

1062. Wittie, Robert (1613?–1684). ΟΥΡΟΝΟΣΚΟΠΙΑ; *or, A Survey of the Heavens: A Plain Description of the Admirable Fabrick and Motions of the Heavenly Bodies*. To Which Is Added the Gout-Raptures, Augmented & Improved. In Englishe, Latine, and Greek Lyrick Verse. London: Printed by J. M. for the Author, 1681. 158 pp. [MS/NUC 670:221]

The book belonged to Lovecraft's father. The Greek title transliterates to *Ouronoskopia*.

1063. [Wolcot, John (1738–1819).] *The Works of Peter Pindar, Esq.* Philadelphia: M. W. Woodward & Co., 1835. viii, 460 pp. [MS/NUC 670:590]
Poetry by a late Augustan.

1064. Wood, Clement (1888–1950). *Hints on Writing Poetry.* Girard, KS: Haldeman-Julius Co., 1924. 64 pp. [OCLC]
In a letter to MWM (27–29 July 1929; *MWM* 223) HPL writes: "You'll find a swell paragraph on this subject in Clement Wood's booklet on poetry-writing in the *Haldeman-Julius* series." *ET* 91 *FLB* 143

1065. Wood, John George (1827–1889). *The Illustrated Natural History.* London: George Routledge & Co., 1853–72. [MS/NUC 672:299–301]
CE 2.195

1066. Woodberry, George E[dward] (1855–1930). *Edgar Allan Poe.* Boston: Houghton Mifflin, 1885. ix, 354 pp. [MS/NUC 672:451]

1067. Woodhouselee, Alexander Fraser Tytler, Lord (1747–1813). *Essay on the Principles of Translation.* <1791> London: J. M. Dent; New York: E. P. Dutton (Everyman's Library), [1907]. xiv, 239 pp. [MS/NUC 672:594]

1068. Wordsworth, William (1771–1850). *The Poetical Works of William Wordsworth.* Boston: Phillips, Sampson & Co., 1859. 539 pp. [MS/NUC 673:698]

1069. Wright, S[ydney] Fowler (1874–1965). *Deluge: A Romance.* New York: Cosmopolitan Book Corp., 1928. 395 pp. [HPL/MS/NUC 675:450]
Given to HPL by R. H. Barlow (*OFF* 77n1).

1070. ———. *The World Below.* New York: Longmans, Green, 1930. viii, 344 pp. [HPL/MS/NUC 675:453]
Given to HPL by Ernest A. Edkins. *SL* 5.415 *ES* 537 *OFF* 50 *MF* 527 *JVS* 121, 125

1071. Wyllarde, Dolf (1871–1950). *Stories of Strange Happenings.* London: Mills & Boon, 1930. 286 pp. [HPL/MS/Tuck 2:471]
Contents: "I Heard Voices . . ."; The Passion of Susan Tremlett; "Hear It Unaware"; The Ten Talents; Yesterday; The Changeling; The Benefit of the Doubt; The Sinless Sinner; Nothing.

1072. Xenophon (428?–354? B.C.E.). *The Anabasis of Xenophon.* With an Interlinear Translation . . . on the Hamiltonian System, as Improved by

Thomas Clark. Philadelphia: DeSilver & Sons, [1887]. 564 pp. [MS/NUC 677:206]

SL 1.184 *MF* 583

1073. Yonge, Charlotte Mary (1823–1901). *Young Folks' History of England.* <1879> Jersey City, NJ: Barr-Dinwiddie, n.d. [MS/BC]

A children's history by a prolific British novelist.

1074. Young, Charles Augustus (1834–1908). *The Elements of Astronomy: A Textbook.* <1889> Rev. ed. Boston: Ginn & Co., 1903. x, 464 pp. [MS/NUC 679:231]

1075. ———. *Lessons in Astronomy Including Uranography.* Boston: Ginn & Co., 1893. ix, 357 pp. [MS/NUC 679:232]

1076. ———. *Lessons in Astronomy Including Uranography.* Rev. ed. Boston: Ginn & Co., 1903. ix, 420 pp. [MS/NUC 679:232]

SL 2.39 *FLB* 157

1077. Young, John Russell (1841–1899). *Around the World with General Grant: A Narrative of the Visit of General U. S. Grant, Ex-President of the United States, to Various Countries in Europe, Asia, and Africa, in 1877, 1878, 1879.* New York: American News Co., 1879. 2 vols. [MS/NUC 679:450]

Addenda

1078. *Beowulf.*

No ed. cited by HPL: "In his [Arthur Leeds'] shop—The Half Moon, in Surf Ave., the principal street [in Coney Island]—I found a copy of the ancient Saxon epic of Beowulf (in a good school translation) for 10¢; hence purchased it, since I have always wished for a copy of my own" (HPL to Lillian D. Clark, 8[–10] July 1931; *LFF*).

1079. *The British Novelist: Forming a Choice Collection of the Best Novels in the English Language . . .* Embellished with engravings on wood. London: J. Limbird, 1823–32. 1 vol. [OCLC]

Contents: Julia de Roubigné, by [Henry Mackenzie]; Nature and Art, by Mrs. [Elizabeth] Inchbald; The History of Nourjahad, the Persian, by Mrs. [Frances] Sheridan; Solyman and Almena, by Dr. [John] Langhorne; Almoran and Hamet, by Dr. [John] Hawkesworth; Edward, by Dr. [John] Moore; Zeluco, by Dr. [John] Moore.

See HPL to Donald Wandrei, [25 November 1927]: "[Eino] Railo says he has never been able to consult a copy of Moore's 'Zeluco'. Well—*I own 'Zeluco'*—albeit in a cheap form bound up with a lot of other early material" (*MTS* 188).

1080. [Chicago Tribune.] *The Linebook, 1926.* Edited by Richard Henry Little (d. 1946). Chicago: Chicago Tribune, 1926. [NUC 106:519]

A gift from MWM. See MWM to HPL, 17 December 1926: "In place of a Christmas card I am sending you the Chitrib Linebook, which came out a week or two ago" (TLS, JHL).

1081. [———.] *The Linebook, 1927.* Edited by Richard Henry Little. Chicago: Chicago Tribune, 1927. [NUC 106:519]

Another gift from MWM. See MWM to HPL, 17 December 1927: "Here is the annual offering of myrrh. . . . The Line recently has contained many merry badinage anent the cover design" (TLS, JHL).

1082. Partridge, John [pseud.]. *Merlinus Liberatus: An Almanack for the Year of Our Redemption, 1814.* London: Printed for the Company of Stationers by William Thorne, [1814]. 48 pp. [archive.org]

HPL states in a letter to Wilfred B. Talman (15 January 1929; ALS, JHL) that "I have a British annual for 1814 . . ." There is another British almanac for 1814: Francis Moore, *Vox Stellarum; or, A Loyal Almanack for the Year of Our Human Redemption, 1814* (London: Printed for the Company of Stationers by Luke Hansard & Sons, [1814]).

1083. Quackenbos, G[eorge] P[ayn] (1826–1881). *Advanced Course of Composition and Rhetoric: A Series of Practical Lessons on the Origin, History, and Peculiarities of the English Language.* New York: D. Appleton & Co., 1855–88. 451 pp. [HPL to Edward H. Cole, 14 December 1914 (ALS, JHL/NUC 476:291–92]

No ed. cited by HPL.

1084. Spalding, William (1809–1859). *The History of English Literature; with an Outline of the Origin and Growth of the English Language.* Edinburgh: Oliver & Boyd, 1853. *or* New York: D. Appleton & Co., 1853–89. 413 pp. [HPL to Edward H. Cole, 14 December 1914, (ALS, JHL/NUC 560:176–77]

No ed. cited by HPL.

1085. Wood, Alphonso (1810–1881) and Joel Dorman Steele. *Fourteen Weeks in Botany.* New York: A.S. Barnes & Co., 1879. 318 pp. [HPL to Wilred B. Talman, Friday (December 1931) (ALS, JHL)]/OCLC]

WEIRD &c. ITEMS IN LIBRARY OF H. P. LOVECRAFT

Fiction & Poetry

Andreyev, Leonid	The Red Laugh [#40]
	The Seven Who Were Hanged [#41]
Arlen, Michael	Ghost Stories [#52]
Astor, John Jacob	Journey to Other Worlds [#56]
Austin, F. Britten	On the Borderland [#61]
Baudelaire, Charles-Pierre	Poems (Mod. Lib. Edition) [#78]
Beckford, William	History of the Caliph Vathek [#84–85]
	Episodes of Vathek [#83]
Benson, E. F.	Visible & Invisible [#90]
	Man Who Went Too Far (short) [#91, 356, 629]
Beraud, Henri	Lazarus [#92]
Bierce, Ambrose	In the Midst of Life [#99]
	Can Such Things Be? [#98]
	Monk & Hangman's Daughter (collab.) [#100]
Birch, A. G.	The Moon Terror [#104]
Blackwood, Algernon	Shocks [#111]
	John Silence [#107–8]
	Jimbo [#106]
	Julius Le Vallon [#109]
	The Willows (in anthology) [#603]
	The Lost Valley & Other Stories [#110]
Bligh-Bond, Mary	Avernus [#118]
Brontë, Emily	Wuthering Heights [#666]
Buchan, John	The Runagates' Club [#141]
Bulwer-Lytton, Edward	Zanoni [#145]
	A Strange Story [#145]
	The House & the Brain [#145]
	The Coming Race [#144]
Busson, Paul	The Man Who Was Born Again [#156]
Chambers, Robert W.	The King in Yellow [#184]
	In Search of the Unknown [#183]
Cline, Leonard	The Dark Chamber [#198]
Cowan, Frank	Revi-Lona [#217]
d'Aurevilly, Barbey	Story without a Name [#74]
de la Mare, Walter	The Riddle &c. [#244]
	The Connoisseur &c. [#243]
De Mille, James	MS. Found in a Copper Cylinder [#245]
Disraeli, Benjamin	Alroy [#268]

Doyle, A. Conan	Tales of Twilight & the Unseen [#278]
	Tales of Long Ago [#277]
	The Lost World [#276]
Dunsany, Lord	The Gods of Pegāna [#293]
	Time & the Gods [#289]
	A Dreamer's Tales [#209]
	The Sword of Welleran [#289]
	The Book of Wonder [#289]
	Last Book of Wonder [#295]
	Tales of Three Hemispheres [#298]
	Fifty-One Tales [#291]
	Don Rodriguez [#288]
	King of Elfland's Daughter [#294]
	The Blessing of Pan [#287]
	Five Plays [#292]
	Plays of Gods & Men [#296]
	Plays of Near & Far [#297]
	Travel Tales of Mr. Joseph Jorkens [#299]
Eddison, E. R.	The Worm Ouroboros [#309]
Flaubert, Gustave	Salammbo [#341]
	Temptation of St. Anthony [#342]
Forbes, Esther	A Mirror for Witches [#343]
Fouque, La Motte	Undine [#549]
	Sintram &c. [#549]
Gautier, Theophile	Clarimonde [#365]
	Avatar [#368]
	One of Cleopatra's Nights [#367]
Haggard, H. Rider	She [#411]
Hawthorne, Nathaniel	House of Seven Gables [#430]
	(short tales—scattered)
Hearn, Lafcadio	Kwaidan [#440]
Hugo, Victor	Hans of Iceland [#477]
Huysmans, Joris-Karl	Against the Grain [#483]
Jackson, Charles Loring	The Gold Point [#497]
James, Henry	The Turn of the Screw [#498]
James, Montague Rhodes	Ghost Stories of an Antiquary [#499]
	More Ghost Stories [#500]
	Thin Ghost & Others [#501]
	Warning to the Curious [#502]
King, Basil	The Spreading Dawn [#530]
Kipling, Rudyard	Phantom Rickshaw [#537]
	Mark of the Beast, &c. &c. [#536]

Le Fanu, Joseph Sheridan	House by the Churchyard [#559]
Level, Maurice	Tales of Mystery & Horror [#565]
	Those Who Return [#566]
Lewis, Matthew Gregory	The Monk [#567]
London, Jack	The Star Rover [#579]
MacDonald, George	Lilith [#611]
Machen, Arthur	The House of Souls [#618]
	The Hill of Dreams [#617]
	The Three Impostors [#623]
	The Shining Pyramid [#621]
	The Terror (in magazine) [#174]
McKenna, Stephen	The Oldest God [#624]
Marryat, Capt.	The Phantom Ship [#640]
Marsh, Richard	The Beetle [#642]
Maturin, Charles Robert	Melmoth, the Wanderer (3 vols.) [#646]
Merimee, Prosper	The Venus of Ille [#368]
Merritt, A.	Through the Dragon Glass [#26, 655]
	The Moon-Pool (in magazine) [#26]
	The Face in the Abyss [#654]
	The Dwellers in the Mirage (mag.) [#51]
	Creep, Shadow (bound instal.) [#51]
Moore, Thomas	The Epicurean [#674]
Onions, Oliver	Ghosts in Daylight [#718]
Pain, Barry	An Exchange of Souls [#735]
Pattee, Fred Lewis	House of the Black Ring [#744]
Perutz, Leo	Master of the Day of Judgment [#753]
Poe, Edgar Allan	Complete tales & poems [#769]
Quiller-Couch, A.	Wandering Heath [#786]
	Noughts & Crosses [#784]
	Old Fires & Profitable Ghosts [#785]
Radcliffe, Ann	Mysteries of Udolpho [#787]
Reeve, Clara	The Old English Baron [#793]
Rohmer, Sax	Brood of the Witch Queen [#811]
Russell, W. Clark	The Frozen Pirate [#821]
	The Flying Dutchman [#820]
Savile, Frank	Beyond the Great South Wall [#828]
Shelley, Mary W.	Frankenstein [#864]
Shiel, M. P.	The Purple Cloud [#871]
	Prince Zaleski [#870]
	The Lord of the Sea [#869]
Sinclair, May	The Intercessor & Others [#874]
Sitwell, Osbert	The Man Who Lost Himself [#876]

Smith, Clark Ashton	The Star-Treader [#884]
	Odes & Sonnets [#882]
	Ebony & Crystal [#881]
	Sandalwood [#883]
	Double Shadow &c. [#880]
Stevenson, R. L.	Jekyll & Hyde (& others) [#922]
Stoker, Bram	Dracula [#926]
Toksvig, Signe	The Last Devil [#973]
Verne, Jules	20,000 Leagues under the Sea [#996]
	From the Earth to the Moon [#995]
	(others in magazines)
Wakefield, H. R.	They Return at Evening [#1002]
	Others Who Return [#1003]
Walpole, Horace	The Castle of Otranto [#1007]
Webster, J. Provand	The Oracle of Baal [#1019]
Wells, H. G.	First Men in the Moon [#1027]
	(others in magazines) [#32]
White, Edward Lucas	Song of the Sirens, &c. [#1051]
	Lukundoo, &c. [#1049]
Wilde, Oscar	The Picture of Dorian Gray [#1051]
	Fairy Tales [#1049]
Wilkins-Freeman, Mary E.	The Wind in the Rosebush [#354]
Wright, S.	Deluge [#1069]
	The World Below [#1070]
Wyllarde, Dolf	Stories of Strange Happenings [#1071]

Anthologies

Asbury, Herbert	Not at Night [#54]
Asquith & others	My Grimmest Nightmare [#55]
French, Joseph Lewis	Best Psychic Stories [#355]
Gawsworth, John	Strange Assembly [#370]
Hammett, Dashiell	Creeps by Night [#421]
Harré, T. Everett	Beware after Dark [#425]
Hutchinson (pub.)	Fifty Years of Ghost Stories [#333]
Lynch, Bohun	Best Ghost Stories [#603]
McSpadden, J. Walker	Famous Psychic Stories [#629]
Neale, Arthur	Great Weird Stories [#700]
Rudwin, Maximilian	Devil Stories [#816]
Saintsbury, George	Tales of Mystery (Radcliffe, Lewis, Maturin extracts) [#824]
Sayers, Dorothy L.	Omnibus of Crime [#830]
Tales from the German (Hoffmann, Hauff, &c.) [#730]	
Terrible Tales (Italian) [#950]	

Lock & Key Library (12 vols.) [#429]
Masterpieces of Mystery (3 vols.) [#356]

Selwyn & Blount "Not at Night" series
{
- Not at Night [#963]
- Gruesome Cargoes [#962]
- You'll Need a Night Light [#966]
- By Daylight Only [#960]
- Switch on the Light [#965]
- Grim Death [#961]
}

Pub. by Philip Allan
{
- Creeps [#223]
- Shudders [#873]
}

Treatise

Birkhead, Edith   The Tale of Terror [#105]

Mythology, Folklore, Occult

	Arabian Nights' Entertainments [#49]
Baring-Gould, S.	Curious Myths of the Middle Ages [#75]
Blakeborough, R.	Hand of Glory &c. [#116]
Book of the Dead	tr. Sir E. Wallis Budge [#121]
Bulfinch, Thomas	Age of Fable [#142]
Fiske, John	Myths & Myth-Makers [#338]
Flammarion, Camille	Haunted Houses [#340]
Grimm	Fairy Tales [#405]
Houdini, Harry	Magician among the Spirits [#470]
Ingram, John H.	Haunted Homes & Family Legends [#489]
Jung-Stilling, J. H.	Theory of Pneumatology [#521]
MacPhilpin, John	Miracles at Knock [#628]
Scott, Walter	Demonology & Witchcraft [#840]
Spence, Lewis	Encyclopaedia of Occultism [#898]

Magazine Files

Amazing Stories	1926–7 [#32]
Fantasy Fan	complete [#325]
Fantasy Magazine	since Jan. 1934 [#326]
Marvel Tales	complete [#644]
Phantagraph	complete [#755]
Strange Tales	complete [#930]
Weird Tales	complete [#1026]

INDEXES

A. Names

Abbott, David P. 428
Abbott, Jacob 1
Abbott, Lyman 2
Abney, Captain W. De W. 3
Abramson, Ben 39n
Adams, John 4
Addison, Joseph 5–12, 417, 728
Adlington, William 48
Aesop 13–14
Agassiz, Louis 15
Ahlhauser, William C. 16
Aiken, Conrad 421–22
Aikin, John 16, 360
Ainger, Alfred 548
Airne, C. W. 18–23
Alan, A. J. 830
Alarcon, Pedro de 428
Albe, Edmund Edward Fournier d' 340
Alcott, Louisa May 24
Alden, Abner 25
Alden, Priscilla 903
Allen, Hervey 27, 765
Allen, John 28
Allen, Joseph H. 30–31
Allen, T. P. 29
Allen, William F. 29–32
Allinson, Alfred 816
Anderson, A. 117
Anderson, Jessie Macmillan 38
Anderson, Sir Robert 356
Andrews, Ethan Allan 39
Andreyev, Leonid Nikolaevich 40, 425
Angell, James Burrill 41
Annandale, Charles 703
Ansted, David Thomas 42
Anthon, Charles 45–46, 890
Anthony, R. 54, 960, 964, 966
Appleton, John Howard 47
Apuleius, Lucius 48, 428
Arbuthnot, John 50
Archer, William 356
Arlen, Michael 52, 830

Armstrong, Terence Ian Fytton. *See* Gawsworth, John
Arnold, Benedict 452
Arnold, Sir Edwin 53, 632
Arnold, Matthew 977
Arnold, Thomas 7
Arnot, Robert 648
Asbury, Herbert 54
Asquith, Lady Cynthia 55, 111n
Astor, John Jacob 56
Astor, William Waldorf 700
Atherton, Gertrude 425
Atlee, Benge 962
Austen, Jane 56–60
Austin, F. Britten 61
Austin, George Lowell 62
Austin, John Osborne 63–65
Austin, L. F. 700
Avebury, John Lubbock, baron 66
Aytoun, W. E. 384

Bache, Franklin 984
Backus, W. Elwyn 421
Bacon, Dolores 67
Bacon, Edgar Mayhew 68
Bacon, Mary Schell Hoke. *See* Bacon, Dolores
Bacon, Victor E. 907
Baird, Edwin 1026
Baird, James S. S. 69
Baker, George 575
Baker, La Fayette Charles 70
Baker, Ray Stannard. *See* Grayson, David
Baldwin, F. Lee 51
Baldwin, James 71
Balzac, Honoré de 428
Bancroft, George 72
Banks, Louis Albert 73
Barbey d'Aurevilly, Jules 74
Barford, George 250
Baring, Maurice 603
Baring-Gould, S. 75
Barker, Elsa 355
Barker, Ernest 1028

Barlow, R. H. 580n, 585n, 589n, 592n, 655n, 768n, 864n, 1069n
Barsony, Etienne 428
Bartlett, John 76
Bartlett, John Russell 77
Bates, Harry 930
Bateson, W. 323
Baudelaire, Charles Pierre 78–79
Bayly, George W. 425
Bayne, Samuel G. 80
Beardsley, Aubrey 81
Beattie, James 771
Beaumont, Francis 82, 528
Beckford, William 83–85
Beddoes, Thomas Lovell 897
Beeding, Francis 962
Beerbohm, Max 86–87
Beers, D. G., & Co. 88
Beeton, Samuel Orchart 89
Bell, Clara 974
Beloe, William 446
Benét, Stephen Vincent 421–22
Benson, E. F. 90–91, 333, 356, 425, 603, 629, 830
Benson, Theodora 55
Benton, Paul 54, 966
Béraud, Henri 92
Beresford, J. D. 830
Bergsoe, Jorgen Wilhelm 428
Bernays, Jakob 600
Besant, Sir Walter 93–94, 667
Betts, Ernest 55
Bickerstaff, Isaac 800
Bieber, I. W. 573
Bierce, Ambrose 98–101, 184n, 333, 355, 395, 428, 629, 830
Bierstadt, Edward Hale 102
Bingham, Caleb 104
Binney, Cecil 333
Binns, Archie 963
Birch, A. G. 104
Birkhead, Edith 105
Birkin, Charles 223, 873
Bishop, Zealia 335n, 964–65
Blackwood, Algernon 55, 106–11, 333, 355–56, 559n, 603, 700
Blaine, Mahlon 85
Blair, Hugh 113

Blaisdell, Albert F. 114
Blake, William 115
Blakeborough, J. Fairfax 116
Blakeborough, Richard 116
Blakeston, Oswell 964
Blashfield, Evangeline W. 629
Blavatsky, Helena 355
Blicher, Steen Steensen 428
Bloomfield, Robert 117
Blumenthal, Walter Hart 703
Boito, Camillo 428
Bolton, Gambier 355
Bond, Mary Bligh 118
Borellus (Petrus Borel) 645n
Borrow, George 122
Boswell, James 124–25, 519
Botta, Anne Charlotte (Lynch) 126
Bouglé, C. 323
Bourget, Paul 428, 648
Bowen, Marjorie 55, 830
Bowring, E. A. 384
Boyd, Ernest 129
Boyd, James R. 524
Braddon, Mary 333
Bradford, Gamaliel, Jr. 605
Bradley, Jack 965
Bradner, Lester 538
Brady, Cyrus Townsend 127
Brady, Matthew 583n
Braithwaite, William Stanley 43
Brandow, John Henry 128
Braybrooke, Lord 751
Brecht, Vincent B. 227
Bregenzer, Don 129
Brett, Reginald Balliol 130
Bridge, Ann 333
Broad, R. F. 965
Brocklesby, John 133
Brontë, Charlotte 134
Brontë, Emily 666
Brougham and Vaux, Henry Brougham, baron 135
Brown, Alice 903
Brown, Charles Brockden 428
Brown, Charles Wilson 538
Browning, Robert 136
Bruce, Isabel 816
Brucker, Johann Jakob 137

Indexes 181

Bruère, Robert Walter 436
Bryant, William Cullen 138–39, 908
Bryce, James, Viscount 120, 140
Buchan, John 141
Buckley, Theodore Alois 463, 999
Budge, Sir E. A. Wallis 121
Bulfinch, Thomas 142
Bullen, John Ravenor 143
Bulwer-Lytton, Edward 144–45, 333, 428
Bunyan, John 146
Burks, Arthur J. 960
Burnaby, William 754
Burnett, Frances Hodgson 147
Burney, Frances (Fanny) 148, 417
Burns, Robert 149
Burrage, A. M. 333, 830
Burritt, Elijah Hinsdale 150–51
Burton, Warren 152
Bury, J. B. 323
Bush, David Van 153–55
Busson, Paul 156
Butler, Gervaise 474n
Butler, Joseph 157
Butler, Samuel 158
Byrd, Mary Emma 159
Byron, Harriet 417

Caballero, Fernán 816
Cabell, James Branch 129, 160
Caesar, C. Julius 161–63
Caldecott, Randolph 492
Callendar, John 801
Calvert, George H. 164
Campbell, Thomas 165
Canby, Henry Seidel 166
Cannon, Peter 84n
Capuana, Luigi 428
Carey, Henry Francis 232–33
Carleton, S. 425
Carleton, Will 167
Carlyle, Thomas 168–69, 596
Carpenter, James 699
Carrel, Alexis 170
Carrington, Hereward 355, 428
Carroll, Ellen M. 171
Carroll, Lewis 172
Carter, Frederick 369
Castle, Egerton 428

Castleman, J. H. 139
Cave, Hugh B. 964
Chalmers, Alexander 131, 175, 518
Chamberlain, Arthur Bensley 176
Chambers, George F. 177–80
Chambers, Robert 181–82
Chambers, Robert W. 98n, 183–84
Chapman, George 461
Charles, Joseph F. 173
Chartres, J. S. 341n
Chase, Thomas 186
Chatrian, Alexandre 428
Chatterton, Thomas 187
Chaucer, Geoffrey 188, 596, 929
Chekhov, Anton 356, 428
Cherbuliez, Victor 428
Chesnutt, Charles W. 189
Chesson, Gordon 964
Chesterfield, Philip Dormer Stanhope, earl of 190
Christie-Murray, Dora 962
Church, Alfred J. 191
Cicero, M. Tullius 192
Claretie, Jules 428
Clark, Franklin Chase 63n, 77n, 569n
Clark, Lillian D. 150n, 401n, 552n, 791n
Clark, Thomas 162, 192, 462, 729, 1072
Clarke, Charles Cowden 9
Clarke, Harry 383, 768
Clarke, James Freeman 193
Clarke, Mary Cowden 194
Clemens, Samuel Langhorne. See Twain, Mark
Cleveland, Charles Dexter 195–96
Clifford, Lucy (Lane) 197
Cline, Leonard 198
Clodd, Edward 199
Clough, A. H. 764
Coates, Walter John 200–203, 590n
Cobb, Irvin S. 421, 425
Colange, Leo de 204
Coleridge, Samuel Taylor 205
Coligny, Gaspard de 93
Collar, William C. 206–7, 441
Collier, John 421
Collins, Arthur 208
Collins, Charles 830

Collins, W. Chiswell 963
Collins, Wilkie 356, 428, 629
Collins, William 175, 771
Collins, William Lucas 209
Collins (William), Sons, & Co. 210
Colter, Eli 966
Colum, Padraic 290
Combe, William. *See* Syntax, Doctor
Comstock, George Cary 212
Conder, Claude Reignier 213
Congreve, William 727
Conrad, Joseph 830
Conyngton, Mary 538
Cook, Oscar 961–62, 964–66
Cook, W. Paul 16n, 83n, 143n, 184n, 593n, 646n, 731n, 792
Cooke, Thomas 449
Cooper, J. G. 1000
Cormack, John 330
Cornell, Sarah S. 214
Corson, Hiram 522
Corte, Matteo della 215
Corvo, Frederick Baron 216
Cotton, John 706
Counselman, Mary Elizabeth 964
Cowan, Frank 217
Cowley, Abraham 466–67, 938
Cowper, William 218–19
Crabb, George 220
Crabbe, George 221, 680
Crackanthorpe, Hubert 369
Craik, Dinah Maria (Mulock). *See* Mulock, Mrs.
Cram, Ralph Adams 356
Crawford, F. Marion 333, 428
Crawford, William L. 644
Creasy, Sir Edward Shepherd 222
Creighton, M. 224
Croker, John Wilson 519
Cromwell, Oliver 426
Cumberland, Richard 225
Cunningham, A. C. 221
Cunningham, Peter 226, 517
Currey, L. W. 471n, 810n
Curtis, George William 227

Daboll, David A. 705n
Daboll, Nathan 705n
Dallas, W. S. 543

Dalton, John Call 229
Dalton, Ormonde M. *See* Leith, W. Compton
Dampier, William 230
Dana, James D. 231
Danforth, Walter Raleigh 513n
Dante Alighieri 232–33, 741n
Dark, Sidney 234–35
Darwin, Charles 236n, 323, 543
Darwin, Erasmus 236, 543
Daudet, Alphonse 816
Davidson, Joseph 999
Davies, Rhys 369
Davis, Andrew Jackson 355
Davis, Owen 237
Davis, Sarah Matilda Henry 238
Davis, William Morris 239
Davis, William Stearns 240
Dealey, James Quayle 538
Dean, Gerald 54, 963
Dearden, Harold 421–22
De Casseres, Benjamin 594n
de Castro, Adolphe 79n, 100n
Defoe, Daniel 241–42, 387n, 980
de la Mare, Walter 243–44, 333, 830
De Mille, James 245
Dennie, John 246
De Puy, W. H. 318
De Quincey, Thomas 247, 428
Derham, William 248
Derleth, August 51n, 54, 55n, 61n, 108n, 110n, 111n, 141n, 156n, 183n, 198n, 249–53, 369n, 498, 588n, 591n, 603n, 642n, 874n, 960, 964–66, 1004n
Deulin, Charles 816
De Windt, Harry 962
Dick, Thomas 255–56
Dickens, Charles 257–67, 428, 700, 830
Disraeli, Benjamin 268
Dixon, Thomas, Jr. 269
Dobson, Austin 270, 322
Dodgson, Charles Luttwidge. *See* Carroll, Lewis
Dodsley, Robert 272
Dold, Elliot 447
Doré, Gustave 205n, 232, 656
Dostoevsky, Feodor 428
Douglas, Aaron 677

Indexes 183

Dowden, Edward 273, 865
Dowe, Jennie E. T. 1040
Downing, Andrew Jackson 274
Doyle, Sir Arthur Conan 275–78, 356, 428, 700
Drake, Joseph Rodman 279
Drake, Samuel Adams 280–82
Dreiser, Theodore 719
Drillien, B. 566
Dryden, John 283–84, 466–67, 728, 764, 1001
Dübner, F. 468
Dumas, Alexandre 285, 428
Duncan, Robert Kennedy 286
Dunsany, Lord 102, 287–300
Durant, Will 301
Durfee, Job 302
Durfee, Thomas 302–3
Durham, Willard Higley 166
Dutt, R. Palme 304
Dwight, John 960
Dwyer, Bernard Austin 620n, 623n
Dyer, John 175
Dyer, Walter Alden 305

Earle, Alice (Morse) 306–7
Eberlein, Harold Donaldson 308
Eddison, E. R. 309
Eddy, Arthur 638n
Eddy, C. M., Jr. 638n
Edholm, C. L. 960
Edkins, Ernest A. 510n, 649n, 767n, 1070n
Edwards, George Wharton 355
Eggleston, George Cary 310
Elck, Arthur 428
Eliot, George Fielding 960, 964
Eliot, T. S. 254
Ellet, Elizabeth Fries (Lummis) 311
Ellis, Annie Raine 148
Ellis, Edward S. 312
Ellis, Havelock 483
Emerson, Ralph Waldo 313–17, 596, 908
Erckmann, Emile 428
Eschenburg, J. J. 319
Esenwein, Joseph Berg 320
Eustace, Robert 700
Evans, Lewis 523

Evelyn, John 321
Everett, Mrs H. D. 322, 873
Ewart, Wilfrid 369
Ewers, Hanns Heinz 421–22
Ex-Private X. *See* Burrage, A. M.

Fadiman, Clifton P. 542
Fairfax, Edward 947
Falconer, William 324
Farington, Joseph 327
Farrar, Frederic William 329
Faulkner, William 421–22
Faunce, William Herbert Perry 538
Feiling, C. A. 730
Fénelon, François de Salignac de la Mothe 330
Fernald, Chester Bailey 356
Fessenden, Thomas G. 331
Field, Edward 332
Fielding, Henry 417
Figuier, Louis 334
Finger, Charles J. 335
Finlay, John H. 220
Fiske, John 336–38
Fiske, N. W. 319
FitzGerald, Edward 339
Flammarion, Camille 340
Flanders, Henry 225
Flaubert, Gustave 341–42
Fleming, Peter 421
Fleming, Walter L. 563
Fletcher, John 81, 528
Fogarty, Thomas 398
Fogazzaro, Antonio 428
Forbes, Allen 907
Forbes, Esther 343
Ford, John 528
Forest, J. 344
Forster, John 345
Foster, Sir Michael 346
Foulke, William Dudley 347
Fowler, William Chauncey 348
France, Anatole 816
Francis, Philip 466–67
Frank, Waldo 350
Fraser, Maxwell 351
Freeman, Edward Augustus 352
Freeman, Mary Eleanor (Wilkins) 353–54, 428, 629

French, Joseph Lewis 355–56
French, Nora May 357
Frere, John Hookham 680
Freund, W. 39
Fricker, Karl 358
Frisbie, R. D. 421
Froissart, Jean 359
Frost, John 360
Funk, I. W. 629

Gabelle, James 798
Gainsborough, Thomas 176
Gall, James 361
Gallagher, Oscar Charles 314
Galpin, Alfred 313n, 884n
Galt, John 362
Gamwell, Annie E. P. 152
Gardner, Henry Brayton 538
Gardner, Mrs. Marinus Willett 791
Garnett, Richard 762, 816
Garrett, Edmund Henry 363
Garth, Sir Samuel 364, 728n
Gaskell, Elizabeth 333, 603
Gaspard de Coligny 93
Gautier, Théophile 356, 365–68
Gavorse, Joseph 934
Gawsworth, John 370
Gay, John 9, 417, 868
Geikie, Sir Archibald 370
George IV (King of England) 478
George, W. L. 333
Gerga, Giovanni 428
Gernsback, Hugo 32
Gibbings, Robert 343
Gibbon, Charles 933
Gibbon, Edward 373–75
Gibson, Charles 902
Gibson, Frank Markey 376
Gifford, William 522–23
Gilfillan, George 9, 776, 866
Gilman, Arthur 377
Gittins, Anthony 333
Gladstone, William Ewart 378
Glasgow, Ellen 425
Gleason, Clarence W. 207
Gleeson, Alice Collins 379
Godfrey, Albert 381
Godfrey, Hollis 380

Goethe, Johann Wolfgang von 317, 382–84, 730
Gogol, Nicolai 816
Goldenweiser, Alex. 886
Goldberg, Isaac 766
Goldsmith, J. *See* Phillips, Sir Richard
Goldsmith, Oliver 345, 385–86, 417
Gonzales, Manoel 387
Goodrich, Charles A. 388
Goodrich, Chauncey A. 1021–22
Goodrich, Samuel Griswold 389–92
Goodyear, W. H. 393
Gorky, Maxim 816
Gorst, H. H. 961
Gould, B. A. 724
Gourmont, Remy de 394
Grainger, James 969
Graham, Stephen 369
Grant, Ulysses S. 1077
Grattan, C. Hartley 395
Gray, Asa 396
Gray, Thomas 397, 417, 771
Grayson, David 398
Grayson, Rupert 960, 962
Green, Anna Katherine 357
Green, John Richard 401
Greene, Albert Gorton 402
Greene, Charles S. 403
Greene, George Washington 8, 889
Greene, Robert 528
Greene, Sonia H. 861n
Greene, Welcome Arnold 403
Greig, James 327
Grieve, Robert 404
Grimm, Jakob Ludwig Karl 405
Grimm, Wilhelm 405
Grimshaw, Beatrice 425
Grimshaw, William 385
Griswold, Rufus Wilmot 406
Groner, August 428
Gudeman, Alfred 407
Guiney, Louise Imogen 903
Guizot, François Pierre Guillaume 408
Gummere, Francis B. 790n
Guy, Joseph, the elder 409
Gwynn, Michael 964

Haeckel, Ernst 323
Hagar, George J. 750

Haggard, Audrey 410
Haggard, H. Rider 411
Hakluyt, Richard 412
Haldane, J. B. S. 413–14
Hale, Edward Everett 415
Hale, Salma 416
Hale, Susan 417
Halifax, Samuel 157
Hall, Frederic Aldin 418
Hallowell, J. O. 857
Hals, Frans 419
Hamilton, Anne 420
Hamilton, Edmond 425, 964–65
Hamilton, James 162, 825
Hamlet, Alice 1049n
Hammett, Dashiell 421–22
Hanfstaengl, F. 419, 695, 799
Hannay, James 454
Hanshew, Mary E. 356
Hanshew, Thomas W. 356
Hapgood, Isabel F. 816
Harkness, Albert 424
Harré, T. Everett 425
Harris, Arthur 587n
Harrison, Frederic 426
Harrison, James A. 427
Hart, Levi 1001
Harvey, William F. 356, 629, 830
Hauff, Wilhelm 428, 730, 816
Hawker, Robert 146
Hawkesworth, John 1079
Hawthorne, Julian 428
Hawthorne, Nathaniel 356, 425, 428–37, 629
Hayden, John A. B. 438
Hayes, Isaac Israel 439
Heald, Hazel 964
Hearn, Lafcadio 342, 355–56, 365, 367, 425, 440
Heatley, H. R. 441
Heighway, Richard 14
Heilig, George William 739
Heller, Louie Regina 442
Help, P. H. 928
Hemans, Felicia Dorothea 443
Henderson, Keith 309
Henley, Samuel 84n
Henneberger, J. C. 445n, 476n

Henry, C. S. 408
Herbert, Edward Herbert, baron 444
Hergesheimer, Joseph 445
Herotodus 428, 446
Herrick, Robert 436
Hersey, Harold 447
Hervey, James 448
Hesiod 449
Heyse, Paul 428
Heywood, Thomas 528
Hiatt, J. M. 966
Hichens, Robert 830
Hickey, William R. 960
Higgins, Lothrop D. 450
Hill, George Canning 451
Hilton, Martha 903
Hinks, Arthur R. 452
Hoag, Jonathan E. 453
Höffding, H. 323
Hoffmann, E. T. A. 428, 730
Hoffsten, Ernest Godfrey 595
Hogarth, William 454
Holbrook, Josiah 455
Holden, Inez 55
Holland, Hester 964
Holland, Josiah Gilbert. *See* Titcomb, Timothy, Esq.
Holliday, Carl 456
Holmes, Oliver Wendell 457–58, 908
Holmes, Prescott 459
Homer 378, 418, 461–64
Hooker, Sir Joseph Dalton 465
Horace (Q. Horatius Flaccus) 466–69, 643
Horne, Charles F. 312
Hornig, Charles D. 324
Houdini, Harry 470
Houtain, J. G. 460
Houtain, Mrs. J. G. 460
Howard, John 471
Howard, John 483
Howard, Robert E. 961
Howe, Daniel Wait 473
Howitt, William 473
Howland, Avis C. 474
Hudson, Stephen 369
Hudson, W. H. 475
Hughes, Rupert 476

Hugo, Victor 477
Huish, Robert 478
Humboldt, Alexander, freiherr von 479
Humelbergius Secundus, Dick 480
Hunt, Leigh 947
Hunt, Violet 333, 830
Hussey, Christopher 481
Hutton, Maurice 482
Huysmans, Joris-Karl 483–84
Hyde, Edna 485

Immerman, Karl 730
Inchbald, Elizabeth 1079
Ingemann, Bernhard Severin 428
Ingram, John H. 488–89, 816
Irving, Henry B. 566
Irving, Washington 386, 428, 491–95, 816
Isham, Norman Morrison 496

Jackson, Andrew 127
Jackson, Charles Loring 497
Jackson, Samuel 521
Jacobs, Joseph 14
Jacobs, W. W. 830
James I (King of England) 680
James, G. P. R. 700
James, Henry 498
James, M. R. 333, 356, 499–502, 603, 629, 830
James, Thomas 13
Jay, Herbert 55
Jebb, R. C. 504
Jefferies, Richard 505
Jelihovsky, Vera 428
Jenks, William 505
Jerdan, William 676
Jerome, Jerome K. 830
Jervis, William Henley 506
Jimerson, Royal W. 960
Joan of Arc 983
Johnson, Clifton 152, 507–8
Johnson, Fanny Kemble 509
Johnson, Gaylord 510
Johnson, Isaac T. 703
Johnson, Morgan 960
Johnson, Samuel 124–25, 175, 371n, 417, 511–18, 605
Johnston, Sir H. H. 1028

Jonson, Ben 466–67, 519, 528
Jokai, Maurus 428
Joshi, S. T. 245n, 453n
Joy, James Richard 520
Joyce, Michael 421–22
Judas Maccabaeus 213
Jung-Stilling, Johann Heinrich 522
Juvenal (D. Junius Juvenalis) 523–24

Kames, Henry Home, Lord 524
Kapfer, A. W. 964
Keats, John 205, 525
Keetels, Jean Gustave 526
Keller, David H. 885, 961, 964
Kellogg, Vernon Lyman 527
Keltie, Sir John Scott 528
Kendrick, Asahel C. 529
Kerruish, Jessie D. 964
King, Basil 530
King, Moses 531–32
King, W. C. 44
Kingdon, N. H. 441
Kinglake, Alexander William 533
Kingsley, Charles 534–35
Kipling, Rudyard 428, 536–37, 700
Kippis, Andrew 157
Kirk, George 74n, 160n, 350n, 413n, 651n, 743n, 882n, 939n
Kirk, William 538
Kittredge, George Lyman 539
Kleiner, Rheinhart 84n, 576n
Kleist, Heinrich von 730
Knight, Charles 947
Knight, Cornelia 540
Knight, William 660
Knowles, James Davis 541
Knox, Ann 55
Koenig, H. C. 586n
Kosztolányi, Dezsö 542
Kraus, Ernst Ludwig 543
Krestovski, Vsevolod Vladimirovitch 429
Kugler, Franz Theodor 544
Kuhns, O. 932
Kuntz, Eugene B. 545

Lactantius, L. Caecilius Firmianus 645n
Lake, J. W. 842
Lamb, Charles 546–48

Lamb, Mary 548
La Motte-Fouqué, Friedrich Heinrich Karl 549, 680
Landon, Perceval 2, 603
Lang, Andrew 49, 428, 767
Langhorne, John 762, 1079
Langhorne, William 762
Langley, Noel 55
Lankester, Sir E. Ray 1028
Lardner, Dionysius 550
Larned, J. N. 551
Larssen, Otto 429
La Spina, Greye 54, 963
Laswell, George D. 552
Laver, James 55
Lawrence, Eugene 892
Lecky, W. E. H. 555
Lederer, Charles 556
Ledge, Warden 964
Lee, Abby 475n
Lee, Guy Carleton 557
Lee, Robert E. 734
Lee, Sarah (Wallis) Bowdich 558
Lee, Vernon 333
Leeds, Arthur 874n
Le Fanu, Joseph Sheridan 333, 559, 830
Leith, W. Compton 559
Leland, Charles Godfrey 560
Lennox, Charlotte 417
Leonard, Sterling A. 562
Leonard-Stuart, Charles 750
Le Queux, William 563
Leroux, Gaston 700
Leslie, Shane 333
Lester, John C. 564
Level, Maurice 565–66, 961
Levitan, Mortimer 963
Lewis, Homer P. 551
Lewis, L. A. 964
Lewis, Matthew Gregory 567, 824n
Lincoln, Charles Henry 872
Liddell, Henry George 568–69
Liggett, Carr 130
Lincoln, Abraham 561, 596
Lincoln, Charles Henry 872
Lincoln, John Larkin 570
Lindsay, Miss B. 571

Lippitt, Charles Warren 572
Little, Richard Henry 1080–81
Livingstone, David 573
Livy (T. Livius) 191, 574–75
Lloyd, Charles. *See* Birkin, Charles
Locker-Lampson, Frederick 576–77
Lohr, Friedrich 578
London, Jack 355, 579
Long, Amelia Reynolds 965
Long, Frank Belknap 54, 342n, 421–22, 579–80, 765n, 824n, 855n, 970n, 940, 963, 965
Longfellow, Henry Wadsworth 62, 582, 908
Lossing, Benson J. 583
Lounsbury, Thomas R. 584
Lovecraft, H. P. 32, 54, 143, 203, 421–22, 425, 453, 460, 545, 562n, 585–92, 715, 940n, 960, 964–66, 1040
Lovecraft, Sarah Susan 24n, 49n, 285n, 526n
Lovecraft, Winfield Scott 974, 1062n
Loveman, Samuel 48n, 101, 129, 217n, 354n, 453n, 485, 545, 575n, 581, 593–94, 601n, 754n, 870n
Lowell, James Russell 595–97, 908
Lowrie, Sarah D. 598
Lubbock, John. *See* Avebury, John Lubbock, baron
Lucian of Samosata 599
Lucilius, C. 522
Lucretius (T. Lucretius Carus) 600
Ludlow, Fitz Hugh 601
Ludlum, Mabel Stewart 598
Lumley, William 85n, 121n, 1036n
Luther, Martin 978
Lyly, John 528
Lynch, Anne C. *See* Botta, Anne Charlotte (Lynch)
Lynch, J. Bernard 602
Lynch, John Gilbert Bohun 603
Lytton, Edward Robert Bulwer Lytton, earl of. *See* Meredith, Owen

Mabbott, Thomas Ollive 765
Macaulay, Thomas Babington 516, 604–6, 679
Macchiavelli, Niccolò 816
Macchioro, Vittorio 607–8

McCord, Joseph 54, 966
McDannald, A. H. 668
Macdonald, Alice Edith (Middleton), Lady 609–10
MacDonald, George 611
Macdonald, Philip 421
Macdonald, William 538, 612
McDougall, Frances Harriet (Whipple) Greene 613
Machen, Arthur 174, 356, 369, 425, 559n, 614–23, 700, 830
McKenna, Stephen 624
Mackenzie, Henry 625, 1079
Macklin, Alys Eyre 566
Macleod, Fiona 355
McNeil, Everett 923n
Macpherson, Hector 626
Macpherson, James 627
MacPhilpin, John 628
Macready, R. G. 54
McSarcasm, Sir Archibald. *See* Shaw, William
McSpadden, J. Walker 629
Macy, William Francis 630
Madden, Cecil 55
Mahaffy, J. P. 633–34
Mais, S. P. B. 635
Major, Dagney 962
Malinowski, Bronislaw 886
Malory, Sir Thomas 636
Mandeville, Sir John 637
Mann, Francis Oscar 816
Mann, Henry 638
Mann, Thomas 542
Marcet, Jane (Haldimand) 639
Marchant, J. R. V. 173
Mariconda, Steven J. 75n, 483n
Markham, Edwin 770
Markham, Harold 960, 962
Marlowe, Christopher 528
Marryat, Florence 356
Marryat, Frederick 640
Marsden, Francis 369
Marsh, John 641
Marsh, Richard 642
Marston, John 528
Martial (M. Valerius Martialis) 643
Martin, Theodore 384

Marzials, Frank T. 83
Masefield, John 816
Massinger, Philip 528
Masson, David 247
Mather, Cotton 645
Matthews, Brander 91, 356, 790n
Matthews, J. Dyott 961
Matthews, J. W. 341n
Mattison, Hiram 150–51
Maturin, Charles Robert 428, 646, 824n
Maunder, Edward Walter 647
Maupassant, Guy de 356, 428, 648, 816
Maurice, Michael 649
Maurois, André 421–22, 650
Mayne, Ethel Colburn 830
Meade, L. T. 700
Meldrum, D. Storrar 362
Melville, Herman 651
Mencken, H. L. 129, 160, 652
Menzel, Adolph 544
Meredith, Owen 653
Mérimée, Prosper 369
Merkel, Rudolf 727
Merritt, A. 26, 51, 654–55
Metcalfe, John 830
Meyrink, Gustav 428
Middleton, Edgar 55
Miles, Hamish 677
Mills, Abraham 113
Mille, Pierre 428
Miller, C. Franklin 960, 963
Miller, Frank Justus 747, 932
Mills, W. Jay 743
Milman, H. H. 375
Milton, John 466–67, 656–57, 771
Minarik, Frank L. 130
Miniter, Edith 659
Minto, William 660
Mirski, Prince 156
Mitchell, David Andrew 661
Mitchell, Edwin Valentine 662
Mitchell, J. Leslie 961
Mitchell, John Ames 663
Mitchell, Samuel Augustus 664–65
Mitford, Mary Russell 666
Mitton, Geraldine Edith 667

Moe, Maurice W. 560n, 562n, 669, 1064n, 1080n, 1081n
Moffett, Cleveland 356
Moffett, Harold Y. 562
Molnar, Ferencz 428
Monnier, Marc 670
Monson, R. A. 55
Montagu, Lady Mary Wortley 417
Montaigne, Michel de 317
Montaut, Henri de 994
Montefiore, G. Frederick 963–64
Montgomery, David Henry 670
Mooney, M. P. 129
Moore, C. L. 584n, 673, 1053n
Moore, John 1079
Moore, Thomas 674–76
Morand, Paul 677
Mordaunt, Elinor 603
More, Hannah 863
Morell, Sir Charles 681
Morey, William C. 678
Morgan, Bassett 54, 425, 960–61, 966
Morgan, C. Lloyd 323
Morison, James Cotter 679
Morley, Christopher 129
Morley, Henry 680, 840
Morris, Gouverneur 425
Morris, Richard 188
Morris, William 682
Morse, Edward S. 683
Morse, Jedidiah 684–85
Morse, Richard Ely 447n, 687, 869n, 871n, 994n, 1037n
Morton, J. B. 55
Morton, James Ferdinand 190n, 453n
Moult, Thomas 156, 688
Mowry, William Augustus 688
Mulock, Mrs. 689–93
Munn, H. Warner 96n, 184n, 960, 964
Munro, H. H. *See* Saki
Munro, Wilfred Harold 694
Murillo, Bartolome Estaban 695
Murphy, Arthur 942
Murray, Gilbert 1028
Murray, Lindley 696–97
Murray, Philip 223, 873
Musaeus, J. H. 730
Muspratt, Rosalie 961

Myers, Ernest 758
Myers, P. V. N. 698

Napoleon Bonaparte 317
Nash, Richard ("Beau") 417
Nash, T. R. 158
Nasmyth, James 699
Neale, Arthur 700
Nepos, Cornelius 701
Nesbit, E. 700
Nevin, John Williamson 702
Newcomb, Simon 711–12
Newton, Douglas 960
Newton, John 146
Nichols, Joel Martin, Jr. 54
Nizida 355
Nodier, Charles 428
North, Lockhart 962
Nuttall, P. A. 470

O'Brien, Edward J. 714–15
O'Brien, Fitz-James 356, 428
O'Donnell, Elliott 223, 873
Oelenschlaeger, Adam 730
Olcott, William Tyler 716
Oliphant, Margaret 333, 629, 830
Oliver, John A. Westwood 717
O'Neail, N. J. 965
Onions, Oliver 333, 718
Oppenheim, E. Phillips 425
Oranio, Alfred 428
Orton, Vrest 143n, 614n, 719
Osborn, Edward Bolland 720–21
Osborn, V. R. 1001
Oulton, L. 962
Overman, Frederick 722
Ovid (P. Ovidius Naso) 723–29
Owen, Frank 731
Oxenford, John 730

Packard, Frederick Adolphus 732–33
Page, Thomas Nelson 734
Paget, Walter 243
Pain, Barry 603, 735, 830
Paine, R. T. 800n
Palgrave, Francis T. 736
Palmarini, I. M. 428
Palmer, Edward Henry 737
Palmer, Herbert E. 370
Parish, Elijah 686

Parker, Richard Green 738
Parkman, Francis 739
Parsons, Theophilus 740
Parsons, Thomas William 741
Partridge, John 1082
Pater, Walter 742
Paterson, William 743
Pattee, Fred Lewis 744
Paul, John. *See* Clemens, Samuel Langhorne
Pearson, James Larkin 745
Peattie, Elia W. 629
Peck, Harry Thurston 746
Peele, George 529
Pellisson, Maurice 747
Pelton, W. F. 748
Pennell, H. Cholmondeley 749
Pepys, Samuel 751
Percival, James Gates 596, 756
Percy, Thomas 752
Perkins, Frederic Beecher 816
Perseus (A. Persius Flaccus) 524
Perutz, Leo 753
Petronius (T. Petronius Arbiter) 754
Phaedrus, C. Julius 466–67
Phelps, William Lyon 953
Philips, Ambrose 175
Philips, George Morris 860
Phillips, Sir Richard 756
Phillips, Susie. *See* Lovecraft, Sarah Susan
Phillips, Whipple Van Buren 152n, 740n
Pierce, Frederick Erastus 166
Pindar 758
Pindar, Peter. *See* Wolcot, John
Pinelli, Bartolommeo 191
Pittenger, William 758–59
Place, Robie Alzada 151
Plarr, Victor 761
Plato 317, 762
Pliny the Younger (C. Plinius Caecilius Secundus) 356, 428
Plutarch 763–64
Poe, Edgar Allan 27, 355–56, 406n, 427n, 428, 488, 559n, 603, 629, 700, 738n, 765–70, 816, 908, 970, 1045, 1066

Poland, William Carey 538
Ponder, Zita I. 54, 966
Poole, Romeo 54, 963, 966
Pope, Alexander 50n, 371n, 417, 458n, 463–64, 466–67, 596, 728, 772
Porter, Noah 1022, 1024
Post, Melvlle Davisson 428
Powers, Paul S. 54, 963, 966
Powys, John Cowper 773
Prescott, William H. 774
Preston, Guy 961, 964
Prime, William Cowper 775
Prince, Walter F. 355
Prior, Matthew 776
Proctor, Richard Anthony 777
Pronti, Domenico 778
Pushkin, Alexander 428
Pyle, Katharine 781

"Q." *See* Quiller-Couch, Sir Arthur
Quackenbos, G. P. 1083
Quackenbos, John D. 782
Quatrafages de Breau, Louis Armand de 783
Quiller-Couch, Sir Arthur 784–86, 830
Quincy, Josiah 596
Quinn, Seabury 55, 964, 966

Radcliffe, Ann 417, 787, 824n
Raeper, William 611n
Raikes, Thomas 540
Rand, William Wilberforce 788
Ransome, Arthur 394
Rascoe, Burton 129
Raschid, Haroun al- 737
Rawlinson, A. A. 962
Raymond, George Lansing 790
Read, Francis 791
Redman, Ben Ray 85, 129
Reedy, William Marion 560
Reeve, Arthur B. 356
Reeve, Clara 793
Renaud, Jean Joseph 964–65
Rennell, James Rennell Rodd, baron 794
Renshaw, Anne Tillery 744n, 795–96
Reynolds, Beatrix 798
Reynolds, Sir Joshua 799
Reynolds, S. E. 55

Rhys, Ernest 939
Rice, James 94
Rich, H. Thompson 54, 963
Richard of Bury 680
Richardson, Charles Francis 803
Richardson, Flavia. *See* Thomson, Christine Campbell
Richardson, Samuel 417, 977
Richman, Irving Berdine 804
Rickford, Katherine 357
Rickword, Edgell 805
Richter, Gisela M. A. 708
Richter, Jean Paul Friedrich 730
Rickford, Katherine 355
Ridley, James. *See* Morell, Sir Charles
Riley, Henry T. 726
Riley, James Whitcomb 806
Rimbaud, Arthur 805
Rimel, Duane W. 51
Robbins, R. J. 54, 964
Robbins, Tod 224, 873
Robert-Houdin, M. 429
Roberts, H. Chalmers 112
Roberts, Morley 830
Roberts, Peter 807
Roberts, R. Ellis 830
Robinson, Edwin Meade 129
Rodd, Rennel. *See* Rennell, James Rennell Rodd, baron
Rogers, Samuel 808–9
Roget, John Lewis 810
Roget, Peter Mark 810
Rohmer, Sax 700, 811, 830
Rolfe, Frederick William. *See* Corvo, Frederick, Baron
Rolfe, William J. 859
Rollin, Charles 812
Roscoe, Sir Henry Enfield 813
Rose, D. Murray 787n
Rosner, Karl 428
Ross, Sir Ronald 369
Rossetti, William Michael 772
Rountree, Richard Jerome 814
Routeledge, Robert 816
Rowan, Victor 54, 963
Rowson, Susanna (Haswell) 815
Royde-Smith, N. 830
Rud, Anthony M. 104

Rudwin, Maximilian 816
Ruoff, Henry W. 817
Ruskin, John 818–19
Russell, W. Clark 820–21
Russell, William 822

Saint-Pierre, Jacques Henri Bernadin de 823
Saintsbury, George 824
Saki 830
Sallust (C. Sallustius Crispus) 825
Saltus, Edgar 368, 826
Sampson, Martin W. 1020
Sargent, Epes 827
Saunders, T. Bailey 833
Savile, Frank Mackenzie 828
Sawyer, Laurie A. 448n
Saxe, John Godfrey 829
Sayers, Dorothy L. 830
Scarborough, Dorothy 355
Schermerhorn, Frank Earle 420n, 933n
Schiller, Friedrich 730
Schisgall, Oscar 960
Schmitz, Leonhard 446, 831
Schoonmaker, Frank 832
Schopenhauer, Arthur 833
Schorer, Mark 965
Schrevel, Cornelius 834
Schultz, David E. 198n, 421n, 645n
Schwalbe, G. 323
Schwartz, Julius 326
Scott, Fred N. 515
Scott, Frederick George 835
Scott, J. Loughran 143
Scott, Robert 569
Scott, Sir Walter 333, 700, 836–44
Scott, William 643
Scudder, Horace E. 845–46
Seabrook, W. R. 422–23
Seccombe, Thomas 772
Seeley, Harry Govier 847
Selden, John 848
Seltzer, Thomas 40
Serviss, Garrett P. 849–51
Seton, William 852
Sewell, Elizabeth M. 853–54
Seymour, G. S. 855
Seymour, St John D. 355
Shackleton, Robert 856

Shakespeare, William 194, 273, 317, 539n, 548, 857–59, 1060
Sharp, William. *See* Macleod, Fiona
Sharpe, William 809
Sharpless, Isaac 860
Shaw, George Bernard 861
Shaw, Thomas B. 862
Shaw, William 863
Sheldon, Elizabeth 961
Sheldon, M. French 341n
Shelley, Mary 864
Shelley, Percy Bysshe 205, 865
Shenstone, William 175, 866
Shepherd, R. H. 546
Sheppard, Alice 185n, 505n, 569n
Sheridan, Frances 1079
Sheridan, Richard Brinsley 867
Sherwin, Oscar 868
Shiel, M. P. 369, 425, 869–71
Shipley, Joseph T. 78n
Shirley, James 528
Shirley, William 873
Shumway, Edgar S. 578
Sidney, Sir Philip 238
Sime, Sidney H. 295
Simmone, T. 993
Sinclair, May 603, 830, 874
Singer, Hedwig 753
Singleton, Esther 875
Sitwell, Sir Osbert 876
Skinner, Charles M. 877–78
Skinner, Conrad Arthur. *See* Maurice, Michael
Slater, John 888
Sliney, B. W. 54
Small, Frank O. 917
Smart, Christopher 466–67
Smellie, William 879
Smith, C. W. 545
Smith, Clark Ashton 83n, 460, 656n, 768n, 880–85, 1022n
Smith, G. Elliot 886
Smith, T. R. 77, 887–88
Smith, Will 54, 964
Smith, Sir William 375, 889–95
Snell, Edmund 962
Snider, Denton Jacques 896
Snow, Royall H. 897

Somerville, William 9
Sonnenschein, A. 358
Spalding, William 1084
Spence, Lewis 898
Spencer, Charles 55
Spencer, Truman J. 899
Spens, H. 762
Spenser, Edmund 900
Spielhagen, Friedrich 428
Spin, T. E. 1018
Spinden, Herbert J. 886, 901
Spofford, Ainsworth Rand 703, 902
Spofford, Harriet Elizabeth (Prescott) 903
Spyri, Johanna 905
Squires, Roy A. 592n
Stacpoole, Henry de Vere 55
Stainforth, F. 867
Stamper, W. J. 963–64, 966
Staples, William Reed 801
Stark, James Henry 906
Starrett, Vincent 104, 621n
Stead, William T. 355
Stedman, Edmund Clarence 908
Steele, Esther Baker 916–17
Steele, George McKendree 909
Steele, Joel Dorman 380n, 911–17, 1085
Steele, Sir Richard 10–12
Steele, Wilbur Daniel 356
Stephens, Moye W. 966
Sterling, George 99, 357n
Sterling, Kenneth 304
Sterne, Laurence 428, 919
Steuben, Baron de 989
Stevans, C. M. 1031
Stevens, Frank 920
Stevenson, Robert Louis 357, 425, 830, 921–23
Stewart, Balfour 924
Stirling, Anna Maria Diana Wilhelmina 925
Stirling, John 469
Stockley, Cynthia 425
Stockwell, George A. 800
Stoddard, Richard Henry 540, 676
Stoker, Bram 333, 830, 926
Stone, Paschal 927

Stone, Richard 965
Stormonth, James 928
Storr, Francis 929
Streatfield, Noel 55
Strong, L. A. G. 421
Stuart, Dorothy Margaret 931
Stuart, Miranda 55
Sturgis, Russell 875
Sudbury, Charles 933
Suetonius (C. Suetonius Tranquillus) 934
Sullivan, Francis Stoughton 935
Sulpicia 969
Surrey, Henry Howard, earl of 936
Surriage, Agnes 903
Suter, Paul 421–22
Sutton, Eric 92
Swanwick, Anne 382
Swedenborg, Emanuel 317
Swift, Jonathan 936–37
Swinburne, Algernon Charles 596, 939
Symmes, Mrs. William B. 940
Symons, Arthur 81
Syntax, Doctor 941

Tacitus, P. Cornelius 942
Talman, Wilfred B. 244n, 623n, 943
Tannahill, Robert 944
Tarbell, Frank Bigelow 945
Tarbell, Ida Minerva 946
Tasso, Torquato 947
Taylor, Bayard 383, 908
Taylor, John 948
Tenniel, John 13, 172
Tennyson, Alfred, Lord 949
Teter, George E. 951
Thackeray, William Makepeace 428, 816, 952–57
Thaxter, Celia (Laughton) 958
Theden, Dietrich 428
Thimm, Franz 959
Thomson, Christine Campbell 54n, 960–66
Thomson, H. 962
Thomson, Hugh 10
Thomson, J. Arthur 323
Thomson, James 219, 967
Thoreau, Henry David 596
Thornsburgh, Zada 1047

Thucydides 209
Thwing, Annie Haven 968
Tibullus, Albius 969
Tickell, Thomas 5
Ticknor, Caroline 970
Tieck, Ludwig 730
Titcomb, Timothy 971
Todd, David Peck 972
Toksvig, Signe 960, 973
Toldridge, Elizabeth 34n, 35n, 37n, 171n, 609n, 798n
Tolstoi, Leo 974
Tomes, Robert 975
Tomlinson, Everett 976
Tracy, R. S. 346
Traill, H. D. 977
Train, Arthur 428
Travers, Martin 48, 754
Treadwell, John H. 978
Trench, Richard Chenevix 979
Trent, William P. 980–81
Trevelyan, Lady 606
Trumbull, John 211
Tuberville, George 726
Tuckerman, Henry T. 862
Tuckey, Janet 983
Turner, Edward 984
Turner, Hawes 929
Twain, Mark 356, 985–87
Tylor, E. B. 334n

Underwood, William 192
Upton, Winslow 990
Upward, Allen 700

Vallings, Gabrielle 55
Van der Velde, C. F. 730
Van Dusen, Washington 991
Van Vechten, Carl 869
Vaughan, L. Brent 992
Velázquez de la Cavena, Mariano 993
Vercoe, Anthony 961, 963
Verelst, Myndart. *See* Saltus, Edgar
Verne, Jules 994–96
Villiers de l'Isle Adam, Philippe-Auguste, comte de 356, 428
Vinal, Harold 997
Vince, Charles 998
Virgil (P. Vergilius Maro) 999–1002

Voltaire (François Marie Arouet) 428
Vorley, L. 55
Voss, Richard 100n

Waggett, P. H. 323
Wakefield, H. Russell 223, 873, 1003–4
Walker, John 1005–6
Walpole, Horace 417, 931, 1007
Walters, Robert 848
Walton, George A. 1008
Wandrei, Donald 420, 1009–10
Wandrei, Howard 1009
Wanostrocht, Nicholas 10011
Ward, Arthur Sarsfield. *See* Rohmer, Sax
Ward, Harold 961, 963
Ware, John 879
Warford, Aaron 1012–13
Warner, Charles Dudley 1014
Warren, David M. 1015
Washington, George 427, 798
Watson, Elkanah 1016
Watson, John Selby 701
Watson, Winslow C. 1016
Watts, Isaac 175
Watts, William Lord 1017
Webb, Thomas William 1018
Webster, J. Provand 1019
Webster, Daniel 631n
Webster, John 529, 1020
Webster, Noah 926n, 1021–23
Weeden, William Babcock 538
Weguelin, J. R. 604
Weigall, Arthur 1025
Weir, Harrison 558
Weismann, August 323
Weiss, Ehrich. *See* Houdini, Harry
Wells, Benjamin W. 981
Wells, H. G. 31, 700, 830, 1027–29
Wessely, Ignaz Emanuel 1030–31
West, Gilbert 175
West, Willis Mason 1032
Westlake, Herbert Francis 1033
Weyman, Stanley J. 428
Wharton, Anthony 962
Wharton, Edith 333
Whipple, Edwin P. 1034
White, Edward Lucas 425, 830, 1035–35
White, Gilbert 1038

White, Gleeson 1039
White, Michael 1040
White, Richard Grant 858, 1041
White, W. B. 1042
White, Walter R. 1043
Whitehead, Henry S. 198n, 677n, 930n, 964, 1003n
Whitehill, Henry W. 962
Whiting, Lilian 1044
Whitman, Sarah Helen 970, 1045–46
Whitman, Walt 908, 1047
Whittaker, J. S. 965
Whittier, John Greenleaf 908, 1048
Whittington, Sir Richard 94
Wiener, Leo 816
Wild, Nathan 328
Wilde, Oscar 793, 1049–52
Wilder, Thornton 1053
Wilkins, Augustus S. 1054
Wilkins, Mary E. *See* Freeman, Mary Eleanor (Wilkins)
Wilkinson, Maude 747
Wilkinson, William Cleaver 1055–56
William I (King of England) ("the Conqueror") 352
Williams, Blanche Colton 1057
Williams, Roger 301, 541
Williams, Roswell. *See* Owen, Frank
Wilson, Colin 1049n
Wilson, D. L. 564
Wilson, George Grafton 538
Wilson, John Fleming 425
Wilson, Rufus Rockwell 1058
Winchell, Alexander 1059
Winsor, G. MacLeod 32
Winter, William 1060
Wister, Owen 1061
Wittie, Robert 1062
Wolcot, John 1063
Wolf, Howard 129
Wollheim, Donald A. 755
Wood, Alphonso 1085
Wood, Clement 1064
Wood, John George 1065
Woodberry, Goerge E. 1066
Woodhouselee, Alexander Fraser Tytler, Lord 1067
Woodward, Arthur 961

Woodward, P. H. 428
Wordsworth, William 1068
Wright, Farnsworth 104, 1026
Wright, S. Fowler 54, 421, 1069–70
Wright, William Aldis 339
Wyllarde, Dolf 1071
Wyss, Johann David 905n

Xenophon 1072
Xerxes (King of Persia) 1

Yeats, William Butler 116
Yonge, Charlotte Mary 1073
Young, Charles Augustus 1074–76
Young, Edward 175, 771
Young, John Russell 1077

Zschokke, Heinrich 730

B. Titles

Against the Grain (Huysmans) 483
Age of Fable, The (Bulfinch) 142
Aids to English Composition (Parker) 738
Alciphron (Moore) 674n
Alroy (Disraeli) 268
"Ancestor, The" (Derleth) 198n
Andivius Hedulio (White) 1035
Apparitions and Miracles at Knock, The (MacPhilpin) 628
Arabian Nights 49, 681
Architecture of Colonial America, The (Eberlein) 308
Astro-Theology (Derham) 248
"Avatar" (Gautier) 368
Avernus (Bond) 118

Beetle, The (Marsh) 642
Best Ghost Stories, The (Lynch) 603
Best Psychic Stories, The (French) 355
Best Short Stories of 1928, The (O'Brien) 715
Beowulf 1078
Beware After Dark! (Harré) 425
Bloody Poet, The (Kosztolányi) 542
Bookfellow Anthology, A (Seymour) 855
Brood of the Witch-Queen (Rohmer) 811
By Daylight Only (Thomson) 960

"Coming of the Terror, The" (Machen) 175

"*Corners and Characters of Rhode Island*" (Laswell) 552
Creep, Shadow! (Merritt) 51
Creeps by Night (Hammett) 421
Curious Myths of the Middle Ages (Baring-Gould) 75
Cyclopedia of the Literature of Amateur Journalism, A (Spencer) 899

Daedalus (Haldane) 413
Dance of the Machines, The (O'Brien) 714
Dark Chamber, The (Cline) 198
Death-Mask and Other Ghosts, The (Everett) 322
Devil Stories (Rudwin) 816
"Diamond Lens, The" (O'Brien) 356
Double Axe, The (Haggard) 410
Down There (Huysmans) 484
Dwellers in the Mirage, The (Merritt) 51

Edgar Poe and His Critics (Whitman) 1045
Elements of Criticism (Kames) 524
Encyclopaedia Britannica 71, 318
Encyclopaedia of Occultism, An (Spence) 898
Eureka (Poe) 770n
Exchange of Souls, An (Pain) 735

Face in the Abyss, The (Merritt) 654
Famous Psychic Stories (McSpadden) 629
Fascism and Social Revolution (Dutt) 304
Friend of Caesar, A (Davis) 240
Frozen Pirate, The (Russell) 821

Geography Made Easy (Morse) 684–85
Geography of the Heavens, The (Burritt) 150–51
Ghosts in Daylight (Onions) 718
Giles Corey, Yeoman (Freeman) 353
Gold Point and Other Strange Stories, The (Jackson) 497
Golden Treasury, The (Palgrave) 736
Great Weird Stories, The (Neale) 700
Green Mansions (Hudson) 475
"Green Tea" (LeFanu) 559n, 830
Grim Death (Thomson) 961
Gruesome Cargoes (Thomson) 962
Guardian, The (Addison) 8

Hadrian the Seventh (Rolfe) 216

"Harbor-Master, The" (Chambers) 183
Hasheesh Eater, The (Ludlow) 601
"Haunted and the Haunters; or, The House and the Brain, The" (Bulwer-Lytton) 145, 428
Hints on Writing Poetry (Wood) 1064
Hints on Writing Short Stories (Finger) 335
"Horla, The" (Maupassant) 356, 428
House of the Black Ring, The (Pattee) 743
How to Revise Your Own Poems (Hamilton) 420

Icebound: A Play (Davis) 237
In Memoriam: Jennie E. T. Dowe (White) 1040
In Search of the Unknown (Chambers) 183
Introduction to Some Elements of Poetry, An (Teter) 951

Jimbo: A Fantasy (Blackwood) 106
John Silence—Physician Extraordinary (Blackwood) 107–8
Journey in Other Worlds, A (Astor) 56
Junior Literature (Leonard-Moffett) 562

King in Yellow, The (Chambers) 184

Last American, The (Mitchell) 663
Last Devil, The (Toksvig) 973
Lazarus (Béraud) 92
Lectures on Rhetoric and Belles Lettres (Blair) 113
"Letter to Sura" (Pliny) 428
Life of Christ, The (Farrar) 329
Light of Asia, The (Arnold) 53
Linebook, The (Little) 1080–81
Little Women (Alcott) 24
Lives of the English Poets (Johnson) 175n, 516
Lock and Key Library, The (Hawthorne) 428
London in 1731 (Gonzales) 387

Magician among the Spirits, A (Houdini) 470
Magnalia Christi Americana (Mather) 645
Man Who Lost Himself, The (Sitwell) 876
Man Who Was Born Again, The (Busson) 156
"Man Who Went Too Far, The" (Benson) 91, 356, 629

Masterpieces of Mystery (French) 356
"Melmoth Reconciled" (Balzac) 428
Melmoth the Wanderer (Maturin) 428, 646
Metamorphoses (Ovid) 726, 728–29
Mirror for Witches, A (Forbes) 343
Modern City: Providence, Rhode Island and Its Activities, A (Kirk) 538
"Moon Pool, The" (Merritt) 26
More Seven Club Tales (Austin) 64
My Grimmest Nightmare (Asquith) 55
Myths and Legends of Our Own Land (Skinner) 878
Myths and Myth-Makers (Fiske) 338

Night (Hersey) 447
Night in the Luxembourg, A (Gourmont) 394
Not at Night! (Asbury) 54
Not at Night (Thomson) 963
"Not at Night" Omnibus, The (Thomson) 964
Not in Our Stars (Maurice) 649

Old Farmer and His Almanack, The (Kittredge) 539
Old World Footprints (Symmes) 940
Oldest God, The (McKenna) 624
Omnibus of Crime, The (Sayers) 830
On the Borderland (Austin) 61
"Ooze" (Rud) 104
Open Polar Sea, The (Hayes) 439
Oracle of Baal, The (Webster) 1019
Our Natupski Neighbors (Miniter) 659
Ouronoskopia (Wittie) 1062

"Penelope" (Starrett) 104
"Phantom Bus, The" (Backus) 421
Phantom Ship, The (Marryat) 640
Plan de Paris (Forest) 344
Poe's Helen (Ticknor) 970
Poems of Ossian, The (Macpherson) 627
Poetry as a Representative Art (Raymond) 790
Providence Plantations for Two Hundred and Fifty Years, The (Greene) 403

Reader, The (Alden) 25
Recueil choisi de traits historiques (Wanostrocht) 1011
"Red Brain, The" (Wandrei) 421

Red Laugh, The (Andreyev) 40
Reliques of Ancient English Poetry (Percy) 752
Revi-Lona (Cowan) 217
Rhode-Island Tales, and Tales of Old Times (Howland) 474
"Rose for Emily, A" (Faulkner) 421–22
Rose Leaf and Apple Leaf (Rennell) 794
Round-Table in Poictesme, A (Bregenzer-Loveman) 129
Runagates Club, The (Buchan) 141

Select Works of the British Poets (Aikin) 17
"Sin-Eater, The" (Sharp) 355
Sirenica (Leith) 560
Song Celestial, The (Mahabharata) 632
Spectator, The (Addison-Steele-et al.) 7, 11–12
"Spider, The" (Ewers) 421–22
State of Rhode Island and Providence Plantations at the End of the Century (Field) 332
Stories of Strange Happenings (Wyllarde) 1071
Story of Philosophy, The (Durant) 301
Story without a Name, The (Barbey d'Aurevilly) 74
Strange Assembly (Gawsworth) 369
Strange Manuscript Found in a Copper Cylinder, A (De Mille) 245
Strange Story, A (Bulwer-Lytton) 145
Swiss Family Robinson, The (Wyss) 905n
Switch On the Light (Thomson) 965
Sword of Welleran, The (Dunsany) 290

Tale of Terror, The (Birkhead) 105
Tales from Blackwood 112
Tales from the German (Oxenford-Feiling) 730
Tales of Mystery (Saintsbury) 824
Tales of Mystery and Horror (Level) 565
Tales of the Genii (Morell) 681
Tatler, The (Addison) 8
Theory of Pneumatology (Jung-Stilling) 521
Those Who Return (Level) 566
Thoughts and Pictures (Kuntz) 545
"Through the Dragon Glass" (Merritt) 26, 655
"Thurnley Abbey" (Landon) 603

Time and the Gods (Dunsany) 288
Tomb of Perneb, The 709
"Torture by Hope, The" (Villiers de l'Isle Adam) 356, 429
Turn of the Screw, The (James) 499
Two Gentlemen in Touraine (Sudbury) 933

Undine (La Motte-Fouqué) 549

Vathek (Beckford) 84–85
"Venus of Ille, The" (Mérimée) 368

Wanderings in Roman Britain (Weigall) 1025
Waste Land, The (Eliot) 254
"Weigher of Souls, The" (Maurois) 649
Weird Tales 54n, 104n, 425n, 731n, 1026
Well Bred Speech (Renshaw) 796
"Wendigo, The" (Blackwood) 110
"Werewolf, The" (Marryat) 640n
Westminster Street, Providence, as It Was about 1824 (Read) 791
White Fire (Bullen) 143
Wieland (Brown) 428
"Willows, The" (Blackwood) 602
Wind in the Rose-Bush and Other Stories of the Supernatural, The (Freeman) 354
Wind That Tramps the World, The (Owen) 731
Worm Ouroboros, The (Eddison) 309
Writing the Short-Story (Esenwein) 320
Wuthering Heights (Brontë) 666

You'll Need a Night Light (Thomson) 966
Young Chemist, The (Appleton) 47

Zanoni (Bulwer-Lytton) 145

C. Works by Lovecraft

Alfredo 82
"Allowable Rhyme, The" 158
At the Mountains of Madness 245, 821, 871
Azathoth 84

"Battle That Ended the Century" (Lovecraft–Barlow) 51
"Beyond the Wall of Sleep" 98, 850
"Biographical Notice" 715
"Bookstall, The" 364

"C. S. A. 1861–1865: To the Starry Cross of the SOUTH" 671
"Call of Cthulhu, The" 425
"Canal, The" 203
Case of Charles Dexter Ward, The 645
Cats of Ulthar, The 585
Charleston 586
Club of the Seven Dreamers, The 64
"Colour out of Space, The" 32
Commonplace Book 78, 99, 111, 141, 198, 290, 298, 318, 340, 421, 430–32, 436, 645, 742, 1059
Crime of Crimes, The 587
"Curse of Yig, The" (Lovecraft–Bishop) 964–65
Dream-Quest of Unknown Kadath, The 84
"Dunwich Horror, The" 104, 110, 318, 878
"Epistle to the Rt. Hon[ble.] Maurice Winter Moe . . ., An" 951
"Festival, The" 645
"Fragment on Whitman" 1047
Further Criticism of Poetry 588
"Gems from *In a Minor Key*" 604
"Haunter of the Dark, The" 422
"Herbert West—Reanimator" 461
"History of the 'Necronomicon'" 84
"Horror at Red Hook, The" 54, 81, 318, 966
"Horror in the Museum, The" (Lovecraft–Heald) 964
"Hound, The" 483
"Hypnos" 78
"In a Major Key" 1047
"In Memoriam: J. E. T. D." 1040
"Introduction" (to *The Poetical Works of Jonathan E. Hoag*) 453
Looking Backward 589
"Lord Dunsany and His Work" 298
"Lurking Fear, The" 460
Materialist Today, The 590
"Mound, The" (Lovecraft–Bishop) 245
"Music of Erich Zann, The" 344, 421–22

"Observations on Several Parts of America" 562
"Outsider, The" 1049
"Ovid's Metamorphoses" 726
"Pickman's Model" 960, 964
"Preface" (to *Old World Footprints*) 940
"Preface" (to *White Fire*) 142
"Prophecy of Capys Secundus, The" 604
"Rats in the Walls, The" 75, 355, 754
"Shadow out of Time, The" 92, 318, 735
"Shadow over Innsmouth, The" 183
Shadow over Innsmouth, The 591
"Shunned House, The" 358, 878
Shunned House, The 592
"Singer of Ethereal Moods and Fancies, A" 1040
"Sleepy Hollow To-day" 562
"Suggestions for a Reading Guide" 796
"Sunset" 398
Supernatural Horror in Literature 48–49, 75, 83–84, 90–91, 98–99, 101, 105–7, 110–11, 136, 141, 145, 149, 174, 183–84, 198, 205, 243–44, 278, 288, 290, 292, 296, 325, 3412, 354, 356, 365, 367–68, 382, 384, 411, 421, 428, 430–32, 435–37, 440, 477, 495, 498–502, 525, 536–37, 549, 565, 567, 611, 615, 617–18, 621–23, 627, 636, 640, 642, 646, 648, 666, 674–75, 735, 744, 787, 792–93, 811, 824, 840, 857, 864, 871, 874, 880, 922, 926, 1003–4, 1007, 1020, 1036–37, 1051
"Thing on the Doorstep, The" 735
"To Mr. Kleiner, on Receiving from Him the Poetical Works of Addison, Gay, and Somerville" 9
"Transition of Juan Romero, The" 774
"Trap, The" (Lovecraft-Whitehead) 930
"Under the Pyramids" (Lovecraft–Houdini) 709
"Unknown City in the Ocean, The" 631
"Waste Paper" 254

Indexes 199

"Whisperer in Darkness, The" 98, 783
"With a Copy of Wilde's Fairy Tales" 1049
"Year Off, A" 576

D. Publishers

Allan, Philip 223, 322, 873
ARRA Press 655
Auburn Journal 880–81, 883
Book Club of California 882
Clarendon Press (Oxford University Press) 7, 188
Colophon Club 129
Cook, W. Paul 16, 581, 593, 1040. *See also* Recluse Press
Dragon-Fly Press (R. H. Barlow) 580, 585
Driftwind Press 200–203, 590
Everyman's Library (Dent/Dutton) 12, 82, 124–25, 257, 373, 410, 519, 636, 752, 762, 922, 937, 1067
Fantasy Publications (William L. Crawford) 885
Fetter, George G., Co. 588
Gilliss Press 707–9
Great Western Railway Co. 351, 635
Green-Leach, Leacy N. 34–37
Haldeman-Julius Co. 91, 335, 394, 536, 766, 773, 833, 1064
Harris, A. 587
Kenyon Press 669, 814, 951
Kirk, George 101
Koenig, H. C. 586
Loring & Mussey 249–51, 253, 662
Modern Library (Boni & Liveright) 40, 78, 81, 98–99, 115, 288, 290, 323, 342, 355, 366, 742, 934, 939, 1049–52
Mosher, Thomas Bird 560, 794
Oxford University Press. *See* Clarendon Press; World's Classics
Parker, Charles A. A. 485
Popular Fiction Publishing Co. 104

Recluse Press (W. Paul Cook) 143, 592, 940, 1010
Rhode Island imprints: 47, 63–65, 126, 302, 380, 401, 403–4, 496, 532, 552, 572, 613, 638, 694, 779, 791, 800–802, 943, 1043, 1046
Selwyn & Blount 960–66
Smith, Charles W. 545, 589
Strange Co. 357
Tousey, Frank 3, 28, 1012–13
Visionary Publishing Co. 591
World's Classics (Oxford University Press) 1002

E. Subjects

Africa 573
African Americans 189, 677
Almanacs 271, 328, 331, 381, 486, 539, 553–54, 658, 705, 800, 904, 982, 1082
Amateur Journalism 16, 485, 545, 588–89, 602, 659, 745, 899, 991, 1040
American Language 77, 652
American Literature
 Drama 237, 353, 1053
 Essays and Belles Lettres 101, 227, 313, 315–17, 398, 457, 595–96, 766, 770, 981, 986
 Fiction
  18th century 456
  19th century 24, 100, 189, 227, 429–37, 491–92, 494–95, 601, 651, 663, 689–93, 835, 985, 987
  20th century 160, 250, 252, 269, 350, 445, 476, 602, 659, 715, 998
 Poetry
  18th century 211, 981
  19th century 138–39, 167, 211, 279, 314, 458, 582, 597, 741, 767, 806, 829, 1046–48
  20th century 34–37, 43–44, 143, 153–55, 171, 200–203, 254, 357, 447, 453, 485, 509, 545, 580–81, 587, 593–94, 687, 745, 855, 881–84, 943, 991, 997, 1009–10

Anthologies 203, 406, 442, 798, 855, 981
Magazines 792
Criticism 27, 62, 129, 395, 488, 588, 714, 719, 862, 908, 970
see also Weird Fiction—American
Anglo-Saxon literature 1078
Anthropology 199, 334, 783, 886
Architecture 274, 308, 887–88, 896
Arctic and Antarctic Regions 358, 439, 459, 828
Aristocracy (English) 208
Arithmetic 389, 1008
Art 81, 556
18th century 454, 799
Furniture 305, 875
Greek 945
Mediaeval 394
Museum Handbooks 123, 707–9
Pottery 775
Renaissance 419, 695
Roman 393
Criticism of 176, 455, 549, 818, 945
Astronomy 80, 150–51, 159, 177–79, 193, 212, 248, 255–56, 361, 376, 409, 452, 626, 647, 683, 699, 711–12, 716–17, 777, 849–51, 860, 910, 972, 1018, 1042, 1062, 1074–76
Atlases 88, 423, 664, 789
Astronomical 150, 361, 990

Bermuda 906
Biology 528
Boston, MA 404, 531, 845, 856, 968
Botany 396, 466, 1085
Buddhism 53
Business 740

Charleston, SC 586
Chemistry 47, 286, 380, 812, 911, 984
Chess 661
Christianity 2, 95–97, 157, 248, 329, 471, 505, 641, 645, 702, 748, 978
Civil War (American) 402, 557, 561, 583, 734
Conduct 164, 795
Cookery 481
Country Life 504

Debating 760

Dictionaries
Bible 732–33, 788, 895
Biographical 89, 704
Classical 29, 45, 69, 319, 746, 890–91, 894
English 512, 928, 1005, 1021–24
Greek 568, 834
Italian 1031
Latin 39, 173, 834, 893, 1030
Spanish 992
Education 152
Egypt 121, 709, 812, 945
Elocution 25, 796, 822, 1006
Encyclopaedias 72, 185, 204, 228, 318, 668, 703, 750, 817, 898
England
Description and Travel 124, 351, 399, 481, 490, 635, 667, 907, 1038–39
History 18, 208, 260, 390, 400, 520, 551, 925, 927, 935, 1061, 1072
Ancient 21, 1025
Mediaeval 20, 22, 95, 352
16th century 23, 1060
17th century 23, 426
18th century 19, 130, 417, 478
19th century 19, 479
Scotland 515, 610–11
see also London
English Language 25, 38, 220, 348, 584, 796, 810, 827, 979, 1041, 1078, 1083
see also American Language; Dictionaries—English
English Literature (General) 371, 797
Drama
Renaissance 82, 284, 519, 528, 857–59, 1020
18th century 387, 867
19th century 1050
20th century 292, 296–97, 861
Criticism of 102, 194, 274, 548
Essays and Belles Lettres
Renaissance 848
17th century 322, 444, 657, 751
18th century 5, 7–12, 50, 124, 131, 190, 327, 373, 386, 448, 511, 513, 515–18, 938, 948

19th century 169, 225, 247, 257, 339, 540, 546–47, 606, 676, 809, 819, 948
20th century 87, 614–16, 622
Criticism of 113, 125, 238, 345, 605, 679
Fiction
  Renaissance 636
  17th century 146
  18th century 122, 148, 241–42, 514, 625, 815, 919, 937, 1079
  19th century 57–60, 112, 134–35, 147, 172, 258–59, 261–68, 276, 362, 653, 666, 742, 836–39, 841, 843–44, 921, 923, 952, 954–57, 1049, 1051, 1068, 1079
  20th century 87, 197, 216, 475, 617, 620
  Criticism of 980
Poetry
  Renaissance 188, 752, 900, 929, 936
  17th century 17, 158, 283, 364, 656, 771
  18th century 5, 9, 17, 115, 117, 149, 166, 175, 187, 205, 218–19, 221, 236, 272, 324, 360, 397, 627, 675, 771–72, 776, 808, 866, 944, 967, 1063
  19th century 115, 136, 165, 205, 221, 270, 360, 443, 525, 534, 545, 575–76, 604, 675, 682, 749, 761, 794, 808, 842, 865, 939, 949, 1049, 1052
  Criticism of 517, 868, 897
Anthologies 17, 112, 175, 182, 195–96, 272, 372, 528, 660, 680, 696–97, 736, 749, 752
Magazines 112, 371–72, 672
Criticism of (General) 862, 863, 953, 1034, 1084
see also Weird Fiction—British
Evolution 323
France
  Description and Travel 300, 933, 975
  History 93, 168, 391, 506, 916, 946, 983

  see also Paris
French language 526, 1011
French Literature 78–79, 285, 341–42, 365–68, 394, 477, 483–84, 565–66, 648, 650, 823, 994–96, 1011
  History and Criticism 805

Geography 29, 42, 46, 69, 214, 239, 664, 684–85, 756, 1015
Geology 231, 370, 779, 847, 915, 1059
German Language 959
German Literature 382–84, 549, 730, 753, 905
Germany 544
Greece (Ancient)
  Description and Travel 186
  History 385, 392, 438, 482, 633–34, 678, 698, 720, 812, 831, 854, 889
  in Literature 410, 418, 435, 437, 534
Greek Language 529, 1055
  see also Dictionaries—Greek
Greek Literature
  Texts 462, 1072
  Translations and Paraphrases 13–14, 446, 449, 461–64, 599, 758, 762–64, 1072
  Criticism of 209, 378, 503, 782

Haunted Houses 340, 489
Hinduism 53
Historical Fiction 63, 240, 267, 341, 410, 476, 542, 1035
History (General) 120, 130, 222, 312, 359, 408, 555, 812, 1028–29, 1032
Hygiene 229, 346

Iceland 1017
Immigrants 807
Indians (American) 487
Inventors 1013
Ireland 757
Isle of Shoals 958
Israel 213
Italian Literature 232–33, 932, 947, 950
  see also Dictionaries—Italian
Italy 6, 257, 563

Journalism 1080–81

Ku Klux Klan 564

Landscape Gardening 274

Latin Language 30–31, 1056
  see also Dictionaries—Latin
Latin Literature
  Texts 162–63, 192, 207, 407, 468–69, 522, 574, 600, 643, 701, 724, 727, 729, 825, 969, 1000–1
  Translations and Paraphrases 48, 161–63, 191–92, 441, 466–67, 469, 522–23, 574–75, 643, 701, 723, 725–26, 728–29, 754, 825, 934, 942, 969, 999, 1001–2
  Criticism of 206, 424, 782, 932
Letters and Diaries 79, 101, 190, 321, 327, 339, 488, 751
Literary Criticism (General) 524, 616, 773, 803, 977, 1057
  see also Writing
Literature (General) 562, 680, 902
London
  Description and Travel 210, 226, 234–35, 387, 473, 619, 1033
  History 988
  in Literature 242, 576–77
Magic Lanterns 28
Manuscripts 132
Meteorology 133, 180
Mexico 773, 901
Middle Ages 75, 721
Military History 222
Mineralogy 722
Music 455, 814
Mystery and Detective Stories 249, 251, 253, 765
Mythology and Folklore 49, 75, 116, 338, 405, 632, 681, 877–78
  Classical 29, 69, 142
Nantucket 630–31
Natural History 15, 66, 181, 510, 639, 879, 1038, 1065
New England
  Churches 67
  Description and Travel 281–82, 507, 907
  History 415, 645, 686
  Houses 491
  Legends 280, 508
  in Literature 705, 903
New York City 349, 493, 709, 1058

Nova Scotia 1014
Occultism 521, 628, 898
Oratory 103, 442, 827
Paris, France 344, 1044
Persia 1
Philadelphia 598
Philology, Classical 570
Philosophy 590, 833
  History of 137, 301, 330
Photography 3
Physics 450, 913, 924
Physiology 114, 229, 346, 912
Poetry (General) 420, 669, 736, 790, 951, 1064
Politics 303, 688, 909
Pompeii 215, 607–8, 670
Providence, RI
  Description and Travel 88, 532, 537, 1043
  History 332, 403, 496, 638, 791, 801
Providence Journal, The 780
Psychology 170
Quotations 76
Religion 157, 826
  see also Buddhism; Christianity; Hinduism; Jesus Christ
Rhetoric 796, 1006, 1078
Rhode Island
  Description and Travel 67, 88, 552, 694
  History 41, 67, 332, 379, 540, 572, 613, 779, 781, 801, 804, 853
  Literature 63–65, 126, 302–3, 401, 474, 802
Rome (Ancient)
  Description and Travel 246, 778, 1054
  History 224, 307, 374–75, 377, 568, 578, 698, 720, 747, 831, 892, 917
  in Literature 240, 542, 604, 1035
Rome (Modern) 246
Russia 347
Russian Literature 973–74
Science (General) 413–14, 550, 1012
Science Fiction 32, 56, 579, 994–96, 1027, 1069–70

Secret Service (United States) 70, 759
Self-Help 795, 971
Sirens 560
Spanish language 993
  see also Dictionaries—Spanish
Spiritualism 471, 521, 614, 628
Stonehenge 920
Translation 1067
Travel 4, 230, 412, 479, 532, 573, 637, 713, 832, 941, 986, 1077
United States
  History 33, 72–73, 127, 363, 388, 416, 427, 612, 671, 918
    Colonial and Revolutionary 128, 306, 308, 310–11, 337, 451, 472, 493, 739, 743, 846, 872, 976, 989, 1016
    Politics 140, 336, 1060
    see also Civil War—American
Weird Fiction
  American 26, 51, 91, 98–99, 183–84, 198, 217, 343, 354, 430, 440, 497–98, 529, 585, 591–92, 649, 654–55, 673, 731, 744, 768–69, 880, 885, 1009–10, 1019, 1036–37
  Canadian 245

British 52, 61, 83–85, 90, 91, 106–11, 118, 141, 144–45, 174, 243–44, 275, 277–78, 287–99, 309, 322, 411, 500–502, 536–37, 559, 567, 611, 618, 621, 623, 624, 640, 642, 646, 674, 718, 735, 784–86, 793, 811, 820–21, 864, 869–71, 874, 876, 922, 926, 1003–4, 1007, 1071
French 74, 92, 156, 342, 365, 367–68, 477, 483–84, 565–66, 650
German 549, 753
Italian 950
Russian 40, 973
Anthologies 54–55, 104, 223, 333, 355–56, 369, 421–22, 425, 428, 603, 629, 700, 730, 816, 824, 830, 873, 960–66
Magazines 325–26, 460, 644, 755, 930, 1026
Criticism of 105
Witch Trials (Salem) 343, 353
Witchcraft 840
World War I 300, 587
Writing 166, 320, 335, 420, 662, 738, 1057, 1064
Zoology 558, 571, 852, 914

CPSIA information can be obtained
at www.ICGtesting.com
Printed in the USA
BVOW09s1000020418
512247BV00026B/938/P